LOOKING OUT, LOOKING IN

Anthology of Latino Poetry

Edited by William Luis

Arte Público Press
Houston, Texas

For Tammie, Gabriel and Diego

Looking Out, Looking In: Anthology of Latino Poetry is made possible through grants from the National Endowment for the Arts and the City of Houston through the Houston Arts Alliance.

Recovering the past, creating the future

Arte Público Press
University of Houston
4902 Gulf Fwy, Rm 100
Houston, Texas 77204-2004

Cover illustration by Alfredo M. Arreguín
Cover design by Mora Des¡gn

Luis, Williams
    Looking out, looking in : anthology of Latino poetry / by William Luis, editor.
        pages cm
    ISBN 978-1-55885-761-2 (alk. paper)
    1. American poetry—Hispanic American authors. 2. American poetry—19th century. 3. American poetry—20th century. I. Luis, William, editor of compilation.
    PS591.H58L66 2013
    811'.54080868—dc23

                                                                    2012046343
                                                                    CIP

12 13 14 15 16 17 18   10 9 8 7 6 5 4 3 2 1

Table of Contents

Latino Poetry and Distinctiveness

William Luis
Gertrude Conaway Vanderbilt Professor of Spanish
Vanderbilt University

I

Latino literature, written by authors of Spanish-speaking descent—living and writing in the United States—is experiencing a literary Boom. The increased population of Hispanics and Latinos has created a significant pool of writers with exceptional works. Readers, whether they are of Latino, Hispanic, European, African or Asian descent, are drawn to these writings and await anxiously to be mesmerized by the fascinating, intricate, and at times somber worlds writers place before them. Indeed, Latino literature has invaded the U.S. literature, culture and market place. This literary production already counts with two Pulitzer Prize winners, Oscar Hijuelos (1990) and Junot Díaz (2008), and Díaz was awarded a prestigious MacArthur Genius Fellowship for 2012. These and many others writers are recipients of countless literary awards. Some have already reached international notoriety, and their works have been translated into many world languages. Publishing houses, literary agents and academic journals are competing to claim their own writers. Undeniably, Latino literature is experiencing a Boom similar to the one seen with Latin American literature of the 1960s that bought to a world audience works such as Gabriel García Márquez's *One Hundred Years of Solitude* (1967). However, the Latino one is distinctive. It is written in Spanish but mainly in English and gathers different geographic spaces, time periods, cultures, languages, races, sex and gender orientations, and perspectives, therefore breaking with the binary structure common to many writers. Latino literature has already set the groundwork for becoming the literature of the twenty-first century.

Within Latino writings, poetry is a fundamental avenue for expressing the Latino experience. Latino poetry belongs to the tradition of Classical Western oral and written aesthetic expressions that can be traced to the dawn of civilization. From its inception and to the present, poetry provides insights into the different stages, periods, trends, moods and movements of cultures, associated with the classic, the baroque, the romantic, the realist, the modern or the postmodern period. In the early stages, Homer's *The Odyssey* described Ulysses' ten-year journey home to Ithaca after the fall of Troy, detailing his challenges with what many centuries later Pliny the Elder would classify as members of the Monstrous Races.

Critics have assessed this idiosyncratic form of communication equally as long as poets have composed poems. In Western culture, Plato was critical of poets. He did not value their contributions; on the contrary, he considered their societal role to be of no merit, and even excluded them, I would add unfairly, from the construction of his Republic. For him, philosophy was more valuable than an imitative art form. Aristotle also contemplated the significance of poetry. In the *Art of Poetry*, he addressed the issue of poets and their imaginative works, but paid particular attention to use of the meters, establishing important distinctions between the epic, the comic and the tragic forms, later known as epic poetry, lyric poetry and dramatic poetry; and to the latter he incorporated the comic and tragic as subgenres. Whether we side with one master critic or the other, each responded to the poetic concerns prevalent during the society in which he lived.

Latino poetry belongs to the tradition of Western and world cultures. In the contemporary period it represents the wants, desires, pain, struggles, violence, exile, migration, downfalls, births and rebirths, and successes of Latinos and their respective communities. Though the lives of Latinos are intrinsically tied to the culture of their parents' Spanish-speaking country of origin, they are also influenced by events unfolding in the adopted homeland of the United States, a space that for many has been transformed into a place of permanence. Gloria Anzaldúa refers to this space as a borderland/frontera, where different cultures come together, coexist, intermingle and convey new meaning and signification. Tato Laviera defines it as "nideaquinideallá" (neither from here nor there), thus suggesting that no place is also a location of identity.

There have been attempts to trace the origins of Latino literature to the early Spanish colonial period, and more specifically to a geographic space that would later become the southern or southwestern part of the United States. While this may be the case, Latino writing more aptly belongs to a literature that developed as the United States expanded its borders to become a continental mainland. Latinos are an integral part of the United States, whether they were absorbed into what later became the growing and geographically expanding nation or for political or economic reasons migrated to the adopted country where many have lived for generations.

Latino literature in general and poetry in particular gains meaning as a narrative of resistance and cultural opposition within the context of the United States. Latino people are actively involved in creating cultural, linguistic, political, gender and racial spaces in which they are agents of their own writing process, which uniquely allows them to describe events not from a singular but a multilayered point of view. According to Luis Valdez's *Las dos caras del patrón*, Corky Gonzales' "I am Joaquín," and Anzaldúa's *Borderlands / La Frontera*, it includes the voices of the oppressor but favors those of the oppressed. Certainly, these floating signifiers take into account factors such as parents' country of origin, time of migration or exile, place of residence in the United States, educational and economic status, race, gender, sexual orientation and class, among others. And the language of communication plays a fundamental role. Generally speaking, Hispanics traveling to or living in the United States, tend to foster the language and culture of their parent's country of origin. Those who were born or raised in the United States feel more comfortable in the language and culture of their adopted homeland, and they are mainly dominant English speakers. This is not to discount that there are families, communities or cities that foster the parents' language, and these authors are also bilingual. Most Latino authors write in English, some express themselves in Spanish and a few insist on using Spanglish or Caló.

The general tendency is to interchange the terms Hispanic and Latino, but there are discernable differences between the two. A more accurate representation takes into account their similarities, but also underscores their distinctions. Much of the present confusion is generated by bureaucrats and responds to how the U.S. government officials define race and Hispanics. Intentionally or not, government administrators, with little knowledge about the inner workings of culture, armed with their legislations, are producing or defining and redefining aspects of U.S. culture. For the consistency of record keeping and data presentation, the Office of Management and Budget Directive No. 14 mandates that the Census Bureau use four race categories—white, black, American Indian and Alaska Native, and Asian and Pacific Islander—and two ethnic categories: Hispanic and non-Hispanic. Combined, they produce eight ethnic-race categories. So, according to the Census Bureau Hispanics can be white, black, American Indian and Alaskan Native, and Asian and Pacific Islander. If we accept these categorizations, most Hispanics are whites, fewer are blacks and an even smaller number are American Indian and Asian. Of course, the Census does not take into account the mixture that exists in many Spanish-speaking countries, how race is determined in the country of origin and impacts the statistical compilation, how some Hispanics and Latinos identify with African American culture, and how some even prefer to consider themselves more African Americans rather than Hispanic, perhaps knowing that some white Hispanics can also be racist. The census does not consider that some Hispanic Amerindians (or American Indians) do not speak Spanish, which for them is a foreign language imposed upon them by those who continue to speak the language and practice the culture of the imperial power, Spain, which subjugated their people. And if they are classified as non-Hispanic Amerindians, are we not erasing important distinctions between them and the Native American population of the United States?

In a society in which whites are more successful than blacks, it is much easier for blacks, mulattos or mestizos to pass for or even become "white" on paper. However, after the Black Power Movement of the decade of the sixties, many mulattos and mestizos, who supported the Civil Rights and Black Power movements, considered themselves black. The categories are not stable, and they fluctuate. As I mentioned, someone who is mulatto or mestizo in a Hispanic country can also be white in the United States. Or someone of the same racial mixture may be drawn to identifying himself as black. Finally, the Census Bureau does not make any distinction between Hispanics and Latinos, and assumes that Latinos will embrace the Hispanic terminology, when in fact Afro-Latinos are more inclined to seek refuge among African Americans. The Bureau neither takes into consideration the increasingly popular term Raza used by Latinos in the Southwest, which tends to be inclusive and provides unity to the many self-identified categories, such as Chicanos/as, gays, queers, lesbians of color, transgender, etc. The surveys favor Hispanics over Latinos, even though a large portion of the English-speaking Hispanic community prefers the term Latino. I remember as a child growing up in New York City, the operative classifications at that time were white, black (probably negro) and Puerto Rican, as if the latter were also a race. I never knew how to identify myself since I was black, white and spoke Spanish but was not Puerto Rican, though I identified with Puerto Rican culture and politics. And where would I situate my Chinese heritage? Should I have ignored it? Administrators, who do not have a clear sense of how culture develops, impose a particular and narrow understanding of culture on the rest of the population. For indeed Latino culture and identity are not singular but plural.

The Hispanic print culture in the United States of the nineteenth century provides important clues. Exiles seeking freedom in the Untied States wrote back to their home country to combat the ideology of the governing power, but also responded to the needs of the Cuban community in the adopted homeland. This was the case with Félix Varela's *El Habanero*, published in Philadelphia (1824-1826), which supported Cuban independence from Spain, and circulated clandestinely in the island. Valera and *El Habanero* were not an isolated event; there was also *El Mensajero Semanal* and *El Mercurio de Nueva York*, both published in New York in 1828. Indeed, New York became a center for the development of exile print media that attempted to influence the political discourse both home and abroad. In Cuba, Cirilo Villaverde contributed to New York's *La Verdad* (1848-185?), which promoted U.S. annexation of Cuba. In exile in the United States, he and Manuel Antonio Marino published the bilingual *El Independiente: Órgano de la Democracia Cubana* in New Orleans; Villaverde also wrote anonymously for New York's *La Voz de la América: Órgano Político de las Repúblicas Hispano-americanas y de las Antillas Españolas* (1865-1867), *La Ilustración American* (1866-1870) and *El Espejo* (1873-1893), as well as others from cities like New Orleans, Tampa and Philadelphia, all expressing a perspective censored by the Spanish Courts in Cuba and Puerto Rico.

Not all Cubans in exile shared the same goals. While *La Verdad* supported the U.S. purchase of Cuba and expeditions into countries south of the U.S. border, *El Mulato* (1854-?), founded by Carlos de Colins, Lorenzo Alló and Juan Clemente Zenea, proposed independence with the emancipation of slaves. It is ironic, as Nicolás Kanellos points out, that the editorial exchanges between the two papers questioned whether freedom could be obtained in a country that denies liberty to all. *La Voz de América*, under the direction of Cuban Juan Manuel Macías and Puerto Rican José Bassora, promoted a united front that gathered all the various political positions: the slave holder, the freedman and the slave, and encouraged them to fight the Spanish colonial power.

Hispanics in the United States use a national term and a broader one as a way of addressing a community with a common language and similar cultures, in a country that has resisted their integration into mainstream society. This position is peculiar since Hispanics, like Mexicans, Cubans and Puerto Ricans, have been a part of U.S. history, politics and culture since the beginning of the nineteenth century, when the United States acquired Florida, occupied Cuba, Puerto Rico, Texas and the southwestern part of the expanding nation state. In the early U.S. Spanish-speaking publications, writers desiring to address more than a singular national identity, considered

Hispano an appropriate term to bring together groups that sought common linguistic, political and cultural links with other Spanish-speaking nationals. The Cuban José Martí envisioned the concept of *Nuestra América* as an oppositional space within his country of residence. Martí was a member of the club Las Dos Antillas (1892-1898), a political organization whose objective was to liberate both Cuba and Puerto Rico from Spain. This was the same club to which the Afro-Puerto Rican Arturo Alfonso Schomberg belonged. Martí and the Puerto Rican Arturo Pachín Marín were members of the Cuban Liberation Army. They resided in the United States and both met untimely deaths fighting to free Cuba from the Spanish Crown.

A perfunctory reading of Kanellos and Martell's *Hispanic Periodicals in the United States, Origins to 1960: A Brief History and Comprehensive Bibliography* shows that of the more than 1,700 records contained in the book, the most common identity is one that addresses a particular nationality, whether it is Cuban, Mexican, Puerto Rican, Chilean or other. However, the preferred nomenclature when referring to *Hispanos* (Hispanics) in the early publications in Spanish is Hispano-Americano (Spanish American) or Hispano-América (Spanish America), used in newspapers like *El Correo Hispano-Americano* (1868) of New York; *Hispano-América* (1917-1934) of San Francisco; *El Hispano-Americano* (1893) of El Paso, Texas; *El Hispano-Americano* (1890-1920) of Las Vegas, New Mexico; *El Hispano-Americano* (1909-19uu) of Mora, New Mexico; *El Hispano-Americano* (1905-19uu) of Roy, New Mexico; *El Hispano-Americano* (1913) of Belen, New Mexico; *El Hispano-Americano* (1914-1937) of San Diego; and *El Hispano-Americano* (1891-1uuu) of Socorro, New Mexico. All were published in Spanish except for those in Mora, Roy and San Diego; they were released in Spanish and English. There is also *Cultura Hispánica* of New York (1926-19uu), listed as a Spanish-language monthly publication. In this and other variants, *Hispano* refers to the Spanish language and traditions, and Hispano Americano to those same customs present in Spanish or Hispanic America; and they were meant to address the needs of a Spanish-speaking population in the city of origin.

In the twentieth century the word Latino or Latin appears as a reference to Latin America but more appropriately to the journal *Latino-Americano* in Alice, Texas (1933-19uu); in El Paso, Texas (1891); in New Orleans (1930-19uu); and *Latinoamericano* in Phoenix (1934-19uu), all in Spanish-language publications. However, the term Latino is present in *La Gaceta* (1922-present) of Tampa, but here more as a reference to the languages derived from Latin, which is the case of Italian. Also *El Heraldo Latino* of New York (1923-19uu) promoted an international scope in Spanish with respect to *Latino América* (Latin America).

In recent years, the term Hispanic is used to classify an overwhelming number of people from Spanish America and the Caribbean moving north to their new home. However, these newly arrived immigrants or exiles do not consider themselves to be Hispanics. Rather, they are Cubans, Colombians, Venezuelans or Nicaraguans with their own distinct national identities. As new arrivals, they are bound to identify with their country of origin, though many U.S. citizens erase the new immigrant's national identity and classify them as Hispanics. With time, and awareness of the political, cultural, racial and economic conditions of Spanish-speakers in the United States, these foreign nationals tend to accept a Hispanic identity. Under Ramón La Villa, the New York weekly publication *Gráfico* (1927) publicized injustices committed against Hispanics and was subtitled *"Semanario defensor de la Raza Hispana"* (weekly defender of the Hispanic race); under Adolfo Rodrígues, it was known as *"Defensa de la Colonia Hispano Americana"* (defense of the Hispanic-American community); and under Bernardo Vega, it was subtitled *"Semanario Defensor de la Raza"* (weekly defender of the race), which recalls the original subtitle but dropped the word *Hispana* to highlight the concept of race. Schomburg, Evelio Grillo and Piri Thomas, among other dark-skinned Puerto Ricans, Cubans, Dominicans and Hispanics like Panamanians, also identify with African Americans and their culture.

All Hispanics have been grouped into the same category because they speak the same Spanish language, but there may be other reasons as well. Since there are many different countries in Spanish America, for a U.S. citizen who insists on an insular vision of the nation, it is easier to classify all Spanish-speaking "foreigners" as Hispanics, rather than to distinguish between each national identity, something that school children in Spain or Latin America learn early in school. Yet there may be other reasons. Someone from Europe is identified by his national origin, French, German, Russian, etcetera. But Hispanic becomes a catchall word that erases difference and is used to identify Spanish-speaking foreigners or immigrants, even though many are citizens of the United States. This type of classification also fosters an insular U.S. identity. A problem arises when Spanish- and English-speakers use the same word but with different meanings and partake in the same conversation; oftentimes the speaker uses the term within a particular frame of reference and the listener interprets the same word, which is also spelled the same way in the other language, but understands it in different cultural and historic contexts. Both use the word correctly but contextualize it differently.

As a U.S. term in English, Latino is of recent usage. As I have argued elsewhere, prior to its presence in the decade of the sixties, Latin was another popular word employed to identify people of Spanish or Spanish-

American heritage, but it did not pertain to people of Portuguese, French or Italian descent, as the language Latin would denote in Spanish and English. For example, Latin (as in Latin Jazz or Latin Tinge or Latin Thing) was used to refer to Latin or Caribbean sounds during the Big Band era in which many Hispanic or Latin (or Latino) musicians began to enter the mainstream.

Indeed, Latin (Cuban) sounds had become popular with the first recordings of RCA Victor and Columbia records, featuring the magical sounds of the Son, as performed by the Sexteto Habanero and the Septeto Ignacio Piñeiro. These were the sounds that the Cuban Liberation Army gathered from the eastern mountains of Cuba and played in Havana, as Miguel Matamoro's unforgettable "Son de la loma" ("Son of the mountain") describes so eloquently. Later, U.S. citizens traveling to Cuba after the Spanish-American War discovered the same melodies. Shortly thereafter, these and other musical compositions made their way onto the mainland, where they were welcomed by both Hispanic and mainstream audiences. Hispanic and Latin musicians in the United States popularized them. So, Moisés Simon's "El manisero" ("The Peanut Vendor"), Chano Pozo's "Manteca" ("Lard"), a contribution to Dizzy Gillepsie's band, Desi Arnarz performances on the *I Love Lucy Show*, Pérez Prado's Mambo, as well as Xaviour Cugart's music to Bing Crosby and Bob Hope movies, moved rapidly across the nations soundscape. But if these musicians responded to the Hispanic with Latin music, other musicians would justify the traditional use of the term Latin, when taking into account the music of Carmen Miranda, and composer Antonio Carlos Jobim, and other Brazilian musical traditions in vogue. Perhaps for this reason the Latin was also appropriated by Hispanics who felt more comfortable in their adopted homeland than in the culture of their parents' country of origin, in particular those living in the northeast.

In U.S. print culture, Latino does not appear until much later. After *El Amigo del Hogar* (Friend of the home, Indiana Harbor, 1925) ceased publication, it was republished some twenty-five years later as *The Latin Times* (1956), mainly as a newspaper for English readers, in support of the Mexican American and Puerto Rican communities of East Chicago. The transition between Latin and Latino is evident in Pedro Pietri's "Puerto Rican Obituary," about the deaths of Juan, Miguel, Milagros, Olga and Manuel. Toward the end of the poem, when referring to the positive aspects of Puerto Rico and Puerto Rican identity, the poetic voice exclaims:

If only they
had turned off the televisions
If only they

had used the white supremacy bibles
for toilet paper purpose
and make their *latin* souls
the only religion of their race (emphasis added)

The poem was well known in the New York City of the sixties, many years before it was published in *Palante: The Young Lords Party*, in 1971. In subsequent editions of the poem, Pietri changed "latin" for "latino."

As I have also argued, Latino is also a Spanglish word; it is formed from the popular English word Latin. The word is borrowed from the English and pronounced in Spanish with a final "o" to produce the hybrid Latino, which coincides with the spelling of the Spanish *latino* (whose vowel sounds are much fuller) but is pronounced not with a Spanish but with an English intonation.

There was indeed a Hispanic or Latino community that was influenced by U.S. politics and culture. Some Mexican-American practices came to the attention of a mainstream audience with the Zoot Suiters, whose customs and traditions received underserved publicity during the Los Angeles riots of the 1940s. Many were discriminated against for adopting their own music, manners of speaking, dancing and dressing, characterized by their baggy clothing. The riots began with the Sleepy Lagoon incident of 1942, when the death of José Díaz was blamed on Hank Leyva and other innocent Mexican Americans identified as Pachucos, or gang members. The War Production Board banned the suits, which it deemed extravagant in times of rationing, and even unpatriotic. After the trial in which the Pachucos were found guilty, other incidents erupted between them and Military servicemen, who went on a rampage attacking Mexican Americans, but also African Americans and Filipinos. The police went on the attack, arresting as many as 600 Mexican Americans but no sailor or military personnel was detained. Eventually, the guilty charge was overturned, but the attacks on the Zoot Suiters spread to other cities like New York, Philadelphia and Detroit. In the *Labyrinth of Solitude*, Nobel Laureate Octavio Paz describes the Pachucos as outsiders of both Mexican and U.S. mainstream societies. For Paz, the visitor who traveled throughout the United States for two years, the Pachuco was a symbol of resistance and rejected access to white dominant culture. The Pachucos, who were kept at the margins of mainstream society, created a hybrid space for the expression of a new and different culture that also drew on both Mexican and American traditions. Other groups that followed pressed for their own culture and identity, and articulated a political position that supported their best interests. The most prominent was the Chicano Movement of the 1960s, though Chicanas also demanded a space to recount their own Mexican-American experiences. In New York, the Young Lords Party supported the Puerto Rican and Latino communities of that metropolitan city.

For the purpose of the present anthology, Latino more aptly conveys in a generalized manner the experiences of people of Hispanic descent, who feel more comfortable interacting with the culture and language of their adopted homeland than that of the Hispanic one known to their parents; the latter one, I should add is not forgotten and continues to play an important role in their everyday lives. Many Latinos attempt to negotiate a hybrid identity or in betweenness that incorporates at least two cultures and more, especially if you take into account African American and Amerindian mores. And if we were guided by the definitions provided by the Census, they also include Hispanics and Latinos of Asian descent.

As U.S. terms, Hispanic and Latino became clearer to me when researching "Latino Caribbean Literature" for the *Cambridge History of Latin American Literature*, which became the groundwork for my *Dance Between Two Cultures*. With these and other studies, I observed a distinct difference between the literature of authors writing from their Spanish-speaking country of origin, authors writing in Spanish from abroad in the United States and authors writing in English from the United States. From the perspective of the literature I read, there was a close thematic and linguistic association between authors writing in Spanish, whether they lived in their country of origin or in the United States. This was certainly the case of Cubans living in the United States of the nineteenth century, who became foundational writers of Cuba's national literature, as was the case with the romantic poet José María Heredia, the novelist Cirilo Villaverde and the poet and essayist hero José Martí; all were authors who wrote about their country, Cuba, from the society of the country in which they resided, the United States. It is inconceivable to me how the context of the society can be dismissed from literary works, as many critics have done when considering them foundational writers of their own country's national literature. I continue to argue that it is indispensible to read the society from which they wrote as a necessary texture layer of their works. Be that as it may, this literature is distinct from those authors who feel more at home writing in English and incorporate topics about their parents' country of origin from a different linguistic referent. Jesús Colón's *Puerto Rican in New York and Other Stories*, Piri Thomas' *Down These Mean Streets* and Evelio Grillo's *Black Cuban, Black American: A Memoir* incorporate the U.S. cultural landscape into their writings. These Latinos are those born or raised and educated in the United States, and have had to negotiate the pressures exerted on them by the culture of their adopted country, which has also become theirs. While there are Hispanic writers who incorporate the culture of the country of residence into their Spanish works, for Latino authors the mainland culture becomes an inherent characteristic of their works.

Some Hispanic and Latino similarities do not mean that all Hispanics and Latinos are alike. On the contrary, the differences are as important—and in some cases more important—than their similarities, even among those who come from the same country. For example, while some may argue that all Cubans are alike, there are noteworthy differences between Cubans who traveled to and live in United States before Castro's rise to power, and exiles fleeing the communist island. There are also important distinctions between those who left with the first wave of exiles (1959-1961) and those who sought freedom during the Mariel Boatlift (1980), and between the latter and rafters during the turn of the century. To be certain, many Cuban exiles leaving through a second country, such as Mexico or Spain, whether they stay or use it as a stepping-stone to enter the United States do not identify with the stereotypical Miami Cubans. There are even Miami Cubans who do not support other Miami Cubans, who favor the U.S. boycott of the island. This position became evident during the Elián González affair of 2000. Though some may be critical of the Castro government, they welcome a dialogue between the two neighboring countries. More likely than not, they may even be willing to return to the island and support the family they left behind.

Important distinctions are determined by the exile period but also by the city or place of residence, even when departing during the same period. There are dissimilarities between Cubans who reside in Miami and those who live in New York City or even Chicago or any other Midwestern or west coast cities. The early Miami Cubans maintain a fixed identity in opposition to the Castro government, some believing they would soon return to the island. However, those living in New York participate in a broader identity and community that include Cubans who lived in New York prior to the Revolution, but also other Hispanics, in their majority Puerto Ricans, Dominicans and African Americans.

Similarly, there are differences between Puerto Ricans who left the island after receiving citizenship in 1917 and peasants of modest means from the interior who departed after Operation Bootstrap in the late forties and early fifties, between them and the better educated and more affluent travelers, who enrolled in U.S. undergraduate and postgraduate degrees. And then, there are those Afro-Latinos who tend to identify with their national group but have also forged a strong link with the African American community.

There are differences between Mexican Americans who made their way north after the turn of the twentieth century and those who arrived during César Chávez's unionization of farm workers in the decade of the sixties and seventies, and between them and those Mexican Americans who live in states like New Mexico, Arizona and Colorado and trace their descendants to the time they lived in Mexico, that is before the signing of the Treaty of Guadalupe Hidalgo of 1848. There are differences between Chicanos living in Los Angeles, and those living in other cities across the U.S. borderland, like El Paso, between them and those living in rural communities, and other Central Americans residing in the same cities.

Though the term Latino refers to specific groups, it also defies any type of categorization, as I outlined in my essay for *The Other Latin@*, eds. Blas Falconer and Lorraine López. In "Latino Identity and the Desiring Machine," I apply the flows and interruptions proposed by Deleuze and Guattari's *Anti-Oedipus* to the majority groups who compose the Latino experience: Chicanos, Cuban Americans, Dominican Americans and Mainland Puerto Ricans. But I also allude to other combinations that link the prominent groups to new ones, such as Guatemalans, Panamanians and Colombians to name a few, and the latter to even those who have little Hispanic or Latino ancestry or none at all, but who have tangential connections to Latinos. I am referring to non-Latinos who grew up in Latino neighborhoods, accept Latino culture or support Latino racial and gender politics. These "non-Latinos" are also Latinos, and they provide new and groundbreaking ways of imagining Latinos and the Latino experience. With time, Peruvians or Chileans and Spaniards, who become involved in political, economic, racial, gender and social issues in the culture of their adopted homeland, they can also become Latinos, just as Anglo Americans can, and anyone else, including Asians. Latinos defy a single categorization, and propose identity as multiple, for one can be Latino, Hispanic, Chicano/a, of European, African, Asian and Amerindian descent.

II*

Latino writers are at the forefront of a new literature that is transnational, transcultural, multilingual, multiracial and hemispheric, to mention a few categories that come to mind. The present anthology gathers contributions of Latino poets from the four largest Hispanic and Latino groups resid-

---

*Most but not all poems referenced in the introduction are included in the anthology.

ing in the United States: Chicanos/as, Cuban Americans, Dominican Americans and Mainland Puerto Ricans. I have chosen to highlight the historical and cultural contexts that reflect the lives of those whose continuous contributions can be traced from the mid-nineteenth and early twentieth centuries, when the United States moved westward and became a two ocean power, securing its borders with Mexico to the south, and to the Caribbean islands to the southeast, or to the Caribbean floating borderlands. History justifies this selection since these groups had become an integral part of the present definition of the United States. Though history is important, the selection builds on the past and focuses on the present. It provides a snapshot of what we can now proclaim to be a Latino literary Boom.

Hispanics and Latinos are a significant economic, political, cultural and linguistic group and are the largest "minority" in the United States. The United States has the second largest Spanish-speaking population in the world; it is more numerous than Spain, Argentina or Venezuela and is only second to Mexico. According to the 2010 Census, of the four mentioned groups, Mexican Americans make up 63% or 31.8 million of the Hispanic and Latino populations, while Puerto Ricans comprise 4.6%, Cubans 1.8% and Dominicans 1.4%. If I were to edit an anthology of poetry that reflects the percentages of Latinos, the reader would be presented with a work of mainly Chicano poetry, with some representation of other groups. However, there are significant Cuban American, Puerto Rican American and Dominican American writers, though Dominicans occupy the smallest section.

Language is indeed an important factor when assessing Latino poetry. Latino writers feel more at ease writing in English than in Spanish, but the second generation of Cuban American writers, or the 1.5 generation, as proposed by Gustavo Pérez Firmat's *Life on the Hyphen*—whose parents maintained Cuban culture alive, believing that they would soon return to the island—also write in Spanish. Spanish also becomes a medium of expression for Dominican writers who travel regularly to their parent's country and nurture their Spanish, and Chicana/os who frequently cross the U.S. Mexican border and/or live in the borderlands.

Other poets write about their shifting linguistic skills or competency, as they move from one culture and language referent to another, and have continued to do so many years after their arrival in the United States. Such is the case with Pat Mora's "Elena," when recognizing at the outset of her poem that "My Spanish isn't enough." She proceeds to explain how her Spanish once was sufficient, and how her children were fluent in Spanish when living in Mexico. But as high school students in the United States, her children feel more at ease speaking English. These cultural and linguistic shifts isolate her from them and her drunken husband, who also wants the speaker to remain in her traditional place. Nevertheless, she continues to make the effort in the event her children need help. And she is successful since she writes her poem in English.

In preparing the anthology, I noted that "Elena," in its many Spanish and English manifestations, which include "Helena," is the most popular name used by Latino poets. In Franklin Gutiérrez's "Helena," the speaker observes an identity shift from the "Helena" of the Dominican Republic to "Helen" in the United States. If the first responded to the traditions of her culture of origin, the other one has forgotten her past, and has accepted an American boyfriend and way of life. The poem was written in Spanish and translated by Daisy Cocco De Filippis.

In "Bilingual Sestina," Julia Alvarez struggles with thinking in Spanish and writing in English:

Gladys, Rosario, Altagracia—the sounds of Spanish
wash over me like warm island waters as I say
your soothing names: a child again learning the *nombres*
of things you point to in the world before English
turned *sol, tierra, cielo, luna* to vocabulary works—
sun, earth, sky, moon. Language closed.

English is her dominant language, but it is insufficient to express Spanish words and ideas that do not mean the same in the adult culture. English sounds so mundane and ordinary in comparison to the melodic and beautiful images crafted by her childhood Spanish. The early names are associated with Gladys and the innocence of her childhood:

Gladys, I summon you back by saying your *nombre*.
Open up again the house of slated windows closed
since childhood, where *palabras* left behind for English
stand dusty and awkward in neglected Spanish.
Rosario, muse of *el patio*, sing in me and through me say
that world again, begin first with those first words

For Alvarez language is associated with that early, primordial stage, connected to Spanish, which she attempts to recapture as an adult and express in English, but with the same difficulty experienced by anyone attempting to uncover the past.

For Tato Laviera, neither language by itself is sufficient to express the cultural hybrid spaces he occupies. Rather, both languages are necessary to communicate the complexity of the Latino experience in an urban environment, which also includes social and educational variables. Not all immigrants or exiles held privileged positions in their countries of origin. In fact, most who migrated did so for economic reasons, hoping to better their situation in the adopted country, even though they romanticized the country of origin, often forgetting the reasons for leaving. Laviera's "melao" points to a cyclical structure that persists both at home and abroad. Back in Santurce, Melao grew up "speaking spanish streets." Twenty years later, at the age of twenty-nine, he speaks "Santurce spanish streets / en español." However, his son answers "in black american soul english / talk with native sounds / and primitive urban salsa beats." Melao remembers that back home he was criticized for his "arrabal black spanish," just as his son is criticized in certain circles for his speech. But regardless of what any one says, whether he is dominant in Spanish or English, Melao and Melanito are proud of the mixture of Spanglish, which they accept.

In "my graduation speech," Laviera confesses not having learned to speak any one language correctly: "hablo lo inglés matao / hablo lo español matao / no sé leer ninguno bien / so it is, Spanglish to matao / what I digo / ¡ay, virgen, yo no sé hablar!" The poetic voice is eloquent in his expression, but he struggles to fit into a mold that obligates him to express himself in a standard language, which he and many traditional scholars associate with a proper education. But his hybrid language allows him to articulate different and more complete expressions.

José Antonio Burciaga also recognizes the same multicultural and multilingual perspective voiced by Laviera, except in Burciaga's case it applies to his particular social-linguistic and geographic context:

Español entre inglés
entre náhuatl, entre caló.
¡Qué locura!
Mi mente en espiral asciende a las nubes
bien suave siento cuatro lenguas en mi boca.
Sueños torcidos caen
y siento una xóchitl brotar
de cuatro diferentes vidas.

For him, the four lives are represented by four distinct languages with their own culture: Náhuatl, English, Spanish and Caló.

Margarita Cota-Cárdenas also experiences a crisis of identity in which she embraces her plural self with humor: "chicana macana," "gringa marrana," "mera gabacha," "pocha biscocha," "india mocha." She is U.S. American, White, Mexican living in the United States and Amerindian.

Gustavo Pérez Firmat writes from a different perspective. He knows who he is, but everyone else does not; they consistently change his identity and mispronounce his name: Gustazo Perez, Gustavio Penley, Gary Porris, Gus Perry, Gustaf Pirey. He is Gustavo Pérez but he has acquired multiple identities.

Language is a concern among Latino writers, but there are other topics that affect their lives as well. Many are the product of some type of uprooting, whether it is defined by exile or migration. We saw how Mora's and Laviera's poems highlight a geographic displacement, in one case from Mexico, and the other from Puerto Rico, to the United States, where they experience a different culture. Though they may have traveled for economic opportunities, the children were not asked or consulted with the decision made, and in this respect their experiences can mimic those of the children of political exiles. This idea is conveyed in *Poems of Exile and Other Concerns*, which gathers poems by Dominican American writers who, with the exception of Alvarez, migrated after the fall of Trujillo, the dictator of the Dominican Republic from 1930-1961. Their migratory experience is an exile of sorts. Alvarez left her parents' country of origin as an exile, as she conveys it in her poem whose title denotes the family condition. "Exile" captures the feelings of her childhood the night her father and family escaped from the Dominican Republic, a topic first discussed in *How the García Girls Lost Their Accents*. In the poem the reader is exposed to the mystery and secrecy surrounding this event, masked as a trip to the beach. The speaker swimming in the ocean replaces the actual flight, waiting in a deserted airport until dawn, when the plane arrived to take them to freedom. What follows is their transformative life in the United States, as they attempt to absorb and adjust to their new surroundings, described by the activities of a lively city: escalators, department stores and people with "blond hair and blue eyes." The city is a sharp contrast to the lonely evening before the family became exiles. In this other environment, the beach scene takes place behind a department store window; it is artificial and distant from the one familiar to them. Though the poem ends with an uncertain note about their future, it is not difficult to understand that they had to flee the country to survive, but the old culture and memories will always remain in their hearts.

While Alvarez's poem communicates nostalgia of the past, Cuban writers are obsessed, rightly so, with their exile condition. Exile becomes a concern for Ricardo Pau-Llosa. In "Exile," like in Alvarez's poem, Pau-Llosa compares the present with the past; birds that fly in circles are juxtaposed to those that fly in a straight line. The present is devout of meaning while an earlier time is full of life and significance. The harmony of his childhood past, that is, between man and nature, and man and woman, and man and poetry, is absent in the present. But the lost past can only be recovered through writing. The "infernal" present creates the need to write about the past.

Pablo Medina is also haunted by his past. In "The Exile," the speaker again returns to a place of origin, to an abandoned house and yard, without people, where time has stood still. The past is associated with trees, sugarcane fields, smokehouse and a voice emanating form the river asking for communion with the speaker. The river is contrasted with the stagnant water from the well, and the sound of the rocks as they splash at the bottom, never to be recovered. At the end, the poet closes the gate behind him and recognizes that his memories belong in the past. However, it is important for the poetic voice to visit or revisit the past in order for him to move forward.

Elías Miguel Muñoz's poem about exile is entitled "Returning," a title that could also be applicable to the exile poems written by Alvarez, Pau-Llosa and Medina. Muñoz recalls a moment before exile, full of childhood impressions about apples and chewing gum, rather than the traditional rice and beans, which are placed to one side. The past is also associated with the eternal summer, dark skin and *quimbumbia* and *yuca*, traditional Cuban foods associated with the African and Ameridian cultures, respectively, and the folkloric clothing of conga players. Where if the other poets looked to the past with nostalgia, Muñoz wants to flee from the past, which offers no consolation for him. He already knew he had to abandon the past in order to accept the future. For him, there is nothing to return to. The freedom of chewing away until we had no teeth, and speaking of things lost or never possessed, also includes the idea of dreaming about returning. It is the constant leaving and returning that marks this exile's experience.

In Richard Blanco's "America," the family maintained Cuban culture alive by eating roast pork on every holiday; but as their stay became longer, he was exposed to U.S. culture, and one day, in 1976, the family prepared turkey for Thanksgiving. He then came to the realization that his life indeed had changed. After everyone left, and the furniture had been returned to its place:

In the warm and appropriate
of my room that night

I hung like a chrysalis
realizing I lived in a country
I didn't know,
waiting for a home
I never knew, and a name to give myself.

The poetic voice understands that the past is closed off to him. Now he is faced with integrating himself into the life and culture of his adopted homeland.

José Kozer looks at exile from a different perspective. For Kozer, exile is another step in a broader concept he calls "Diaspora." In this poem, the speaker's father, "a dusty Jew," goes about his routine of bringing a loaf of bread to the house, an act that perhaps he or his own father and his father repeated in a different country before arriving in Cuba, and will continue to repeat when he leaves the island for the new country of residence.

Puerto Rican writers have attempted to return to their native Puerto Rico, a space they envisioned as a paradise of sorts. This idea is evident in Pedro Pietri's "Puerto Rican Obituary," which describes the harsh U.S. environment that rejects Puerto Ricans and Puerto Rican culture, and proposes a return to Puerto Rican island culture and identity. Pietri concludes his poem with the following stanza.

Juan, Miguel, Milagros, Olga, Manuel
will right now be doing their own thing
where beautiful people sing
and dance and work together
where the wind is a stranger
to miserable weather conditions
where you do not need a dictionary
to communicate with your people
Aquí Se Habla Español all the time
Aquí you salute your flag first
Aquí there are no dial soap commercials
Aquí everybody smells good
Aquí tv dinners do not have a future
Aquí the men and women admire desire
And never get tired of each other
Aquí Qué Paso Power is what's happening
Aquí to be called negrito
Means to be called LOVE

For Pietri, the United States represents and produces death, a word that is repeated more than thirty times. A return to Puerto Rico signifies redemption, expressed by the Spanish word "Aquí" reiterated eight times at the end of the poem.

For others, the past has been closed to them by island culture that considers them foreigners in their own land. They, for example, are accused of not speaking proper Spanish and of being contaminated by U.S. culture, though U.S. culture is also present on the island. Mariposa in "Ode to the DiaspoRican" highlights the conflict of being Puerto Rican in the United States:

> Some people say that I'm not the real thing
> Boricua, that is
> cuz I wasn't born on the enchanted island
> cuz I was born on the mainland
> north of Spanish Harlem
> cuz I was born in the Bronx . . .
> some people think that I'm not bonafide
> cuz my playground was a concrete jungle
> cuz my Rio Grande de Loiza was the Bronx River
> cuz my Fajardo was City Island
> my Luquillo, Orchard Beach
> and summer nights were filled with city noises
> instead of coquís
> and Puerto Rico
> was just some paradise
> that we only saw in pictures.

Mariposa ends her poem by enlightening readers with the lines suggesting that Puerto Rican "is a state of mind / a state of heart", thus referring to the Puerto Rican saying: "Tengo a Puerto Rico en mi corazón" (Puerto Rico is in my heart), which is where it really matters.

Writers like Miguel Piñero and Judith Ortiz Cofer have distanced themselves from the past and have embraced their present in the United States, as evident with Medina and Muñoz. In Piñero's case, in "A Lower East Side Poem," he prefers to be with the drug addicts, prostitutes and other criminals of the Lower East Side. If New York City or the Lower East Side is Hell and Puerto Rico is Paradise, then Piñero prefers to be in Hell. When he died, he did not want to receive a proper burial in Puerto Rico or in the Long Island Cemetery, but preferred his ashes to be scattered throughout the Lower East Side. Piñero expressed a similar concern about

Puerto Rico in "This Is Not the Place Where I Was Born," thus rejecting Puerto Rico as a place of origin.

Ortiz Cofer's "The Idea of Islands" is composed as an interview in which the speaker refers to Puerto Rico and the Caribbean as her place of birth; she also talks about Atlanta, which for her has become a port city. When asked about her place of birth, the poetic voice first takes us to Atlanta and then to her island. Ortiz Cofer objects to a Paradise, where life was simpler and food was abundant, ". . . Fruit could be plucked / from trees languishing under the weight / of their own fecundity. The thick sea / spewed out fish that crawled into the pots" and everyone lived without worries. The speaker's island is the biblical Paradise on Earth. But unlike Adam and Eve, the poetic voice does not want to remain there; rather, she prefers to be rescued or escape. She is ambitious and does not want things to be handed to her nor does she have any desire to eat mangos three times a day. She does not have to be ejected from Paradise; on the contrary, she is ready to leave on her own. The speaker wants to distance herself from the past, and the present is her calling. She does not need the physical island because she possesses the metaphorical one, as she transforms Atlanta into an island image.

For Jimmy Santiago Baca, the return is not to another country but to a familiar space of his past, "Pinos Wells." In the present it is an abandoned pueblo, with crumbling adobe homes. His memories are like the pictures of the photo albums his grandmother shared with him on Saturday afternoons. The six o'clock mass, Lionel's hamburger stand, the alley behind Jack's Package Liquors, the telephone ringing on Walter street, the red tractors he watched in Santa Fe, the time his mother and father abandoned him, when he made love to Lolita, who when her father found out, slashed her wrist, and others, are vivid pictures of his memory album. But his journey to recover the past is also to understand the present, of redemption, a return to the origin, to earth and nature:

I have been lost from you Mother Earth.
No longer
does your language or rain wear away my thoughts,
nor your language of fresh morning air
wear away my bones.
But when I return, I will become your child again,
let your green alfalfa hands take me,
let your maíz roots plunge into me
and give myself to you again,
with the crane, the elm tree and the sun.

Chicanas/os express a generalized concern for the earth, whether the poems pertain to harvest, migrant workers or an appreciation for the land, as is conveyed in Ana Castillo's "Napa, California." The latter considers the person as a part of nature, who desires to interact with the land, and not exploit it. Lorna Dee Cervantes communicates a similar concern except that she uses a different historical and cultural context. In "Heritage," she attempts to access her Amerindian past. She travels to Oaxaca but her brown body and lack of the local language separates her from the town's people who call her Puta. Though she is taken aback by the response of the locals, she—as someone in the present—cannot or should not be blamed because "'Es la culpa de los antepasados,'" the fault of the ancestors. The past is physically and culturally inaccessible to her.

There is a sense of indignation by the way Latinos are treated in the adopted country. This idea is evident in Pedro Pietri's "Puerto Rican Obituary," where hard work in the country of residence is not enough for Puerto Ricans to obtain the American Dream. Rather, hard work only produces isolation, cultural destruction and physical and metaphorical deaths. Miguel Algarín describes it as a "Mongo Affair," Alusita, in "cornfields thaw out," points to "the beat-packing houses / back Mexicans—mojo's what they call us." The tradition of slaughtering beasts is compared to the stagnant life: "nothing much is different in this barrio / big foot and bigotry squatted," but optimism even if it is momentarily, still reigns. No voice is stronger than that of Gloria Anzaldúa's "El sonavabiche," a poem that describes the painful relationship between the men in uniform and the supervisors and the workers looking to make a living:

> So common a sight no one
> notices
> blood rushes to my face
> twelve years I'd sat on the memory
> the anger scorching me
> my throat so tight I can
> barely get the words out.

At the farm, the workers attempt to escape from the men in uniform, who hunt them with rifles, walkie-talkies, as if they were animals. The Chicano, who also controls the workers at the migrant camp north of Muncie, Indiana, is also a sonavabitche who exploits them "from sunup to dark— 15 hours sometimes. / *Como mulas los trabaja / no saben cómo hacer la perra.*" The farm workers are treated almost as slaves; they are not allowed to rest or pray on Sunday or write letters to their families, and receive half their wages because they have eaten the other half. They are transported across the country in crowded conditions like animals unable to relieve themselves. On payday, the sonavabiche calls the migra, who arrests them. The poetic voice, a woman, threatens the big man, is able to stare him down, demands two weeks of wages, including Saturdays and Sundays, fifteen hours a day, in return for her silence. Though she has no contacts in Washington, D.C., she uses her intelligence to effectively scare and get him to pay her. What the male workers were not able to accomplish, she as a woman, who has witness the mistreatment of workers for years, with a command of English, is able to defeat the big man.

Anzaldúa conveys her individuality; she attacks the sonavabiche, but she is also critical of her own culture, and establishes differentness from la Raza, her own people. In *"Cihuatlyotl*, Woman Alone," she becomes independent of her family and culture, which invaded her desire to be different. She has erected barriers, kicked and clawed, as pieces of her were being severed: ". . . And as I grew you hacked away / at the pieces of me that were different / attached your tentacles to my face and breasts / put a lock between my legs . . ." She had to separate herself from her past to survive and return to her true essence, to a past and a state before the imposition of cultural values that were antithetical to her core being: ". . . I remain who I am, multiple / and one of the herd, yet not of it." She is a part of the past, of the ancients, and is covered by the odor of the current headlines. She is who she is.

Abelardo "Lalo" Delgado is judgmental of his country of residence, in "Stupid America: and The Chicano Manifesto," in which America is personified and critical of poets who do not conform to a standard vision of literature. Though he recognizes that Chicanos are also gifted, he seems to agree with Stupid America that their talents will be lost unless they expressed them on paper.

Latinas are leading in defining the traditional Hispanic gender values associated with the old culture. As their male counterparts, they also have concerns about the life in the country of origin. However, in the adopted homeland, Latinas experience a sense of cultural and sexual liberation that separates them from those of their traditional counterparts. This change was evident in the Chicana platform during the heydays of the Chicano Movement and the Young Lords Party, when Latinas opposed the macho behavior of their comrades in arms and demanded to be treated with respect, as individuals, beyond their sexual and cultural roles. The change is not limited to Chicanas and Puerto Ricans, but becomes an inherent component in the lives of all Latinas.

Whereas Pablo Medina, Pau-Llosa and Muñoz must return to the past in order to come to terms with it, the women poets have already adopted to their new environment. Just like Ortiz Cofer chose Atlanta over the island of Puerto Rico, and even Nuyorican poets like Piñero and Laviera accept their adopted environment, Berta Sánchez-Bello embraces the city of Elizabeth, New Jersey, as permanence and another origin with new meanings: a pregnant blond, a would-be prostitute, five happy bums recovering from a hangover, women shop, men have no place to go, a fourteen-year-old Adonis jumping to the tracks, an ancient woman located on the third floor and Cuban workers never stop dreaming or swearing.

In Carolina Hospital's "Dear Tía," a poem written as a letter to her aunt in Cuba, the poetic voice explains why she does not write; it is not because she misses her voice, her smile or the pride the aunt felt when they called her "my mother." She can no longer feel her soft skin, her laughter and smell of her body; rather, she states: "I write because I cannot remember at all." The past, once origin, represented by the surrogate mother, has been closed to her, and the act of writing is a way of creating memories where memories no longer exist. Writing creates or invents a different type of memory. The poetic voice experiences pain, but the pain does not derive from the nostalgia for the past, in which the aunt had attained the status of the speaker's mother. The discomfort is caused by not experiencing the pain of remembering or forgetting. It comes from an absence of memory. The act of writing the poem is a means of remembering the past, not as origin, but as a (re)creation of it. The absence produces a void and thus launches the poetic voice into writing to satisfy something that cannot be filled. The past is a fabrication of the present.

For Magali Alabau, while her parents argue at midnight in a hotel how their lives have changed, the poetic voice is clear about the past: "Cuba is a trunk bound with straps, / full of the forbidden. / a box I don't open / because from it, one by one, emerges / evils." It is best to leave the past where it belongs because the present offers many more future possibilities.

Women living and writing in the new homeland experience a sense of freedom previously unknown in the Hispanic traditional culture. As a whole, they look to define a new role for Latinas. However, though Latinas are freer to express their ideas and feelings, some celebrate the fifteen-century Roman Lucrezia Borgia, and others the seventeenth-century Spanish colonial (Mexican) nun, Sor Juana Inés de la Cruz, as precursors, and pay tribute to them. Lucrezia Borgia, whose family had been associated with ruthless politics and sexual corruption, was married many times for political gain, and may have even had an incestuous relationship with one of her brothers. In Carlota Caufield's "Letter from Lucrezia Borgia to Her Confessor," the speaker express-es to her confessor her bodily desires. In Caufield's case, "My punishment now / is twentieth-century freedom." One can assume that traditional culture has molded the individual by assigning them roles that may or may not feel comfortable. Women have had to subject themselves to values promoted by patriarchal society. So the question becomes, how can freedom be a punish-ment? Freedom is a new concept for women familiar with old structures of society that has dictated a behavior familiar to them. But freedom—in some respects—knows no boundaries and mistakes can be easily made. If one believes in the pure concept of freedom, perhaps women will follow their hearts and fall into danger that could be considered a form of punishment. This is not to say that in traditional society women did not follow their hearts, but they were taught lessons that would help them avert some of the down-falls. With an idealized form of freedom, only experiences can be your guide. The other interpretation is that her punishment is freedom, therefore there is no "real" punishment, perhaps an acceptance or denial of responsibility, and this is due to the life women like Lucrezia Borgia lived, which allowed oth-ers to enjoy their freedom.

Sor Juana indeed is a symbol for women attempting to create their own paths, and Alicia Gaspar de Alba goes as far as celebrating her as the first feminist. In her "Sor Juana's Litany in the Subjunctive," she unveils the speaker's sexuality. Trapped in a physical and religious cell, the poetic "I" wants to rub herself against the Other and work toward the center of plea-sure, first by starting with the calf, then by laying her cheeks against his thigh, then by tasting "the bread, the blood, the salt / between your legs / as I taste mine." These images of desire are counter posed to those she wants to forget, in which the priest and the devil share common interests. In this version of Sor Juana's life, she wants to transform herself into a bee and free herself, for the other is more important than ". . . that black / cloth, that rosary, that crucifix—" because "nothing could save you / from my sting." The word or concept of salvation is relevant here as expressed in the next to the last line. Traditionally, you can be saved if you are pious. But in the poem salvation is not the issue, for salvation is a hindrance to anoth-er salvation, which is the unity between the poetic voice and her lover. The sting is her way of injecting him with what she also wants for herself.

In "Confessions," Gaspar de Alba is even harder on the hypocrisy of reli-gion and the priesthood; she knows that confessing her sins produce excite-ment in the priest who, after all, is a man. What the priest does is no differ-ent from what ordinary men or lesbians who rape women do. In her confession, she recounts the loss of her innocence to the priest as ". . . you slipped / unannounced, / quiet as Gabriel, / into that virgin / place between / my eleven-year-old thighs." As she confesses their sexual encounter, she transforms herself into the blood and body of Christ and invites him to partake of this holy sacrament, to eat and drink the body and blood of Christ:

> Come, Father, eat
> of this body, drink of this
> blood, as if the only memory
> left in our puckered history
> were curled under
> the tongue
> green seed
> sprouting planets.

The twentieth-century freedom to which Caufield refers takes other forms of sexual expressivity. In "for tito," Sandra María Esteves celebrates his "machoness," as she repeats "macho machete," "macho paciencia" and "macho soledad," which create a union between the two bodies described as "growing and pounding / with all the desire you're your drum / pounding with my womb / planting seeds in the night." The "you" and the "I" produce a "we" of unity and communion between tito and the poetic voice: "together / we reap mystical surgarcane in the ghetto / where all the palm trees grow ripe / and rich with coconut milk." The poem can be read as a unity by means of the male symbol.

Esteves, however, is better known for redefining the role of the Puerto Rican woman in two poems, "My Name Is María Christina" and "So Your Name Is Not María Cristina." In the first poem, María Christina combines the qualities of the Virgin Mary and is a female Christ figure; she comes from humble origins, understands the traditions of her people, but is not accepting of all of them: she does not tease the men (perhaps like tito of the above mentioned poem), does not sleep with her brothers and cousins, and does not poison them. However, she is respectful of them and is also a teacher. Though she does not complain about her traditional role, she cooks, nurses the children and determines their values; she says "I am the mother of a new age of warriors." Above all, she teaches, a word that is repeated three times in the sixth stanza, and five times in an eight-stanza poem.

The second poem, "So Your Name Isn't María Cristina," is a poetic answer to Luz María Umpierre's "Response," which is critical of Esteves' first poem. In the second one, Esteves purports to hold some traditional values, and admits that the poetic voice of the early poem was young and full of contradictions. The first María was näive, just beginning her metamorphosis, struggling for explanations, searching for her purpose, discovering new meanings. But the present María has changed; she is older, considers Umpierre as an older sister and understands the long and arduous road taken by her fellow Puerto Rican. Though María claims to have grown and changed with Umpierre's help, there is a tone of gratitude but also defiance in upholding the old values of the earlier poem: "Now she can build her own house / as well as sew, cook, wash, have babies, / even if her name hasn't changed." This other María is a mixture of the old and the new as she expresses in the next to the last stanza of the poem by repeating two lines from the above mentioned stanza: "Now she can build her own house, / even though her name hasn't changed." And she ends with "Thank God, / it was a good thing you were around."

Alina Galliano speaks about her sexuality in relation to the other. Unlike Esteves, who refers to teaching a community, Galliano is concerned with the self. In "VIII" she describes the relationship between the "I" and the "you," in which the other is not always a male. Her poem begins with "You crawl / my throat," and ends with "in case / I ever need you," which shows a resounding emergence of the poetic "I" in firm control of the "you." Galliano's poem allows for more than one interpretation. In the first, the "you" is a real person with whom the poetic voice has an intimate relationship. She is not totally satisfied with this person and invents him into being something he is not, but can meet her sexual needs. The "you" also can be an object or a person treated like an object. The poetic voice describes how she keeps the "you" in the cabinets or in other locations, ready for her use. The inability to identify the other suggests that the "you" is not really important. The focus of the poem is the "I" and her needs. Regardless, the poetic voice relies on her imagination to create or invent a situation that will give her the most pleasure, proposing that her needs could not be satisfied in her current world, only in her imagination.

In Galliano's "VIII" the "you" is a woman to whom the poetic "I" speaks in the third person. At the beginning of the poem the speaker is moved by the other's voice, described as "her shattered / mirrored voice." The broken image refers to the sharpness of the tone and words, which may damage, but also to the reflexive properties of each of the fragmented pieces, in which the speaker can recognize parts of herself. The poetic "I" vanishes in the night searching for words and the other but also her self. The fragrance she preserves is a trace of the other's presence, and the fingers and mouth are the instruments of love that unite the women. The relationship is not one-sided, but mutual, because the other also incorporates the flesh of the "I" into her memory. Just as the "you" moves the speaker, the "I" also believes that the other is influenced by her, for she is concerned about being engraved in the other's memory. The equality between the two women is conveyed by how each is affected by the other. This type of relationship is different from the one often developed between men and women, in which one is superior and the other is subordinate. The symmetry between the women expresses the desire to be recorded in the other's memory and to maintain an open communication. The relationship is mutual and benefits each woman, indicated by the visual contact, embraces and kisses. But this relationship also recalls the one described in "VIII," not because this one may now suggest an affair between two women, but because the one in "XIV" also exists in the imagination. Hearing the shattered voices stimulates the speaker's recollection of the other and her belief that the other feels the same way as she does. And the relationship also unfolds in the memory.

Iraida Iturralde is sexually explicit in her poem "Elephant Ride," in which she equates the trunk of the beastly animal with a phallic.

> The bodies tumble, tear through the curtain
> and then fall silently agape. One sagging muscle
> is lured into erection, hugging warmly
> the sensuous summit, the erotic snapshot
> of a tusk enclaved

The vulva also makes an appearance, described as a ride "Through the cherry-sented garden." The poem continues with the fusion of the two bodies and then "The elephant pours out its mystic's soul." At the end of the ride, the poetic "I" emerges and refers to the other: "Careful. I'm still wet / Don't make a splash."

Gender preference is a topic that is receiving much attention. It opens the dialogue on sexuality and tests the tolerance of both Hispanic and U.S. cultures. In Rafael Campo's "XVI. The Daughter of My Imagination," he proposes an imaginary kingdom of which he is an absolute ruler; perhaps referring to the Fidel Castro we all carry within us. Though he would be in command, the poetic voice will be fare and just, even if his citizens opposed the concept of freedom and liberty. He would institute certain changes: "My laws / concerning homosexuality / and immigration would be kind and just." Unfortunately, his country "In being gay and full of immigrants, / is vanishing where seas and mountains meet." Though this ruler or dictator would impose necessary concepts of freedom for all, in particular gays and immigrants, topics relevant to the culture of the home and adopted countries, it only lives in his imagination.

Rafael Campo's imaginary construct is also carried over imagining the life of the speaker's next-door neighbor. In "Aida," though they are neighbors, the two have never met. The speaker attempts to read or understand the neighbor through certain clues: ". . . I know / he's in there—mud-cake shoes outside to dry, / the early evening opera, the glow / (of candlelight?) his window trades for night—" are just a few signs offered in the first stanza. The speaker even suspects that he is ill with some type of sexual disorder as described by the drugs from the pharmacy: Acyclovir, used for genital herpes; Dilantin (Phenytoin), an anti epileptic drug to control seizures; and AZT (azidothymidine) to inhibit the development of AIDS (acquired immunodeficiency syndrome). The neighbor is not in good health, since he no longer runs. Though the poem offers additional information about his job, it mentions that he is a stockbroker, the third stanza also underscores the topic of loneliness and love: ". . . Not in love, / they say—he seems to live alone. I eat / my dinner hovering above my stove." The two ideas are also associated with the speaker, who desires to meet the neighbor to tell him ". . . that I'm also in love with loneliness." The two have never met but the speaker is certain that his eyes are big, and alive, like poetry, but also full of tears. The speaker is certain because he is projecting his own circumstance onto his neighbor. In fact, the speaker is in love with the neighbor, because to love is to be alone. The ending of the poem suggests that Aida, me, himself, are lovers who are alone and will never meet. We know who "me" and "himself" are in the poem, but who is "Aida," whose name appears in the title of the poem. The name Aida contains the first three letters of the deadly disease, AIDS, and perhaps this immunological disease unites the neighbor with the poetic voice; all three are tied together.

Race, in its many manifestations, is a recurring topic that continues to gain ground in literature and literary criticism, not only because it is tied to slavery and the historical past, but many Hispanics and Latinos are multiracial and of African descent. Magdalena Gómez's "Mestiza Legacy" traces the downfall to slavery and the slave trade. The cleaning is without redemption:

this is a ceremony
which is no ceremony;

it is meaning without healing,
it is death without joy,

it is life without sorrow,
it is dance without spirit;

it is only clean.

The stanza is repeated twice except that the last word "clean" is replaced by "ceremony." The issue of race touches the lives of many who live or visit the United States and is also present in "It Happens While Presidents Play Golf." The title appears to be a reference to President Eisenhower, who went to play golf when Castro visited the United States in 1959, and allowed Nixon to meet with the bearded leader, whom Nixon immediately accused of being a communist. However in Gómez's poem, Norberto arrives on the Florida shore in 1952, that is, after Batista takes over the government from the elected Carlos Prío Socarrás. Shortly after his arrival, Norberto encounters racism, when he is denied service "at the whites only restaurant," and "he was duly informed / that the nigger chow hole / was across the street." Unlike other Cuban exiles, Norberto speaks positively of Fidel, who in 1953 stormed the Moncada Barracks and started a revolution that culminated in the Castro triumph of 1959. Norberto leaves, possibly he returns to Cuba, but not without invoking the blessings of Yemayá (the Virgin of Regla) and Changó (Saint Barbara), two African deities, one of the sea and the other of thunder and lightning, respectively.

In Nancy Mercado's "In My Perfect Puerto Rico," she begins by referring to her lineage, "My gray mother" and "My black grandfather." In Felipe Luciano's "Jíbaro My Petty Nigger," he associates his country folk, who attempts to abandon his identity, with the black love of African American culture. For Martín Espada, "Niggerlips" was his high school name. Douglas drove his car near black children "to point an unloaded gun, / to scare niggers / like crows off a tree." Racism is also present in Puerto Rico as the poetic voice tells us that his great-grandfather was also black, a shoemaker his family kept a secret and failed to bleach his copper skin that turned a fly in milk. He ends the poem with a sense of pride as he places all the main ideas in the last stanza:

So Niggerlips has the mouth
of his great-grandfather,
the song he must have sung
as he pounded the leather and nails,
the heat that courses through copper,
the stubbornness of a fly in milk,

and all you have, Douglas,
is that unloaded gun.

The white and "powerful" Douglas has been defeated, and Niggerlips has triumphed.

For Tato Laviera's "Negro Bembón," whose title means "niggerlips," race is also a matter of pride. Though many tend to believe that Puerto Rico is a harmonic blend of races, Laviera breaks with that stereotype and shows how a popular song, *Negro bembón*, written by Bobby Capó and made popular by Ismael Miranda, with music by Rafael Cortijo, celebrates the killing of a thick-lipped man for no other reason than having, as Espada would say, niggerlips. Laviera reproduces the words of the song, incorporates his own lines, as if singing a duet in a different voice and tone, and undermines the original lyrics. In the song the policeman retracts his lips when he finds out the reason for the assassination. Though the assassin was in custody, the cultural norms are much stronger than the law, but Laviera embraces the racial and derogatory colonial classifications used to marginalize blacks and ends his poem with the following lines:

> Sacude bemba gloriosa
> "esconde la bemba" nunca
> más soy un majestuoso
> BEMBÓN

Afro-Cuban or Caribbean religion is present in the works of Laviera, but also Hernández Cruz, Nancy Mercado and Anzaldúa, and their mixture of religions and cultures already signals a new and different space for Latino and Afro-Latino identity.

III

Latino poetry counts with few long (or epic) poems that tell the story of a people. For example, in Spanish-American literature Alonso Ercilla y Zúñiga's *La araucana* tells the story of its Amerindian chief, Caupolicán; Pablo Neruda's "The Heights of Macchu Picchu" uncovers the physical structure of the Inca Empire but also the men who died building it; and in U.S. literature Walt Whitman's "Song of My Self," describes the troubles of a nation in crisis as seen from the poetic "I." It is not my contention to claim that Latino poetry can seek parity with world literatures, but to show that it does follow a literary tradition evident from the dawn of poetry and already encompasses important poets and poems. Latino literature also has at least two long poems that should be acknowledged: Corky Gonzales' "I am Joaquín" and Tato Laviera's "Jesús Papote."

"I am Joaquín" is an epic poem of foundation that recreates history and myth from a Chicano perspective to understand a moment in the present. It can be read by stanza but more appropriately by dividing it by sections that repeat "I am Joaquín," insisting that the poetic voice is an ordinary citizen by the name of Joaquín but also Joaquín Murrieta, a nineteenth-century folk hero who opposed U.S. authority in the Southwest, and anyone else who reads the poem and assumes the voice of the speaker. The poem is circular or cyclical: It starts out in contemporary society, transports the reader to an earlier time and concludes in the present. At the outset of the poem, Gringo society confuses, manipulates and destroys the speaker, in a manner that recalls the contemporary stage of Neruda's "The Heights of Macchu Picchu." The same situation occurred with his forefathers, who were confronted with choosing between economic or spiritual and cultural survival. They made the right decision, and now it is the speaker's turn to decide his future. However, his decision appears to be more difficult than that of his forefathers, since he must consider the economic benefits of Gringo society or the spiritual rewards of his culture. In search of clarity, the speaker uncovers and reconstructs the historical past.

In reconstructing history, origin is not associated with the history of the original thirteen colonies, or with Columbus' encounter. Rather it is found in Aztec civilization, present before the arrival of the Spaniards:

I am Cuauhtémoc
proud and Noble
leader of men,
king of an empire

The speaker is Cuauhtémoc, however, his "I" is not singular but multiple. Just as he represents Cuauhtémoc, he is also the Maya Prince and Nezahualcóyotl, the Great leader of the Chichimecas. In addition, the speaker is their enemy: "I am the sword and flame of Cortez / the despot." The poetic "I" embodies both sides of the encounter. He is the victor and the vanquished. But the speaker seizes the opportunity to voice a proud past of Amerindians that Europeans had silenced.

The poetic voice is born of conflict between the Spaniards and the Aztecs. Out of this tense union emerge Spaniards, Indians and Mestizos, who according to the teachings of the Christian church, are all God's children. Regardless of the subtext, they are also engaged in a battle for freedom. In the nineteenth century, the struggle is against Spanish colonialism. The speaker is a descendent of fighters: Hidalgo, who fought for Mexican independence in 1810, and after his death, Morelos, Matamoros and Guerrero, leading to Mexican independence in 1821. Conversely, the historical transition for independence did not bring the intended results, and the fight continued. During the period of the republic, he became Don Benito Juárez, who fought, between 1863 and 1867, against Maximiliano's attempt to make Mexico a French colony.

Section two highlights the twentieth century, as the history of struggle continues with liberators like Pancho Villa and Emiliano Zapata, who supported the peasants against dictator Porfirio Díaz. From this perspective, the speaker is also the mountain Indians: the Yaqui / Tarahumara / Chaula / Zapotec / Mestizo, an identity that does not exclude the Español. The speaker is the victim and victor, he has killed and he has been killed, the despot Díaz and Huerta, and the democratic Madero. His identity is not limited to male representation, but also include women. Though he is Juan Diego, to whom the Virgin of Guadalupe appeared, he is also the virgin, and her Aztec equivalent Tonatzin. The struggle takes place in Mexico and the United States, and is directed against this country's government. Joaquín is, above all, Joaquín Murrieta and Alfrego Baca, and the Espinoza brothers, in their fight for justice against U.S. exploitation. In the present he is the *campesinos*, as well as the fat political coyote. The speaker is inferior like the Indian, and as a Mestizo he must overcome his new designation. His lower status leads him to reject his father and mother, and assimilate into North American society. He is both a traitor and a savior (of his brother). The poem does not divide Mexico and the United States but considers both countries as one geographic space.

In part three Joaquín is a sacrificial being. He has bled throughout history; beginning with the sacrificial alters of the Aztecs, and continuing with the blood of slaves and masters, *campesinos* and *hacendados*, and all those who have given their lives defending Mexican dignity. In the present, he bleeds in the barrios, prisons and wars, in Normandy, Korea and Vietnam. The bleeding is physical and cultural. The Court of Justice has condemned Joaquín's culture, which has been raped by U.S. government and citizens, as the Treaty of Guadalupe Hidalgo suggests. Mexicans became foreigners in their own land. Outsiders claimed mines on Mexican lands, but also "Our art / our literature / our music, they ignored." The revolution is physical and cultural and includes the great Mexican muralists: "The art of our great señores / Diego Rivera / Siqueiros / Orozco is but / another act of revolution." The music of Mariachi and Corridos convey the souls and passions of a people. The speaker is also the woman, who represents the Llorona, because of the historical pain she feels for her dead sons, who died "on battlefield, or on the barbwire / of social strife."

Section Four contains a significant change. Whereas before there was a space separating the stanzas organized by "I Am Joaquín," there is unity of meaning and purpose as the next two are integrated into the previous one. Joaquín realizes that he is a fighter, and he knows that he has to battle for his future, his children and his culture. His fight is historical, dating to the Reconquista of Spain. He has also survived slavery, and contemporary society's exploitation. Music of pride and jubilation announces the most recent struggle. He is "La Raza! / Mejicano! / Español! / Latino! / Hispano! Chicano! / or whatever I call myself." Though one's name or identity is important, all have been isolated by mainstream society, and the cause of one is also the other's struggle.

Section Five describes a Joaquín who has found himself and the physical and spiritual strength to make him invincible. He is a new warrior, which brings together the Aztec Prince and the Christian Christ. Chicanos embody these two extremes, but with them they will be victorious. If contemporary society at the outset of the poem confused Joaquín, in the historical reconstruction the confusion is expressed by the coming together of very different traditions, represented by Aztec and Spanish, Mexican and North American cultures. However, the reconstruction of history has given Joaquín an insight into his past and present. With the unity of the stanzas, the confusion becomes strength, as Joaquín's purpose and struggle are now clear to him:

I SHALL ENDURE!
I Will Endure! (emphasis in the original)

Joaquín's self-awareness is also conveyed in the insistent affirmation of "I Am Joaquín," which appears five times, thus dividing the poem into five parts, the number of states that define the Southwest.

While the Chicano movement expressed the history of a people who have fought throughout the centuries for freedom, it would be a mistake to group all Chicano writing under a single rubric. Chicanas represent the most notable change in Chicano literature, as they define a position that emerges from the Chicano movement, and takes it to a totally different level of identity and self-awareness. Anzaldua's *Borderlands / La Frontera* best represents the Chicana feminist writings of discovery and self-awareness. Just as "I Am Joaquín" is a poem of coming to terms with who you are, in *Borderlands / La Frontera* Anzaldúa accepts who she is and finds meaning and identity in being different: A Chicana lesbian of color. However, a study of Anzaldúa's work is beyond the scope of this introduction.

Laviera's "Jesús Papote" is a long poem whose structure follows the birth of the poetic voice, which also coincides with the birth of Christ. If Christ were to become incarnate in the contemporary period, he would be a Puerto Rican born in an abandoned lot in the Lower East Side of Manhattan. His father is unknown and his mother is a prostitute, with a heroine addiction. In this poem, Laviera describes the trials and tribulations of a people who have been battered and beaten both at home and abroad. The speaker is a fetus conceived on Easter Sunday and born midnight on Christmas Eve.

As the given name indicates, "Jesús Papote" is a Christ figure, and the poem reconstructs the sacred birth of our Lord. There are similarities and differences between the Biblical figure and Laviera's poetic voice. Christ was proclaimed the Savior; son of the Virgin Mary married to Joseph; conceived by the Holy Ghost; and delivered in a manger. Jesús Papote does not have an identity. He was not planned; his mother is far from being a virgin, is addicted to drugs and does not know the father of her child. Similar to the story about Mary, Joseph and the manger, Laviera's prostitute gives birth on a cold winter day in an abandoned lot on the Lower East Side. The Archangel Gabriel did not proclaim the annunciation of the coming of Jesús Papote; rather, he was the answer to his grandmother's prayers. But like Christ, Jesús Papote is a special being; there is something mystical about him, especially for those living in New York City and "contemporary poets felt the spirit in the air."

Christ was born in humble surroundings to reflect the condition of those in need of salvation. Jesús Papote responds to similar circumstances of his times. When Jesus returns, he will be a Puerto Rican, for Puerto Ricans are the new chosen people; as in the past, in the present they are persecuted. Jesús Papote is a victim of his social and economic environment:

> i was addicted i was beaten i was kicked i was punched
> i slept in empty cellars broken stairways i was infected
> i was injected spermed with many relations
> i ran from police jails i was high every day of life.

Like our Lord, Jesús Papote had to be exposed to these circumstances to understand the plight of his people.

Laviera gives voice to the fetus in the womb and takes the reader on a nine-month epic journey that culminates in the birth of the poetic voice. In April, he is conceived on Easter Sunday, his mother has many partners and cannot identify the father; Jesús is the answer to his grandmother's prayers. May, his mother discovers she is pregnant and tries to abort the fetus, first with pills and after by punching herself; she also has syphilis. June, she submits herself to treatment to detoxify her body, and she finally breaks the habit cold turkey. July, she goes to Puerto Rico, a symbol of origin, and she and the fetus travel throughout the island. Life is peaceful, harmony reigns, and the fetus begs her not to leave: "mamita don't go back give birth in island nativeness / tropical greetings nurturing don't / go back." The destiny of Nuyoricans is the harsh reality of a New York cold environment, not the idyllic and mythical Puerto Rico. September, she is back in New York and the dominant image now is to struggle. October, she tries training programs, the fetus also struggling against heroine addiction, and has a relapse; she fights the drug urge. November, the grandmother's prayers are not answered, the dominant theme is "death la muerte," and the mother barely survives. Death, in both Spanish and English, underscores that it is ever present and that superhuman efforts are needed to overcome it. December, the nine-month cycle is completed and Jesús Papote is ready to be born. It has been a difficult journey, struggling in a society that condones, rather than outlaws, destructive ghetto life and the arduous journey mother and son have endured.

Both the fetus and the mother are survivors, and instead of the mother helping the fetus, she draws upon the fetus's strength for her own. Jesús Papote assumes an active role in the birthing process and even instructs his mother on what to do:

Mami Mami push push i'm coming out celestial barkings
Mami Mami push i don't want to die she slept
Mami Mami push i want to live she slept cough
Mami Mami i have the ability to love cough cough
Mami Mami fight with me again she slept she slept
Mami Mami i'm coming out out out push push push push
Mami Mami can you feel me can you hear me push push
push push empuja empuja cough cough push push push
empuja empuja Mami cough cough push push i am fighting
i am fighting push push nature nature i have a will
to live to denounce you nature i am fighting by myself
your sweeping beasts your widowing backbone

yearnings your howling cemetery steps your
death-cold inhuman palms Mami Mami wake up
this is my birthday little mornings king,
david sang, cough cough cough push push
why do I have to eulogize myself
nobody is listening i am invisible
why tell me why do i have to be
the one the one to acclaim that?

As a conscious, thinking, and spiritual being, the fetus tries to revive his mother from her addiction and instructs her to push. The fetus has become his mother's own midwife. He does not want to die, he does not want her to die either; he is a fighter and must fight from the very beginning, the womb, and will continue to fight and persist throughout his life. From the moment of inception, the fetus becomes a leader of his mother, and his people. After his birth, the newborn also expresses and develops his voice and identity. His first words after birth are pronounced in both Spanish and English, in the third person plural, "We, nosotros." Jesús Papote is the voice of the Puerto Rican and Hispanic and Latino people, and all the people who live in the ghetto, whether they speak one language or the other. Jesús Papote represents the past and the future, not only because Hispanics are the largest minority, but because they are multiethnic, multilingual, multiracial and multicultural. Jesús Papote is crucified before he was born; his crucifixion began in the womb.

If Corky Gonzales' "I Am Joaquín" is based on history and myth, Laviera's "Jesús Papote" is constructed around Christian but also cultural and spiritual beliefs that include "the faith of all beliefs," "this land," "the elders," "english," "my community" and above all "god." Laviera's speaker is also a redeemer and a savior. He understands his mother's condition, does not blame her and is proud to be her son. Jesús Papote has come into the world to save his mother and other Puerto Ricans and Latinos. She draws from his strengths and liberates herself from her oppressive condition: she gets up, breaks the umbilical cord and joins the celebration of the birth of Christ and her own Jesús Papote. The ringing of the bell is a celebration of Christmas in the pagan and religious sense of the word. They are the bells of Santa Claus but also of the church where Jesús Papote is present for everyone to see.

Jesús Papote is the messiah for which Puerto Ricans have been waiting. He is not some mythical figure that only those indoctrinated into religion could understand in the abstract; he is born of the same conditions many living the ghetto experience can acknowledge. Jesús Papote speaks of his condition to theirs. It is important to underscore that the struggle for survival does not originate at birth or after adolescence, but at the moment of conception; those living in poverty and in drug-infested neighborhoods have been marked and condemned before they are born. Jesús Papote is a survivor who gives strength to his mother and to all who need help in overcoming the great odds against them. And like Jesús Papote, the poet has an obligation to develop a voice for his people. For Laviera and his character, it is not a question of something they want to do; rather it is something they must do. Their mission is to save the Latino community.

IV

The task of compiling the present anthology has not been an easy one. As it is widely known, anthologies select writers and works of merit and through time, many of these names and works, which stand the test of time, are repeated in future anthologies, therefore assuring the authors' immortality. In this work, I have followed the practice of my predecessors, but I have also deviated from their tasks. I reviewed all the anthologies available, general ones such as the *Norton Anthology of Latino Literature*, *The Anthology of Hispanic Literature of the U.S.*, *Paper Dance*, *The Chicano/Latino Literary Prize*, *In Other Words: Literature by Latinas of the United States*; and more specific ones highlighting the writings of each particular group: For Puerto Rico I consulted such anthologies as *Puerto Rican Writers at Home in the U.S.*, *Puerto Rican Poetry: An Anthology*, *Aloud: Voices from the Nuyorican Poets Café* and *Nuyorican Poetry*; for Cuban Americas, *Little Havana Blues*, *Poetas cubanas en Nueva York*, *Cuban American Writers: Los Atrevidos*; for Dominican Americans, *Exile Writers and Other Concerns*; and for Chicanas/os, *Literatura Chicana*, *Fiesta in Aztlán* and *The Floating Borderlands*. While our selections coincided with some of the ones made by other editors, I also reviewed the poetry of numerous writers beyond the anthologies, many of them already known to me, and prepared additional selections from individual works. This is particularly the case with younger or lesser-known writers. In a few cases, I invited authors to provide me with a selection of some of their most representative works. These include Ricardo Pau-Llosa, Martín Espada, Julia Alvarez, Willy Perdomo and Nancy Mercado, among others. In a few cases, my invitation was not answered.

In order to provide a broad representation of Latino poetry, rather than offer one or two poems by many different authors, I have decided to focus on the largest Latino groups, which are made up by Chicanos, Cuban

Americans, Puerto Rican Americans and Dominican American. The purpose is not necessarily to address questions about the existence of other Latino groups, whose presence has been underscored in the *The Other Latin@*, but to show the diversity within these four groups. While it is a generalized tendency to group all Latinos in one category, or present them according to national or ethnic groups, my goal is to show the rich diversity within the groups. They, at times, are divided by genre and sexual orientation, but also by geographic location, or politics, or racial identity, or other.

Our main criteria, as outlined at the outset of this introduction, is to consider primarily the works of Latinos who write mainly in English for an English-speaking or bilingual audience. While many Latinos write in Spanish and English, and still others write in Spanglish or Caló, in our selection we opted to feature those works that are attempting to broaden the U.S. canon. All of the selected writers live in the United States, and their works are an integral part of this country's literature. In some cases the author provided both the Spanish and English versions of the poems, and though our intent is to reach an English-speaking audience, the Spanish reads more smoothly, so we opted to include the Spanish as well.

The anthology has been long overdue, and it is time to get it into the readers' hands. I want to thank Nicolás Kanellos for asking me to edit this anthology for Arte Público Press, which was made possible by a grant from the National Endowment for the Humanities. I also want to recognize all those writers and poets whose contributions made this work possible, and a special thanks to my assistant Elizabeth Eiland for her invaluable help made this work possible, to R.J. Boutelle and Sarah Becker for their support in compiling the biographical notes and to Carmen Cañete for reading an early version of the introduction.

Works Cited

Anzaldúa, Gloria. *Borderlands / La Frontera*. San Francisco: Aunt Lute Press, 1987. Print.

Friedman, John Block. *The Monstrous Races in Medieval Art and Thought*. Cambridge: Harvard UP, 1981. Print.

Kanellos, Nicolás, and Helvetia Martell. *Hispanic Periodicals in the United States, Origins to 1960: A Brief History and Comprehensive Bibliography*. Houston: Arte Público Press, 2; Print.

Laviera, Tato. *Mixturao*. Houston: Arte Público Press, 2008. Print.

Luis, William. *Dance Between Two Cultures: Latino Caribbean Literature Written in the United States*. Nashville: Vanderbilt UP, 1997. Print.

_____. "Foreword" and "Afterword: Latino Identity and the Desiring-Machine." *The Other Latin@: Writing Against a Singular Identity*. Eds. Blas Falconer and Lorraine López. Tucson: U of Arizona P, 2011. vii-ix and 145-55. Print.

Obregón Pagán, Eduardo. *Murder at the Sleepy Lagoon: Zoot Suits, Race, and Riot in Wartime L.A.* Chapel Hill: U of North Carolina P., 2004. Print.

Paz, Octavio. *The Labyrinth of Solitude*. New York: Grove Press, 1994. Print.

Pérez Firmat, Gustavo. *Life on the Hyphen: The Cuban-American Way*. Austin: U of Texas P, 1994. Print.

Roberts, John Storm. *The Latin Tinge: The Impact of Latin American Music on the United States*. New York: Oxford UP, 1979. Print.

Young Lords Party and Michael Abramson. *Palante. Young Lords Party*. New York: McGraw-Hill, 1971. Print.

Looking Out, Looking In
Anthology of Latino Poetry

Jack Agüeros ──────────────────────────────

Psalm for the Next Millennium

Lord,
I dreamt it was the year 3001
and we still didn't know
what to do with homeless people,
poor people, odd people or sick people.

So City Hall
paid for a giant flying saucer and filled it with
the Strange, the Homeless, the Left-Handed,
the Ill, the Poor, the Poor, the Poor
and the people who combed their hair this way
instead of that way, and a few more poor.

And I was ordered to fly them out and
leave them anywhere but here.

And I did, because in the year 3001
we all wore T-shirts that said
"ME! ME! ME!"
and on the back "GREED IS GOOD."

But every time I got near a new planet
angry aliens screamed, "not in our galaxy," "not in our
solar system,"
"not in our Milky Way," "not on our Super Nova,"
so I sped back to earth, and mistakenly landed in City Hall Park
where all the policemen were racial profiling for minority astronauts
and they nailed me for double parking,
jaywalking and speaking Spanish
because in my excitement I said, *Caramba, carajo!*

Lord, don't laugh,
double parking carried the death penalty,
jaywalking called for the confiscation
of both my feet and all my toes,
speaking Spanish was punishable by the
murderous sentence of English Only,
and when I went before the judge

1

he looked like my current mayor
and he was washing his hands
and I repeated, "*Caramba, carajo,*" and woke up.

But Lord,
I woke up sad instead of happy,
and I woke up wondering
if it might not be better
wandering in outer space
than living in this world
where I'm supposed to ignore
the everywhere-I-look facts:
a few rich have most of the wealth
and the poor have all the poverty.

~~~~~~

Sonnets for the Four Horsemen of the Apocalypse: Long Time among Us

I. Sonnet for the Elegant Rider

The way I get it is, that when the world is about to end
four horsemen will come thundering down from somewhere.
One will ride a red horse, and his name will be War.
One will ride a white horse and his name I don't get
since it's Captivity. Does that mean slavery? I don't
want to guess about these things, but translations can
be treacherous. One will ride a black horse and be named
Famine. I get that. Now here's another part that leaves
me scratching my head—one will ride a pale horse, and
since when is pale a color? He is named Death, and I
think this translator has him on the wrong horse. Death,
I know, rides the white horse, which symbolizes his purity.

You see, the future tense is wrong, since nothing is as now, or
as inevitable, or so personally elegant and apocalyptic as Death.

2

II. Sonnet for You, Familiar Famine

Nobody's waiting for any apocalypse to meet you, Famine!

We know you. There isn't a corner of our round world
where you don't politely accompany someone to bed each
night. In some families, you're the only one sitting
at the table when the dinner bell tolls. "He's not so
bad," say people who have plenty and easily tolerate you.
They argue that small portions are good for us, and
are just what we deserve. There's an activist side to
you, Famine. You've been known to bring down governments,
yet you never get any credit for your political reforms.

Don't make the mistake I used to make of thinking fat
people are immune to Famine. Famine has this other ugly
side. Famine knows that the more you eat the more you
long. That side bears his other frightening name, Emptiness.

III. Sonnet for Red-Horsed War

Obvious symbolism; let's call it blood-colored; admit
War jumped the gun on the apocalypse a long time ago.

Isn't it shy Peace that deserves free transportation?

What horse would Peace ride? Peace is usually put on a
Dove, but is so rare it ought to ride the extinct Dodo
of lost feathers we infer, and song we never heard.
War is vulgar, in your face and favors harsh words.
Rides recklessly, and lately has even learned to fly;
drops pink mushrooms, enjoys ugly phrases like body
count and megacorpse. Generals love War, worship it by
sanctifying pentagons. When War shakes your hand, he
rips it from your arm; shoot and burn is his lullaby.

Like Kronos, War dines napkinless on his raw sons or
any burned flesh. Look, War is apocalypse all the time.

3

Captivity, I have taken your white horse. Punctilious
Death rides it better. Dubious, I try to look you in
your eye. Are you something like old-time slavery, or
are you like its clever cousin, colonialism? Are you
the same as "occupied," like when a bigger bird takes
over your nest, shits and you still have to sweep? Or
when you struggle like the bottom fish snouting in the
deep cold water and the suck fish goes by scaled in his
neon colors, living off dividends, thinking banking is
work? Captivity, you look like Ireland and Puerto Rico!

Four horsemen of the apocalypse, why should anyone fear
your arrival, when you have already grown gray among us
too familiar and so contemptible? And you, Captivity, you

remind me of a working man who has to be his own horse.

A Mongo Affair

On the corner by the plaza
in front of
the entrance to González-Padín
in old San Juan,
a black Puerto Rican talks
about "the race"
he talks of boricuas
who are in New York on welfare
and on lines waiting for food stamps,
"yes, it's true, they've been taken out
and sent abroad, and those that
went over tell me that they're
doing better over there than here;
they tell me they get money
and medical aid
that their rent is paid
that their clothes get bought
that their teeth get fixed,
is that true?"
on the corner by the entrance to González- Padín
I have to admit that he has been
lied to, misled,
that I know that all the goodies
he named humiliate the receiver,
that a man is demoralized
when his woman and children
beg for weekly checks,
that even the fucking a man does
on a government-bought mattress
draws the blood from his cock,
cockless, sin espina dorsal,
mongo—that's it!
a welfare fuck is a mongo affair!
mongo means flojo
mongo means bloodless
mongo means soft
mongo cannot penetrate
mongo can only tease,

5

but it can't tickle
the juice of the earth-vagina
mongo es el bicho Taíno
porque murió
mongo es el borinqueño
who's been moved
to the inner-city jungles
of north american cities,
mongo is the rican who survives
in the tar jungle of Chicago
who cleans, weeps, crawls,
gets ripped off,
sucks the eighty-dollars-a-week
from the syphilitic
down deep frustrated
northern man—
viejo negro africano,
Africa Puerto Rico,
sitting on department store entrances
don't believe the deadly game
of northern cities paved with gold and plenty,
don't believe the fetching dream
of life improvement in New York
the only thing you'll find in Boston
is a soft leather shoe up your ass,
viejo, anciano africano, Washington
will send you in your old age
to clean the battlefields
in Korea and Vietnam;
you'll be carrying a sack,
and into that canvas
you'll pitch las uñas
los intestinos
las piernas
los bichos mongos
of Puerto Rican soldiers
put at the front to face
¡sí!
to face the bullets, bombs, missiles,
¡sí! the artillery
¡sí!
to face the violent hatred of Nazi Germany

to confront the hungry anger of the world,
viejo negro,
viejo puertorriqueño
the north offers us pain
and everlasting humiliation,
IT DOES NOT COUGH UP
THE EASY LIFE: THAT IS A LIE,
viejo que has visto la isla
perder sus hijos
are there guns to deal with
genocide, expatriation?
are there arms to hold
the exodus of borinqueños
from Borinquen?
we have been moved
we have been shipped
we have been parcel posted
first by water, then by air
el correo has special prices
for the "low island element" to be
removed, then dumped
into the inner-city ghettos
viejo, viejo, viejo
we are the minority
here in Borinquen,
we, the Puerto Ricans,
the original men and women of this island,
are in the minority
I writhe with pain
I jump with anger
I know
I see
I am "la minoría de la isla,"
viejo, viejo anciano,
do you hear me?
there are no more Puerto Ricans
in Borinquen
I am the minority everywhere
I am among the few in all societies
I belong to a tribe of nomads
that roam the world without
a place to call a home,

there is no place that is ALL MINE;
there is no place that I can
call mi casa,
I, yo, Miguel ¡Me oyes, viejo!
I, yo, Miguel
el hijo de María Socorro y Miguel
is homeless, has been homeless,
will be homeless
in the to be
and the to come
Miguelito, Lucky, Bimbo
you like me have lost
your home,
and to the first idealist
I meet
I'll say,
don't lie to me
don't fill me full of vain
disturbing love for an island
filled with Burger Kings,
for I know there are no cuchifritos
in Borinquen
I remember last night
viejito lindo
when your eyes fired me
with trust,
do you hear that?
with trust
and when you said
that you would stand by me
should any danger threaten
I halfway threw myself
into your arms to weep
mis gracias
I loved you
viejo negro
I would have slept
in your arms
I would have caressed
your curly gray hair
I wanted to touch
your wrinkled face

when your eyes fired me
with trust
viejo corazón puertorriqueño
your feelings cocinan
en mi sangre
el poder de realizarme
and when you whispered
your anger into my ears
when you spoke of
"nosotros los que estamos
preparados con las armas,"
it was talk of future
happiness
my ears had not till
that moment heard such
words of promise and of guts
in all of Puerto Rico,
old man with the golden chain
and the medallion with an indian
on your chest
I love you
I see in you
what has been
what is coming
and will be
and over your grave
I will write
HERE SLEEPS
A MAN
WHO SEES ALL OF
WHAT EXISTS
AND THAT WHICH WILL EXIST.

El jibarito moderno

when he dances latin,
he crosses his legs
right over left,
left over right, light as a bright feather
el jibarito turns on and off
like the furthest
star in the milky way,
when he smiles his upper lip
covers his vacant gums
where his teeth have melted
just like my sugar teeth
dissolved into the chocolate
that made me fat in childhood,
el jibarito moderno
travels light
maybe he's afraid of gravity,
y eso,
hay que velarlo cuando
un bomboncito appears
in the atmosphere,
muchacho,
vélalo y cuídate
porque el jibarito conquista
con su liviana apariencia
y su estoy asfixiado look
that melts the temperature
of la damita in blue,
cuídate, cuídate
porque el jibarito
derrite y consume
sin que te des cuenta,
es como el viento
en una tarde caliente
que acaricia y seca
aliviándote el calor.

Nuyorican Angel of Records

(For Miguel Piñero)

Philosophy met her brother Time
and went for a walk,
when they reached Truth's house,
Lies, Greed and Envy
were visiting
but it took History
to point out to Time
that Truth didn't have her house
in order,
in fact,
she was so lineally sloppy
that History refused
to tell time in her house,
Lies, Greed and Envy
laughed till they urinated Pain
which caused a thunderstorm
of maladies known as Plagues.

Alurista (Alberto Baltazar Urista)

Tarde sobria

tarde sobria
        caminas en el agua pavimento cruel
bolsillos sin papel
        sin ruido tus pasos
        past ortega's store—no dimes to spend
gotta look for jesse
        go down see cindy—la gabacha
go to joe's
        go down see virginia
mañana el jale
pero orita el tiempo es mío
patrol car—he stop me
no time to walk, too young
the man
        he doesn't know my raza is old
on the streets he frisk me
        on the job he kills el jefe
en la tienda no atiende a mi mamá
the man
        he say he wanna marry mi carnala
hell no!
        ella es mujer, no juguete
the man
        he likes to play
        he get a lot o' toys
and he don't know
        que las tardes que me alumbran
y las nubes que me visten
        pertenecen a mi raza
        a mi barrio
along with ortega's store
in the afternoons
        dust built walled castles
as i swim through the smog
        and the smell of the cannery

basin headed man of black-white stroll
    stick in hand don't know
no papers in my pockets
    mi bigote for i.d.
gonna look for jesse—forget the gabacha
    go get joe
to see virginia

do u remember

do u remember
the parody of trembling laughter
through the parks clouded by moonlight
  shadows, do u remember
        the rain
  and the thunder
        mushrooming
        huracanes
do u remember
        under our feet
life sprouted on wet dark
        earth, do u
            remember
the dew of dawn lightening
        while your guts tightened
        the irony grew
        out of asphalt
            and found its
            way into
            neon
        celluloid
        and vinyl cuts
            of memories
        running amok
            on wheels
        burning dinosaur bones
and some roaches
        rolling down a '47 chevy

cornfields thaw out

cornfields thaw out
    belted cross the land as
midwestern thunderclad clouds hover
      in omaha, the meat-packing houses
pack mexicans—mojo's what they call us
    while warm tortillas
      shake off the cold at noon
    down dodge st., down way down Q st.
        into the southside salsa
mornings boil dew
      and the stench of slaughtered beasts
    engulfs the nostrils
    and the thought of carnage prevails
nothing much is different in this barrio
    big foot and bigotry squatted
since then no buffalo hooftracks can be stalked
      even pheasants are weary
      of cowboys plucking feathers
      to adorn their stetson tops
and rabbits dread the wheel
      more than their ancient foe
    coyotes howl and german shepherds bark
      the moonfull spring is
    here, for a while only
for a short, short while
    trees will bloom

Homecoming

When my cousin Carmen married, the guards
of her father's finca took the guests' bracelets
and wedding rings and put them in an armored truck
for safefekeeping while wealthy, dark-skinned men
their plump, white women and spoiled children
bathed in a river whose bottom had been cleaned
for the occasion. She was Uncle's only daughter,
and he wanted to show her husband's family,
a bewildered group of sunburnt Minnesotans,
that she was valued. He sat me at their table
to show off my English, and when he danced with
fondling my shoulder blades beneath my bridesmaid
as if they were breasts, he found me skinny
but pretty at seventeen, and clever.
Come back from that cold place, Vermont, he said
all this is yours! Over his shoulder
a dozen workmen hauled in blocks of ice
to keep the champagne lukewarm and stole
glances at the wedding cake, a doll house duplicate
of the family rancho, the shutters marzipan,
the cobbles almonds. A maiden aunt housekept,
touching up whipped cream roses with a syringe
of eggwhites, rescuing the groom when the heat
melted his chocolate shoes into the frosting.
On too much rum Uncle led me across the dance
dusted with talcum for easy gliding, a smell
of babies underfoot. He twirled me often.
excited by my pleas of dizziness, teasing me,
saying that my merengue had lost its Caribbean.
Above us. Chinese lanterns strung between posts
came on and one snapped off and rose
into a purple postcard sky.
A grandmother cried: "The children all grow up too fast."
The Minnesotans finally broke loose and danced a Charleston
and were pronounced good gringos with latino hearts.
The little sister, freckled with a week of beach,
her hair as blonde as movie stars, was asked
by maids if they could touch her hair or skin,

and she backed off, until it was explained to her,
they meant no harm. *This is all yours,*
Uncle whispered, pressing himself into my dress.
The workmen costumed in their workclothes danced
a workman's jig. The maids went by with trays
of wedding bells and matchbooks monogrammed
with Dick's and Carmen's names. It would be years
before I took the courses that would change my mind
in schools paid for by sugar from the fields around us,
years before l could begin to comprehend
how one does not see the maids when they pass by . . .
—It was too late, or early, to be wise—
The sun was coming up beyond the amber wave
of cane, the roosters crowed, the band struck up
Las Mañanitas, a morning serenade. I had a vision
that I blamed on the champagne,
the fields around us were burning. At last
a yawning bride and groom got up and cut
the wedding cake, but everyone was full
of drink and eggs, roast pig and rice and beans.
Except the maids and workmen,
sitting on stoops behind the sugar house,
ate with their fingers from their open palms
windows, shutters, walls, pillars, doors,
made from the cane they had cut in the fields.

33 is the year that Jesus Christ
embraced His life, the minister teases.
I've come to take the edge of loneliness
by being convinced that maybe god exists,
is with me in the empty bed, with
me for bread and tunafish since recipes
depress me with leftovers, and just is.
"Wasn't he crucified at 33,"
I ask, "depressed, deserted by his friends,
divorced from god, subject to human laws?
Wasn't he the most single finally
at 33, meeting his lonely end?"
Yes, the minister takes my hand, he was.

Secretly I am building in the heart
a delicate structure like one of those
cardhouses or popsickle palaces
kids build, patiently piecing each part
together, fingers pinching a small tube
of glue, eyes straining to perceive what new
thing I am making that takes so much time
to finish if there's finish in these things.
And making it out of nothing but what
are ruins from an earlier effort
and tempted constantly to believe that
a readymade is better, and yet I've
labored with my heart to outlast the heart
with this thing I am creating out of love.

Sometimes the words are so close I am
more who I am when I'm down on paper
than anywhere else as if my life were
practising for the real me I become
unbuttoned from the anecdotal and
unnecessary and undressed down
to the figure of the poem, line by line,
the real text a child could understand.
Why do I get confused living it through?
Those of you, lost and yearning to be free,
who hear these words, take heart from me.
I once was in as many drafts as you.
But briefly, essentially, here I am . . .
Who touches this poem touches a woman.

Dusting

Each morning I wrote my name
on the dusty cabinet, then crossed
the dining room table in script, scrawled
in capitals on the backs of chairs,
practicing signatures like scales
while Mother followed, squirting
linseed from a bumpy can
into a crumpled-up flannel.

She erased my fingerprints
from the bookshelf and rocker,
polished mirrors on the desk
scribbled with my alphabets.
My name was swallowed in the towel
with which she jeweled the table tops.
The grain surfaced in the oak
and the pine grew luminous.
But I refused with every mark
to be like her, anonymous.

～∾∾⌒

Bilingual Sestina

Some things I have to say aren't getting said
in this snowy, blonde, blue-eyed, gum-chewing English:
dawn's early light sifting through the *persianas* closed
the night before by dark-skinned girls whose words
evoke *cama, aposento, sueños* in *nombres*
from that first word I can't translate from Spanish.

Gladys, Rosario, Altagracia—the sounds of Spanish
wash over me like warm island waters as I say
your soothing names: a child again learning the *nombres*
of things you point to in the world before English
turned *sol, tierra, cielo, luna* to vocabulary words—
sun, earth, sky, moon—language closed

like the touch-sensitive *morivivir*, whose leaves closed
when we kids poked them, astonished. Even Spanish
failed us when we realized how frail a word is
when faced with the thing it names. How saying
its name won't always summon up in Spanish or English
the full blown genii from the bottled *nombre*.

Gladys, I summon you back by saying your *nombre*
Open up again the house of slatted windows closed
since childhood, where *palabras* left behind for English
stand dusty and awkward in neglected Spanish.

18

Rosario, muse of *el patio*, sing in me and through me say
that world again, begin first with those first words

you put in my mouth as you pointed to the world—
not Adam, not God, but a country girl numbering
the stars, the blades of grass, warming the sun by saying,
¡Qué calor! as you opened up the morning closed
inside the night util you sang in Spanish,
Éstas son las mañanitas, and listening, in bed, no English

yet in my head to confuse me with translations, no English
doubling the world with synonyms, no dizzying array of words
—the world was simple and intact in Spanish—
luna, sol, casa, luz, flor, as if the *nombres*
were the outer skin of things, as if words were so close
one left a mist of breath on things by saying

their names, an intimacy I now yearn for in English—
words so close to what I meant that I almost hear my Spanish
heart beating, beating inside what I say *en inglés.*

⁓᠁᠁⁓

Exile

The night we fled the country, Papi,
you told me we were going to the beach,
hurried me to get dressed along with the others,
while posted at a window you looked out

at a curfew-darkened Ciudad Trujillo,
speaking in worried whispers to your brothers,
which car to take, who'd be willing to drive it,
what explanation to give should we be discovered . . .

On the way to the beach, you added, eyeing me.
The uncles fell in, chuckling phony chuckles,
What a good time she'll have learning to swim!
Back in my sisters room Mami was packing

19

a hurried bag, allowing one toy apiece,
her red eye's belying her explanation:
a week at the beach so Papi can get some rest.
She dressed us in our best dresses, party shoes.

Something was off, I knew, but I was young
and didn't think adult things could go wrong.
So as we quietly filed out of the house
we wouldn't see again for another decade,

I let myself lie back in deep waters,
my arms out like Jesus' on His cross,
and instead of sinking down like I'd always done,
magically, that night, I could stay up,

floating out past the driveway, past the gates,
in the black Ford, Papi grim at the wheel,
winding through the back roads, stroke by difficult stroke,
out on the highway, heading toward the coast.

Past the checkpoint, we raced toward the airport,
my sisters crying when we turned before
the family beach house, Mami consoling,
there was a better surprise for us!

She couldn't tell, though, until . . . until we got there.
But I had already swum ahead and guessed
some loss much larger than I understood,
more danger than the deep end of the pool.

At the dark, deserted airport we waited.
All night in a fitful sleep, I swam.
At dawn the plane arrived, and as we boarded,
Papi, you turned, your eyes scanned the horizon

as if you were trying to sight a distant swimmer,
your hand frantically waving her back in,
for you knew as we stepped inside the cabin
that part of both of us had been set adrift.

Weeks later, wandering our new city, hand-in-hand,
you tried to explain the wonders: escalators
as moving belts; elevators: pulleys and rope;
blonde hair and blue eyes: a genetic code.

We stopped before a summary display window
at Macy's, *The Worlds Largest Department Store*,
to admire a family outfitted for the beach:
the handsome father, slim and sure of himself,

so unlike you, Papi, with your thick mustache,
your three-piece suit, your fedora hat, your accent.
And by his side a girl; that looked like Heidi
in my storybook waded in colored plastic.

We stood awhile, marveling at America,
both of us trying hard to feel luckier
than we felt, both of us pointing out
the beach pails, the shovels, the sandcastles

no wave would ever topple, the red and blue boats.
And when we backed away, we saw our reflections
superimposed, big eyed, dressed to formally
with all due respect with visitors to this country.

Or like, Papi, two swimmers looking down
at the quiet surface of our island waters,
seeing their faces right before plunging in,
eager, afraid, not yet sure of the outcome.

Hairbands

My husband has given away my hairbands
in my dream to the young women he works with,
my black velvet, my mauve, my patent leather one,
the olive band with the magenta rose
whose paper petals crumple in the drawer,
the flowered crepe, the felt with a rickrack
of vines, the twined mock-tortoise shells.
He says I do not need them, I've cut my hair,
so it no longer falls in my eyes when I read,
or when we are making love and I bend over him.

But no, I tell him, you do not understand,
I want my hairbands even if I don't need them.
These are the trophies of my maidenhood,
the satin dress with buttons down the back,
the scented box with the scalloped photographs.
This is my wild-haired girlhood dazzled with stories
of love, the romantic heroine with the pale, operatic face
who throws herself on the train tracks of men's arms.
These are the chastened girl-selves I gave up
to become the woman who could be married to you.

But every once in a while, I pull them out
of my dresser drawer and touch them to my cheek,
worn velvet and faded silk, *mi tesoro, mi juventud—*
which my husband has passed on to the young women
who hold for him the promise of who I was.
And in my dream I weep real tears that wake me up
to my husband sleeping beside me that deep sleep
that makes me tremble thinking of what is coming.
And I slip out of bed to check that they are still mine,
my crumpled rose, my mauve, my black hairbands.

White-wing Season

The whitemen with their guns
       have come again
       to fill the silence and the sky
with buckshot.

         She shakes out the wrinkles
         snapping the sheets,
         they crack like thunder
            lean on the wind.

The *gringos* pull their caps
       down to their eyes
       hand her the bills,
the green flutter in her hand
will reshingle her roof.

        Once her render arms raised up
     her brother's rifle
        pointed at the cooing sounds
        sprigs and two feathers floated down
          near her feet twitching plumage
          translucent eyelid blinking
          across its eye
          the small opened bill
          blood from its mouth

She pours blueing into the washtub
plunges her arms in
        puncturing the sky.
        She wrings the *sábanas*
        they sail and snap in the wind.
        Startled, plump bodies rise
        from the wooded areas and desert brush.
          The bearing of feathers
          white patches on wings and tail.
          The shots

feathers fall over the fields
cover her roof.

On their way back
        to the midwest
the hunters drop two birds
        on her washboard.

          Her eyes shiny pellets
          watching the wind
          trying to lift their wings.
          Tinges of pink
          small twisted necks
          line the furrows.

She dunks the doves in the boiling pot
        plucks out the feathers

    in her belly a rumble
          the sky reddens then blackens
          a flurry of night rain
          gentle as feathers.

～ℓℯ～ↄ

sus plumas el viento

(for my mother, Amalia)

Swollen feet
tripping on vines in the heat,
palms thick and green-knuckled,
sweat drying on top of old sweat.
She flicks her tongue over upper lip
where the salt stings her cracked mouth.
Stupid Pepita and her jokes and the men licking
her heels,
but only the field boss,
un bolillo, of course, having any.

      Ayer entre las matas de maíz
      she had stumbled upon them:

Pepita on her back
grimacing to the sky,
the anglo buzzing around her like a mosquito,
landing on her, digging in, sucking.
When Pepita came out of the irrigation ditch
some of the men spit on the ground.

She listens to Chula singing *corridos*
making up *los versos* as she
plants down the rows
hoes down the rows
picks down the rows
the chorus resounding for acres and acres
Everyone adding a line
the day crawls a little faster.

She pulls ahead
kicking *terremotes,*
el viento sur secándole el sudor
un ruido de alas humming songs in her head.
Que le dé sus plumas el viento.
The sound of hummingbird wings
in her ears, *pico de chuparrosas.*

She looks up into the sun's glare,
las chuparrosas de los jardines
¿en dónde están de su mamagrande?
but all she sees is the obsidian wind
cut tassels of blood
from the hummingbird's throat.

She husks corn, hefts watermelons.
Bends all the way, digs out strawberries
half-buried in the dirt.
Twelve hours later
roped knots cord her back.

Sudor de sobacos chorriando,
limpia de hierba la siembra
Claws clutching hoe, she tells the
two lead spatulas stirring the sand,

jump into it, *patas*, wallow *en el charco de mierda,*
breathe it in through the soles of your feet.
There was nothing else but surrender.
If she hadn't read all those books
she'd be singing up and down the rows
like the rest.

She stares at her hands
Manos hinchadas, quebradas,
thick and calloused like a man's,
the tracks on her left palm
different from those on the right.
Saca la lima y raspa el azadón
se va a mochar sus manos,
she wants to chop off her hands
cut off her feet
only Indians and *mayates*
have flat feet.

Burlap sack wet around her waist,
stained green from leaves and the smears of worms.
White heat no water no place to pee
the men staring at her ass.

Como una mula,
she shifts 150 pounds of cotton onto her back.
It's either *las labores*
or feet soaking in cold puddles *en bodegas*

cutting   washing   weighing   packaging
broccoli spears carrots cabbages in 12 hours   15
double shift the roar of machines inside her head.
She can always clean shit
out of white folks toilets—the Mexican maid.
You're respected if you can use your head
instead of your back, the women said.
Ay m'ijos, ojalá que hallen trabajo
in air-conditioned offices.

The hoe, she wants to cut off . . .
She folds wounded birds, her hands
into the nest, her armpits

looks up at the Texas sky.
Si el viento le diera sus plumas.

She vows to get out
of the numbing chill, the 110-degree heat.
If the wind would give her feathers for fingers
she would string words and images together.
Pero el viento sur le tiró su saliva
pa' 'trás en la cara.

She sees the obsidian wind
cut tassels of blood
from the hummingbird's throat.
As it falls
the hummingbird shadow
becomes the navel of the Earth.

El sonavabitche

(for Aishe Berger)

Car flowing down a lava of highway
just happened to glance out the window
in time to see brown faces bent backs
like prehisroric boulders in a field
so common a sight no one
notices
blood rushes to my face
twelve years I'd sat on the memory
the anger scorching me
my throat so tight I can
barely get the words out.

I got to the farm
in time to hear the shots
ricochet off barn,
spit into the sand,
in time to see tall men in uniforms
thumping fists on doors
metallic voices yelling Halt!
their hawk eyes constantly shifting.

When I hear the words, "*Corran, muchachos*"
I run back to the car, ducking,
see the glistening faces, arms outflung,
of the *mexicanos* running headlong
through the fields
kicking up clouds of dirt

see them reach the tree-line
foliage opening, swishing closed behind them.
I hear the tussling of bodies, grunts, panting
squeak of leather squawk of walkie-talkies
sun reflecting off gunbarrels
     the world a blinding light
     a great buzzing in my ears
     my knees like aspens in the wind.
     I see that wide cavernous look of the hunted
     the look of hares
     thick limp blue-black hair
     The bare heads humbly bent
     of those who do not speak
     the ember in their eyes extinguished.

I lean on the shanty wall of that migrant camp
north of Muncie, Indiana.
Wets, a voice says.
I turn to see a Chicano pushing
the head of his *muchachita*
back into the naguas of the mother
a tin plate face down on the floor
tortillas scattered around them.
His other hand signals me over.
He too is from *el valle de Tejas*
I had been his kid's teacher.
I'd come to get the grower
to fill up the sewage ditch near the huts
saying it wouldn't do for the children
to play in it.
     Smoke from a cooking fire and
     shirtless *niños* gather around us.

     Mojados, he says again,
     leaning on his chipped Chevy station wagon

Been here two weeks
about a dozen of them.
The *sonavabitche* works them
from sunup to dark—15 hours sometimes.
Como mulas los trabaja
no saben cómo hacer la perra.
Last Sunday they asked for a day off
wanted to pray and rest,
write letters to their *familias.*
¿Y sabes lo que hizo el sonavabitche?
He turns away and spits.
Says he has to hold back half their wages
that they'd eaten the other half:
sack of beans, sack of rice, sack of flour.
Frijoleros sí lo son but no way
could they have eaten that many frijoles.
I nod.

Como le dije, son doce—started out 13
five days packed in the back of a pickup
boarded up tight
fast cross-country run no stops
except to change drivers, to gas up
no food they pissed into their shoes—
those that had guaraches
slept slumped against each other
sabe Dios where they shit.
One smothered to death on the way here.

Miss, you should've seen them when they
stumbled out.
First thing the *sonavabitche* did was clamp
a handkerchief over his nose
then ordered them stripped
hosed them down himself
in front of everybody.
They hobbled about
learning to walk all over again.
Flacos con caras de viejos
aunque la mitá eran jóvenes.

Como le estaba diciendo,
today was payday.
You saw them, la migra came busting in
waving their pinche pistolas.
Said someone made a call,
what you call it? Anonymous.
Guess who? That *sonavabitche,* who else?
Done this three times since we've been coming here
Sepa Dios how many times in between.
  Wets, free labor, *esclavos.*
  Pobres jijos de la chingada.
  This the last time we work for him
  no matter how *fregados* we are
  he said, shaking his head,
  spitting at the ground.
  Vámonos, mujer, empaca el mugrero.

  He hands me a cup of coffee,
  half of it sugar, half of it milk
  my throat so dry I even down the dregs.
  It has to be done.
  Steeling myself
  I take that walk to the big house.

Finally the big man lets me in.
How about a drink? I shake my head.
He looks me over, opens his eyes wide
and smiles, says how sorry he is immigration
is getting so tough
a poor Mexican can't make a living
and they sure do need the work.
My throat so thick the words stick.
He studies me, then says,
Well, what can I do you for?
I want two weeks' wages
including two Saturdays and Sundays,
minimum wage, 15 hours a day.
I'm more startled than he.
Whoa there, sinorita,
wets work for whatever you give them
the season hasn't been good.
Besides most are halfway to Mexico by now.

Two weeks' wages, I say,
the words swelling in my throat.

    Miss, uh, what did you say your name was?
    I fumble for my card.
    You can't do this,
    I haven't broken no law,
    his lidded eyes darken, I step back.
    I'm leaving in two minutes and I want cash
    the whole amount right here in my purse
    when I walk out.
    No hoarseness, no trembling.
    It startled both of us.

You want me telling every single one
of your neighbors what you've been doing
all these years? The mayor, too?
Maybe make a call to Washington?
Slitted eyes studied the card again.
They had no cards, no papers.
I'd seen it over and over.
Work them, then turn them in before paying them.

    Well, now, he was saying,
    I know we can work something out,
    a sweet young thang like yourself.
    Cash, I said. I didn't know anyone in D.C.
    now I didn't have to.
    You want to keep it for yourself?
    That it? His eyes were pin pricks.
    Sweat money, Mister, blood money,
    not my sweat, but same blood.
    Yeah, but who's to say you won't abscond with it?
    If I ever hear that you got illegals on your land
    even a single one, I'm going to come here
    in broad daylight and have you
    hung by your balls.
    He walks slowly to his desk.
    Knees shaking, I count every bill
    taking my time.

Cihuatlyotl, **Woman Alone**

Many years   I have fought off your hands, *Raza*
father mother   church   your rage at my desire to be
with myself, alone.   I have learned
to erect barricades   arch my back against
you   thrust back fingers, sticks   to
shriek no   to kick and claw   my way out of
your heart.   And as I grew   you hacked away
at the pieces   of me   that   were   different
attached your tentacles   to my face and breasts
put a lock between my legs.   I had to do it,
Raza,   turn my back on your crookening finger
beckoning   beckoning   your   soft brown
landscape, tender *nopalitos.*   Oh,   it was hard,
Raza   to cleave flesh from flesh   I risked
us both   bleeding to death.   It took   a long
time   but   I learned   to let
your values   roll off   my body   like water
those I swallow to stay alive   become tumors
in my belly.   I refuse   to be taken over   by
things   people   who fear that hollow
aloneness   beckoning   beckoning.   No self,
only race *vecindad familia.*   My soul   has always
been yours   one spark   in the roar of your fire.
We Mexicans are   collective animals.   This I
accept   but my life's work   requires autonomy
like oxygen.   This lifelong battle has ended,
Raza.   I don't need to flail against   you.
Raza india mexicana norteamericana,   there's no-
thing more you can chop off   or graft on me that
will change my soul.   I remain who I am, multiple
and one   of the herd, yet not of it.   I walk
on the ground of my own being   browned and
hardened by the ages.   I am fully formed   carved
by the hands of the ancients,   drenched with
the stench of today's headlines.   But my own
hands whittle   the final work   me.

⌒ᘒ ᘛ⌒

32

To live in the Borderlands means you*

are neither *hispana india negra española*
ni gabacha, eres mestiza, mulata, half-breed
caught in the crossfire between camps
while carrying all five races on your back
not knowing which side to turn to, run from;

To live in the Borderlands means knowing
    that the *india* in you, betrayed for 500 years,
    is no longer speaking to you,
    that *mexicanas* call you *rajetas*,
    that denying the Anglo inside you
    is as bad as having denied the Indian or Black;

Cuando vives en la frontera
    people walk through you, the wind steals your voice,
    you're a *burra, buey,* scapegoat,
    forerunner of a new race,
    half and half—both woman and man, neither—
    a new gender;

To live in the Borderlands means to
    put *chile* in the borscht,
    eat whole wheat *tortillas*,
    speak Tex-Mex with a Brooklyn accent;
    be stopped by *la migra* at the border checkpoints;

Living in the Borderlands means you fight hard to
    resist the gold elixer beckoning from the bottle,
    the pull of the gun barrel,
    the rope crushing the hollow of your throat;

In the Borderlands
    you are the battleground
    where enemies are kin to each other;
    you are at home, a stranger,
    the border disputes have been settled
    the volley of shots have shattered the truce
    you are wounded, lost in action
    dead, fighting back;

To live in the Borderlands means
    the mill with the razor white teeth wants to shred off
    your olive-red skin, crush out the kernel, your heart
    pound you pinch you roll you out
    smelling like white bread but dead;

To survive the Borderlands
    you must live *sin fronteras*
    be a crossroads.

Don't Give In, Chicanita*

(para Missy Anzaldúa)

Don't give in, *mi prietita*
tighten your belt, endure.
Your lineage is ancient,
your roots like those of the mesquite
firmly planted, digging underground
toward that current, the soul of *tierra madre*—
your origin.

Yes, *m'ijita*, your people were raised *en los ranchos*
here in the Valley near the Rio Grande
you descended from the first cowboy, the *vaquero*,
right smack in the border
in the age before the Gringo when Texas was Mexico
over *en los ranchos los Vergeles y Jesús María*—
Dávila land.
Strong women reared you:
my sister, your mom, my mother and I.

And yes, they've taken our lands.
Not even the cemetery is ours now
where they buried Don Urbano
your great-great-grandfather.
Hard times like fodder we carry
with curved backs we walk.

*Translated from the Spanish by the author

34

But they will never take that pride
of being *mexicana*-Chicana-*tejana*
nor our Indian woman's spirit.
And when the Gringos are gone—
see how they kill one another—
here we'll still be like the horned toad and the lizard
relics of an earlier age
survivors of the First Fire Age—*el Quinto Sol.*

Perhaps we'll be dying of hunger as usual
but we'll be members of a new species
skin tone between black and bronze
second eyelid under the first
with the power to look at the sun through naked eyes.
And alive *m'ijita*, very much alive.

Yes, in a few years or centuries
la Raza will rise up, tongue intact
carrying the best of all the cultures.
That sleeping serpent,
rebellion-(r)evolution, will spring up.
Like old skin will fall the slave ways of
obedience, acceptance, silence.
Like serpent lightning we'll move, little woman.
You'll see.

Immigrant's Voice

I heard an immigrant's voice.
It rubbed the walls of downtown
buildings clean,
wiped the glass of steamy truckstop
windows with its breath
& o.d.'d on caffeine
& cigarettes, dawns before work.

It cleared a fog in January
with its whistle in its jeans,
climbed the flagless pole on the Green & shouted,
itself a mast recited
from the dollar
e pluribus unum e pluribus unum.

It prayed in front of the gates
of Union Trust,
climbed city hall steps—kneecaps to concrete
during unemployment—
& asked the mayor, please, a shot of whiskey
or dope, or a dollar, a mighty dollar.

It cut open its forearm six inches
at his machine operator's job
cutting steel—
his words deep-blue-purple,
but he had to be grateful,
had to be grateful for the work.

It pounded on his lover's breast,
this voice
demanding *where* is the dream?
Where *is* the dream?

It broke into tears at public urinals
& spit on statues on the way home
until sweat poured
from the contour
of the histories.

It gargled the news
nights after suppertime
& crawled shivering into its sleep.
What sleep there could be.
What dreams.

Pinos Wells

Pinos Wells—
an abandoned pueblo now.
The presence of those who lived
in these crumbling adobes
lingers in the air
like a picture
removed
leaves its former presence on the wall.

In corral dust
medicinal bottles
preserve rusty sunshine
that parched this pueblo
30 years ago.
Blackened sheds rust
in diablito barbs.
In barn rafters cobwebs
hang intricate as tablecloths
grandma crocheted for parlors
of wealthy Estancia ranchers.
Now she spins silken spider eggs.

My mind circles warm ashes of memories,
the dark edged images of my history.
On *that* field
l hand-swept smooth
top crust dirt and duned a fort.
Idling sounds of Villa's horse
I reared my body and neighed at weeds.

From the orphanage my tía Jenny
drove me to Pinos Wells
to visit grandma. All Saturday afternoon
her gnarled fingers
flipped open photo album pages
like stage curtains at curtain call
the strange actors of my mestizo familia

bowed before me wearing vaquero costumes,
mechanic overalls and holding hoes in fields.

At the six o'clock mass
with clasped hands I whispered
to the blood-shackled Christ on the cross,
begging company with my past—
given to Christ who would never tell
how under the afternoon sun in Santa Fe
the rooster slept and black ants
formed rosaries over the hard dirt yard,
when . . .

        Sanjo barrio,
            Chucos parked
at Lionel's hamburger stand
to watch Las Baby Dolls
cruise Central avenue
chromed excitement of '57 Chevies
flashing in their eyes.

In the alley behind Jack's Package Liquors
dogs fight for a burrito
dropped from a wino's coat pocket.
The ambulance screams down Edith
into Sanjo where Felipe bleeds red whiskey
through knife wounds.

On Walter street
telephones ring in red-stone apartments
while across Broadway
under Guadalupe bridge
box-car gypsies and Mejicanos swig Tokay.

Corridos—
  chairs splintering on kitchen floors—
    arguing voices in dark porches—
      doors angrily slammed—
        Seagrams bottles shatter on the streets—

I fell
into Sanjo, into my own brown body,

not knowing how to swim
as tongues lashed white spray warning
of storms to come,
                    I prayed.

In Santa Fe as a boy
I watched red tractors crumble dirt,
the black fire of disc blades
upturning burned leaves and cornstalks in their wake,
while I collected green and red commas
of broken glass in my yard,
and romped in mud slop of fallen tomb-trunks
of cottonwoods
that steamed in the dawn by the ditch.
Then,
        the fairytale of my small life
                stopped
when mother and father
abandoned me, and the ancient hillgods of my emotions
in caves of my senses
screamed, and the corn seedling of my heart
withered—like an earth worm out of earth,
I came forth into the dark world of freedom.
I ran from the orphanage at ten,
worked at Roger's Sheet Metal shop.
I'd open the window to let morning breeze
cool my boy body, and shoo
sparrows from their window ledge nest.

At the Conquistador Inn on south Central
I made love to Lolita,
and after her father found out, Lolita
slashed her wrists,
sitting on the toilet, blood scribbling
across the yellow linoleum,
as her brother pushed me aside, lifted her
and drove her away, I nodded goodbye.

Teenage years
I sought the dark connection
of words become actions, of dreams made real,
like Tijerina's courthouse raid,

or César Chávez and thousands of braceros
enduring the bloody stubs of police batons
that beat them as they marched.

I ransacked downtown stores
for winter coats to give my friends,
and the National Guard gassed me
at the Roosevelt Park when we burned
a cop's car to the ground.
He clubbed a Chicana for talking back.

On the West Mesa,
I took long walks and listened for a song
to come to me, song of a better life,
while an old Navajo woman sat on her crate
and groaned wet-lipped at the empty wine bottle,
in front of Louie's Market
and gummy drunks staggered to sun by the wall,
mumbling moans for money.

Vatos in Barelas
leaned into their peacoats
against winter wind, faces tempered
with scars, as they rattled down pebbly alleys
to their connection's house.

At the University of New Mexico
learned Chicanos
lugged book-heavy ideas to bed
and leafed through them sleeplessly,
while I slept under cottonwood trees
along the Río Grande
and cruised with Pedro
drinking whiskey through the Sangre De Cristo
mountains, until we hurled off
a sharp snowy curve one December morning
into a canyon, and I carried his dead body to a farm house.

Months after I headed West
on I-40,
in my battered Karmen Ghia.
Desperate for a new start,

sundown in my face,
I spoke with Earth—

>I have been lost from you, Mother Earth.
>No longer
>does your language of rain wear away my thoughts,
>nor your language of fresh morning air
>wear away my face,
>nor your language of roots and blossoms
>wear away my bones.
>But when l return, I will become your child again,
>let your green alfalfa hands take me,
>let your maíz roots plunge into me
>and give myself to you again,
>with the crane, the elm tree and the sun.

Roots

Ten feet beyond the back door
the cottonwood tree
is a steaming stone of beginning time.
A battle-scarred warrior
whose great branches knock
telephone poles aside, mangle trailers
to meager tin-foil in its grasp,
clip chunks of stucco off my house
so sparrows can nest in gaps,
wreck my car hood, splinter
sections of my rail fence,
all, with uncompromising nostalgia
for warring storms.
I am like this tree
Spanish saddle-makers copied
dressing from.
The dense gray wrath of its bark
is the trackway
shipwrecked captains, shepherds, shepherdesses
barn-burners, fence cutters followed.

Camped here at the foot of Black Mesa,
beneath this cottonwood,
leaned muskets on this trunk,
stuck knife blades into its canyon valley bark
red-beaded tasseled arm sleeves clashing
with each throw, as the knife
pierced cattail or bamboo
pinched in bark.

I come back to myself
near this tree, and think of my roots
in this land—
Papa and me working in the field.
I tell Papa, "Look, here comes someone."
He rises, pulls red handkerchief from back pocket,
takes sombrero off, wipes sweat from brow.
You drive up to our field. Unclip briefcase
on the hood of your new government blue car.
Spread official papers out, point with manicured fingers,
telling Papa what he must do.
He lifts a handful of earth by your polished shoe,
and tells you in Spanish, it carries the way of his life.
Before history books were written,
family blood ran through this land,
thrashed against mountain walls and in streams
fed seeds, and swords, and flowers.
"My heart is a root in this earth!" he said in Spanish, angrily.
You didn't understand Spanish, you told him,
you were not to blame for the way things must be.
The government must have his land.
The Land Grant Deed was no good.
You left a trail of dust in our faces.

I asked Papa how a skinny man like you
could take our land away.
He wept that night, wept a strong cry,
as if blood were pouring from his eyes,
instead of tears. I remember hearing his voice
coming through the walls into my bedroom,
"They twist my arms back and tear the joints,
and they crush my spine with their boots . . ."

In my mind's eye I looked into the man's face
for a long time. I stared at his car for a long time,
and knew as a child I would carry the image
of the enemy in my heart forever.

Henceforth,
I will call this cottonwood
Father.

A Daily Joy to Be Alive

No matter how serene things
may be in my life,
how well things are going,
my body and soul
are two cliff peaks
to fly again each day
or die.

Death draws respect
and fear from the living.
Death offers
no false starts. It is not
a referee with a pop-gun
at the starting line
of a hundred yard dash.

I do not live to retrieve
or multiply what my father lost
or gained.

I continually find myself in the ruins
of new beginnings,
uncoiling the rope of my life
to descend ever deeper into unknown abysses,
tying my heart into a knot
round a tree or boulder,
to ensure I have something that will hold me,
that will not let me fall.

My heart has many thorn-studded slits of flame
springing from the red candle jars.
My dreams flicker and twist

on the altar of this earth,
light wrestling with darkness,
light radiating into darkness,
to widen my day blue,
and all that is wax melts
in the flame—

I can see treetops!

～ι ι～ﾟ

from **Poem VI**

Cruising back from 7-11
esta mañana
in my '56 Chevy truckita,
beat up and rankled
farm truck,
clanking between rows
of new shiny cars—

    "Hey fella! Trees need pruning
    and the grass needs trimming!"
A man yelled down to me
from his 3rd-story balcony.

    "Sorry, I'm not the gardener,"
    I yelled up to him.

Funny how in the Valley
an old truck symbolizes prestige
and in the Heights, poverty.

Worth is determined in the Valley
by age and durability,
and in the Heights, by newness
and impression.

In the Valley,
the atmosphere is soft and worn,
things are shared and passed down.
In the Heights,
the air is blistered with the glaze
of new cars and new homes.

How many days of my life
I have spent fixing up
rusty broken things,
charging up old batteries,
wiring pieces of odds and ends together!
Ah, those lovely bricks
and sticks I found in fields
and took home with me
to make flower boxes!
The old cars I've worked on
endlessly giving them tune-ups,
changing tires, tracing
electrical shorts,
cursing when I've been stranded
between Laguna pueblo and Burque.
It's the process of making-do,
of the life I've lived between
breakdowns and break-ups, that has made life
worth living.

I could not bear a life
with everything perfect.

The Jewish Cemetery in Guanabacoa

I.

Outside of Havana
are the Jews
who won't leave Cuba
until the coming
of the Messiah.

There is the grave
of Sender Kaplan's father
a rabbi's grave
encircled by an iron gate
shaded by a royal palm.

There is the grave
in Hebrew letters
that speak Spanish
words of love and loss.
Ay querida, why so soon?

There is the grave
with a crooked
Star of David.
There is the grave
crumbled like feta.

I go searching
for the grave
of my cousin
who was too rich
to die.

I despair.
I've promised a picture
to my aunt and uncle.
They're rich now in Miami
but not a penny for Fidel.

And then I find it—
the grave of Henry Levin
who died of leukemia
at age twelve
and money couldn't save him.

Poor boy,
he got left behind
with the few living Jews
and all the dead ones
for whom the doves pray.

I reach for my camera
but the shutter won't click.
Through ninety long miles
of burned bridges I've come
and Henry Levin won't smile.

I have to return another day
to Henry Levin's grave
with a friend's camera.
Mine is useless for the rest
of the trip, transfixed, dead.

Only later I learn
why Henry Levin
rejected me
a latecomer
to his grave.

My aunt and uncle were wrong.
Henry Levin is not abandoned.
Your criada, the black woman
who didn't marry to care for him,
tends his grave.

Tere tells me she can't forget
Henry, he died in her arms.
Your family left you, cousin,
so thank God for a black woman
who still visits your little bones.

America

I.

Although Tía Miriam boasted she had discovered
at least half-a-dozen uses for peanut butter—
as a dessert topping for guava shells in heavy syrup,
as a substitute for butter on Cuban toast,
as a hair conditioner—
Mamá never quite knew what to do
with the monthly five-pound jars
handed out by the immigration department
until Brian, my schoolmate, suggested jelly.

II.

There was always pork:
on Christmas Eve and birthdays,
on New Year's Eve,
the Fourth of July
and Thanksgiving Day.
Pork-roasted, fried or broiled,
as well as cauldrons of black beans,
yuca con mojito
and fried plantain chips.
These items required a special visit
to Antonio's Mercado
on the corner of West 163rd and Columbus
where the men in *guayaberas* stood in senate
blaming Kennedy—*"ese hijo de puta,"* they would say,
the mixed bile of Cuban coffee and cigar residue
filling the creases of their wrinkled lips—
as they clung to each other
lying about lost wealth
ashamed of their emptiness
like hollow trees.

III.

By seven
I got suspicious.
We were still here.
Overheard conversations about returning
grew wistful and less frequent.
I had mastered a language
my parents didn't understand.
We didn't live in a two-story house
with a maid named Alice
like the *Brady Bunch*.
We didn't have a wood-panel station wagon
and vacation camping in Colorado.
Dad didn't watch football on Sundays.
None of the girls in the family had hair of gold;
none of my brothers or cousins
were named Greg, Peter or Marsha.
None of the characters
on the *Dick Van Dyke Show* or *Happy Days*
were named Guadalupe, Lázaro or Mercedes.
Patty Duke's family lived in Brooklyn, like us,
but they didn't have pork on Thanksgiving.
They went to Grandma's house in Connecticut
and ate turkey with cranberry sauce,
baked yams, cornbread and pumpkin pie,
just like the pictures I colored
in Mrs. Ross' class
and hung on the refrigerator.

IV.

In 1976
I explained to Abuelita
about the Indians and the Pilgrims,
how Lincoln set the slaves free.
I explained to my parents about
the purple mountain's majesty,
the amber waves of grain,
"one if by land, two if by sea,"

50

the cherry tree, the tea party,
the "masses yearning to be free,"
liberty and justice for all . . .
And finally they agreed—
this Thanksgiving we would have turkey,
as well as pork.

V.

Abuelita prepared the poor fowl
as if committing an act of treason,
harnessing as much enthusiasm
as possible, for my sake.
Mamá prepared candied yams,
following instructions printed
on the back of a marshmallow bag,
and set a frozen pumpkin pie in the oven.
Dad watched WLTV: "*Lo Nuestro.*"
The table was speared with Gladiolus
and the turkey was set at the center
on a plastic silver platter from Woolworth's.
Everyone sat erect in the green velvet dining chairs
we had upholstered with clear vinyl,
except Tío Carlos and Toti,
who were seated in the folding chairs
from the Salvation Army.
I uttered a bilingual improvisation
of a blessing Sister Mary Clare had suggested
and the turkey was passed around
like a game of Russian Roulette.
"DRY," Tío Berto said,
and proceeded to drown the lean slices
with pork fat drippings and cranberry jelly—
"*la mierda roja,*" as he called it.
Faces fell when Mamá proudly presented
her ocher pie; everyone knew pumpkin
was a remedy for ulcers,
not a baked dessert.
Abuelo made three rounds of Cuban coffee
then Tía María and Pepe cleared the living room furniture

51

and put on a Celia Cruz LP.
All the relatives began to *merengue*
over the linoleum of our two-bedroom apartment
sweating rum and coffee
until they remembered
it was 1976 and 46 degrees,
in America.
After repositioning the furniture,
Tío Berto was the last to leave.

VI.

In the warm and appropriate darkness
of my room that night
I hung like a chrysalis
realizing I lived in a country
I didn't know,
waiting for a home
I never knew
and a name
to give myself.

Recipe: Chorizo con Huevo Made
in the Microwave

I won't lie,
it's not the same.

When you taste it
memories of abuelita
feeding wood into the stove
will dim.

You won't smell the black crisp
of tortillas
bubbling on cast iron.
Microwaved,
they are pale and limp as avena—
haven't a shadow of smoke.

There's no eggy lace
to scrape from the pan.
No splatters of grease
on the back of the stove.
Everything is clean:
vaporized
dripless.

It's not the same.

If your mother saw you
she'd raise an eyebrow—
the same one she arched
when, at eight,
you turned down sopa de fideo
for peanut butter and jelly at lunch.

You can turn away
from that eyebrow,
but there's no escaping the snarl

grandma will dish out
from her photo in the mantle.

It's the same hard stare
you closed your eyes to
on the day you brought
that microwave home.

Ni modo, pues.

Get out a plastic dish.
Cook the chorizo on high for 4 minutes.
Crack the eggs.
Fold them in.
Microwave 2 minutes
Stir.
Microwave 2 minutes.
Serve.

Eat your chorizo con huevo
with pale tortillas
Remember grandma eating,
craving chorizo cooked
over an outdoor stove
in a Tucson summer.

As the grease runs into your sleeve,
peer into her mind's eye:
a childhood of dust
swirls around feet;
in her mouth
a futile search
for a relic of grit.

While your mouth is full,
recall that her appetite
ached
for a seasonless sky
suspended, a firmament,
over a horizon of sand.

José Antonio Burciaga————————————————

Poema en tres idiomas y caló

Españotli titlán Englishic,
titlán náhuatl, titlán Caló.
¡Qué locotl!
Mi mente spirals al mixtli,
buti suave I feel cuatro lenguas in mi boca.
Coltic sueños temostli
y siento una xóchitl brotar
from four diferentes vidas.

I yotl distinctamentli recuerdotl
cuandotl, I yotl was a maya,
cuandotl, I yotl was a gachupinchi,
when Cortés se cogió a mi great tatarabuela,
cuandotl andaba en Pachucatlán.

I yotl recordotl el toniatiuh
en mi boca cochi
cihuatl, náhuatl
teocalli, my mouth
micca por el english
e hiriendo mi español
ahora cojo ando en caló
pero no hay pedo
porque todo se vale,
con o sin safos.

[traducción]

Español entre inglés
entre náhuatl, entre caló.
¡Qué locura!
Mi mente en espiral asciende a las nubes
bien suave siento cuatro lenguas en mi boca.
Sueños torcidos caen
y siento una xóchitl brotar
de cuatro diferentes vidas.

Yo indudablemente recuerdo
cuando yo era maya,
cuando yo era gachupín,
cuando Cortés se cogió a mi gran tatarabuela,
cuando andaba en Aztlán.

Yo recuerdo el sol
en mi boca duerme
mi mujer náhuatl,
templo mi boca
muerta por el inglés,
e hiriendo mi español,
ahora cojo ando en caló
pero no hay problema
porque todo se vale,
con o sin seguridad.

Julia de Burgos————————————————————

To Julia de Burgos*

Already people whisper I'm your enemy
because in verse they say I give you to the world.

They lie, Julia de Burgos, they lie. They lie, Julia de Burgos.
The one that rises in my verse is not your voice: it's mine.
You're only the clothing; the essence, though, is me;
and the deepest chasm yawns between the two.

You're the bloodless mannequin of social lies,
and I, the virile spark of human truth.

You, the honey of courtly hypocrisies; not me;
in every verse of mine my heart bare naked lies.

You're just like your world, an egoist; not me,
who put everything at risk to be that which I am.

You're only the serious, the imperious grand dame;
not me; I am life, I am strength, I am woman.

You belong to your husband, to your master; not me;
I belong to no one, or to all, because to all, to everyone,
in my unsullied feeling and my thought I surrender.

You curl your hair and put paint on your face; not me;
it's the wind that combs my hair; it's the sun that colors me.

You're a housewife, resigned and submissive,
tied to all the bigotries of men; not me;
who as Rocinante has bolted, running free,
snuffling horizons of the justice of God.

You in your self rule not; you're ruled by everyone;
in you your husband rules, your parents, relatives,
the priest, the dressmaker, the theater, the casino,

*Translated by Roberto Márquez

57

the car, the jewels, the banquet, the champagne,
the heaven and the hell, and the what-will-they-say.

Not so in me, who am ruled only by my heart,
only by what I think; who me commands is me.
You, aristocratic blossom; and I plebian floret.
You have it all with you and owe it all to all,
while I, my nothing to no one do I owe.

You, fixed to the unchanged ancestral dividend
and I, a one in the sum of the social divider,
we're a duel to the death that fatally approaches.

When the multitudes in riot running rouse
leaving behind injustices' burnt ashes;
when they become the seven virtues' torch;
when, running down the seven sins, the multitudes revolt
against you, against all is inhuman and unjust,
I'll be with them with a torch in my hand.

~‿‿ᖯ

My, Oh My, Oh My of the Nappy-Haired Negress*

Oh my, oh my, oh my, I'm nappy-haired and pure black
kinks in my hair, on my lips Kaffir,
my nose so flat it Mozambiques.

Black of pure tint, I lament and laugh
at the pulsings of being a black statue;
a mass of night in which my white
teeth lightning;
a black vine
winding round all is black,
gives curve to the black nest
in which the raven lies.

Black mass of black in which I form myself,
oh my, oh my, oh my, my figure is all black.

They tell me that my grandfather was a slave
for whom the master paid out thirty gold coins.

*Translated by Roberto Márquez

Oh my, oh my, oh my, that that slave was my grandfather
is my sorrow and my grief.
If he had been the master,
it would have been my shame:
for in men, as in nations,
if to be a slave implies one has no rights,
to be a master implies one has no conscience.

my, oh my, oh my, wash the white King's sins away
in the black Queen's forgiveness.

Oh my, oh my, oh my, that race is on the run
and toward the whites it buzzes and it flies,
to sink in their pure water;
or possibly whiteness will be darkened by the black.

Oh my, oh my, oh my, my black race flees
and merges with the white, becoming bronze,
to be the race of the future,
of America's fraternity!

Poem for My Death*

Before a yearning

To die with mine own self, abandoned and alone,
upon the most dense rock of some deserted isle.
In that instant, to feel an aching for carnations,
the vista a tragic horizon of stone.

My eyes filled with sepulchres for stars,
my passion laid out, exhausted and dispersed.
My fingers like children watching the fading of a cloud,
my reason peopled with enormous sheets.

My pale affections returning to the silence
—even love, a brother consumed along my way!—

*Translated by Roberto Márquez

My name untangling, yellow in the branches,
my hands atwitch to yield me to the grass.

To rise up in that last, integral minute,
and give me to the fields with a star's purity
then fold the leaf that is my simple flesh,
and go down with no smile or witness to inertia.

Let none profane my dying with their weeping,
nor dress me forever in the plain, good earth;
in that unfettered moment let me freely
use the planet's only freedom.

"With what ferocious joy will my bones start
to look for airholes in the russet flesh
while I, yielding, ferally and freely, yielding
to the elements break, all alone, my chains!

Who will detain me with futile fantasies
once my soul begins on fulfilling its task,
making of all my dreams a savory dough
for the frail worm will come knocking at my door?

My weary smallness growing smaller still,
greater by the second and simpler my surrender;
perhaps, turning, my chest will start budding a flower,
my lips possibly become a nourishment for lilies.

What shall I be called when all remains of me
is a memory, upon a rock of a deserted isle?
A carnation wedged between the wind and my own shadow,
death's child and my own, I will be known as poet.

Belonging

I went to Cuba on a raft I made
from scraps of wood, aluminum, some rope.
I knew what I was giving up, but who
could choose his comfort over truth? Besides,
it felt so sleek and dangerous, like sharks
or porno magazines or even thirst—
I hadn't packed or anything, and when
I saw the sea gulls teetering the way
they do, I actually felt giddy. Boy,
it took forever on those swells of sea,
like riding on a brontosaurus back
through time. And when I finally arrived,
it wasn't even bloody! No beach of skulls
to pick over, nothing but the same damn sun,
indifferent but oddly angry, the face
my father wore at dinnertime. I stripped
and sat there naked in an effort to
attract some cannibals, but no one came;
I watched my raft drift slowly back to sea,
and wished I'd thought to bring a book
that told the history of my lost people.

XVI.   The Daughter of My Imagination

My country, if I were a potentate,
would be an island and a continent.
It would be free despite its citizens.
Its mountains would resemble seas; escape
would be impossible, because the seas
would be as vast as mountains. Most of all,
my country would belong to me. My laws
concerning homosexuality
and immigration would be kind and just:
offenders would be subject to a fine
not more in value than a poet's line,
nor less than what my country's freedom cost.

My country, in the end, unfortunate
in being not an island nor a continent,
in being gay and full of immigrants,
is vanishing where seas and mountains meet.

❧

Aida

I've never met the guy next door. I know
he's in there—mud-caked shoes outside to dry,
the early evening opera, the glow
(of candlelight?) his window trades for night—

I think he's ill, since once the pharmacy
delivered his prescriptions to my door:
Acyclovir, Dilantin, AZT.
He doesn't go out running anymore.

I've heard that he's a stockbroker who cheats
a little on his taxes. Not in love,
they say—he seems to live alone. I eat
my dinner hovering above my stove,

and wondering. Why haven't we at least
exchanged a terse hello, or shaken hands?
What reasons for the candlelight? His feet,
I'm guessing by his shoes, are small; I can't

imagine more. I'd like to meet him, once—
Outside, without apartments, questions, shoes.
I'd say that I'm in love with loneliness.
I'd sing like candlelight, I'd sing the blues

until we'd finished all the strawberries.
We've never met, and yet I'm sure his eyes
are generous, alive, like poetry
but melting, brimming with the tears he cries

for all of us: Aida, me, himself,
all lovers who may never meet. My wall—
as infinite and kind-faced as the wealth
of sharing candlelight—it falls, it falls.

62

Not Just Because My Husband Said

if i had no poems left
i would be classified *working-class intelligentsia*
my husband said
having to resort to teaching or research
grow cobwebs, between my ears
if I had no poems left

if i did not sing in the morning
or before i went to bed, i'd be as good as dead
my husband said
struck dumb with morose silence or apathy
my children would distrust me
if i did not sing in the morning

if i could not place on the table
fresh fruit, vegetables tender and green
we would soon grow ill and lean
my husband said
we'd grow weak and mean and useless to our neighbors
if I could not place fresh fruit on the table.

Rincón

We curve along the edge of civilization:
overgrown cane fields, sombreroed men
with saffron skin and machetes
lining the road we share with farm equipment,
tractors, ox carts and those who dare
to bicycle the island with children
strapped to homemade-wooden seats
with hope for a Sunday paseo
un día cenizo y triste que se sienta
en mi garganta como un licor extraño.

And you, a product of the revolution,
my cousin, my brother, my love,
have learned to live with horror,
con dolor y escases, con tus ojos tristes,
and the sixteen-hour night you chase
back to Habana in this choleric air
that blows through the open windows
to touch our shoulders and lick our lips.

It has taken me twenty-five years
to get here, to feel these sunburned vinyl seats
stick to my tourist skin with the adhesive that is sweat,
to hold your child who jumps over the dampness
settling inside us, this car,
while you, fascinated by speed and geometry,
spiral through this ash-gray Sunday,
the confused impurity of my thoughts
as your son reaches for his toy alligator,
a Florida souvenir.

I Brought Abuelo Leopoldo Back from the Dead and Moved Him to Miami

Though he died when I was barely five,
though I remember him only as a dark,
silent figure in the black and white
background of childhood,
though he walked around the house
each afternoon looking for abstractions
he claimed to have left on the kitchen counter or his dresser,
though he scared me into believing
we live in a world inside our heads,
I brought Abuelo Leopoldo back from the dead,
sat across him at the dinner table,
stared at the blue of his Caribbean eyes,
wished for his outdoor skin,
wished I could relive my childhood as an adult,
wished I could touch his raw hands, his wrinkled fingers,
the texture-feel of peaches,
and I know I carry him with me
in the part of the self that stores
all that we do not understand
until we can take it out
and say "This is me;
this is who I am."

Leavings

They sleep in one large room:
Sonia, Tin, Zaida, Hectico, Roly.
And I cut through Peralta's backyard
to their tiny apartment, where at night
Hectico and I find our way to the roof
to count the stars.
Zaida is almost fifteen,
and Sonia and I take the bus downtown
every Sunday to collect discarded ice cream
cups to hold the pasta salad Sonia will make
for her birthday party.
Mother doesn't think we'll be able to go

65

to see her dance in her long, pink dress
as she smiles her way into womanhood.
Aunt Velia has called us to America.
Mother says that means I'll never again
sit on Sonia's tar-papered roof,
that Uncle Armando will move into our house,
and we'll be able to send gum in our letters
like Aunt Velia does now,
that the twins will learn English
before they remember these first
few years.

In dreams Aunt Velia waves,
signaling for us to come,
her tall body wrapped in an airmail
envelope, like a cloak.
Mother waves back, clutching the twins
in her arms, and begs me to hurry,
but I hesitate, knowing Sonia has had
a slow day.

Stolen Kisses Are the Sweetest

Louveciennes, 1932

Henry:

> *Je pense a toi taus le temps.*
> *Anaïs*

The only thing I want to know is
if behind the mirror
your eyes wait for me.
Kiss me quick, my dear,
for life is short.

I love you has taken over
all my *Diaries*.
Let us meet whenever and however we can.
I want your hands
to write all your adventures
in the folds
of my pages,
so that each stroke of your pen
will make
my notebook less virginal.

Letter from Lucrezia Borgia to Her Confessor

Father, if you were a woman
you would understand the reasons
and not make me say so many Ave Marías.
Father, don't you see?
My punishment now
is twentieth-century freedom.

To We Who Were Saved by the Stars

> *Education lifts man's sorrows to a higher plane of regard.*
> *A man's whole life can be a metaphor.*
> —Robert Frost

Nothing has to be ugly. Luck of the dumb
is a casual thing. It gathers its beauty in plain
regard. Animus, not inspiration, lets us go
among the flocks and crows crowded around
the railroad ties. Interchanges of far away
places, tokens of our deep faux pas, our interface
of neither/nor, when we mutter moist goodbye and ice
among the silent stars, it frosts our hearts on
the skids and corners, piles the dust upon our grids
as grimaces pardon us, our indecision, our monuments
to presidents, dead, or drafted boys who might have
married us, Mexican poor, or worse. Our lives could be
a casual thing, a reed among the charlatan drones,
a rooted blade, a compass that wields a clubfoot
round and round, drawing fairy circles in clumps
of sand. Irritate a simple sky and stars fill up
the hemispheres. One by one, the procession
of their birth is a surer song than change
jingling in a rich man's pocket. So knit, you
lint-faced mothers, tat your black holes
into paradise. Gag the grin that forms
along the nap. Pull hard, row slow, a white
boat to your destiny. A man's whole life
may be a metaphor—but a woman's lot
is symbol.

Caminando a solas

I.

Me ha quedado
un olor a sangre fresca
en las manos
y un silencio ancho
en el estómago
del que brotan sólo
a fuerza las palabras
porque he estado muy lejos
distante y ajena
caminando a solas
en predios extraños
entre mariposas
que llevan en la piel
un olor amarillo y tibio,
entre sueños
que se sueñan a sí mismos
y se aniquilan
en el preciso momento
del despertar.

II.
Vengo de lejos
de alcobas sin ventanas,
de una realidad
tan dura como el hielo,
de la enconada lucha
con la soledad y el miedo;
vengo de un libro
entre cuyas páginas
por seis meses
como una rosa herida
he vivido.

III.
Caminando a solas
la luz gira
dentro de su sombra

y el tiempo anida
en el remolino del agua,
en los cuchillos
hay rosas muertas
y vuelan heridas
las palomas,
un niño y una niña
se dan la mano,
en esta noche
en que la obscuridad
es tan profunda
como la herida de luz
que las garras del amor
dejaron en la piel
tanto tiempo dormida.

Caminando a solas
en el paréntesis
entre placer y padecer
no hay mayor gloria
que la ausencia del dolor,
ni mayor pena
que la ausencia del amor.

IV.
A veces se me ocurre
el azul marino
entre las piedras
en donde el agua
dejó grabado
su epitafio
de sal endurecida
   El cirio emite
   su sonido
   cristalino
   y trágico
   El diablo ríe
   El agua se queja
Caminando a solas
a veces se me ocurre
la muerte en pleno mediodía
y en invierno

la voz dulciverde
del verano

V.
El año
La estación
El martirio
El pasajero sin destino
Toda el hambre del mundo
envuelta en hojas de maíz
La sopa de letras crudas
esparcidas por toda la mesa
El vendaval
La miseria
La furia
Y de vez en cuando
un diseño de garzas
en el cristal congelado
de la mañana

Caminando a solas
la hoja filosa del verso
se me hunde en la voz
y mi propio grito me despierta.

VI.
De vez
   en cuando
      es bueno
         bajar
            al sótano
               de la memoria
                  y darnos
               un baño
            de sombra
         para
      aprender
   a ser
luz . . .

71

Walking Alone

I.
An odor
of fresh blood
has stayed on my hands
and in my stomach
a wide silence
from which words spring
only by force
because I've been very far away
distant and alienated
walking alone
in strange places
among butterflies
that carry on their skin
a warm yellow scent,
among dreams
that dream about themselves
and dismantle themselves
at the precise moment
of awakening.

II.
I come from far away
from windowless bedrooms,
from a reality
hard as ice,
from the fierce battle
with loneliness and fear;
I come from a book
between whose pages
I have lived
crushed like a rose
for six months.

III.
Walking alone
the light turns
within its shadow
and time builds a nest
in the whirlpool,

there are dead roses
on the knives
and doves
are flying wounded,
a boy and a girl
hold hands,
in this night
where darkness
is as deep
as the wound of light
left by the claws
of love on skin
so long asleep.

Walking alone
in the parenthesis
between pleasure and suffering
there is no glory greater
than the absence of pain,
no pain greater
than the absence of love.

IV.
Sometimes navy blue
occurs to me
among rocks
where water
has etched
its epitaph
in hardened salt
      The candle emits
      its tragic
      crystalline
      sound
      The devil laughs
      The water sighs
Walking alone
sometimes death
occurs to me at high noon;
and in winter
the greensweet voice
of summer

V.
The year
The season
The martyrdom
The traveller without destination
All the hunger of the world
wrapped in cornhusks
And raw alphabet soup
spilled on the table
The windstorm
The misery
The fury
And from time to time
a design of herons
on the frozen window
of morning

Walking alone
the razor-edge of verse
slices into my voice
and I am wakened by my own cry.

VI.
From time
    to time
        it's good
            to go down
                to the cellar
                    of our memory
                        and bathe
                    ourselves
                in shadow
            in order
        to learn
    to be
light . . .

Labor de retazos

1.
Mientras plancho
una voz adentro
me avisa:
"El alma necesita
arrugas
necesita pliegues
alforzas y otros
motivos de edad".

2.
Sacudo los rincones
El amante sin nombre
cac desdiciéndome:
"Era solamente el azul
válsico del verbo
Yo no la supe en mí".

3.
Mi casa está llena
de un rumor viejo
de un sortilegio cascado
de tanto pronunciarse
que aún embosca rufianes
inadvertidos en la noche.

4.
Hay oros fragmentados
y palabras de mediodía
sobre la hierba.
Frutas de temporada
y sal de roca
en las heridas
que me dejaron
los últimos diez años.

5.
Mi amor
estoy llena de espinas
llena de pétalos.
Llevo la complicada
incomplicación
de la palabra
entre pecho
y espalda.

6.
Me llené de raíces
de ramitas de laurel
de yerbabuena y copal
y platiqué con otros vientres
que cultivaban nogales
pasionarias y azaleas
pero nadie me pudo decir
hacia dónde van
los gitanos
cuando se marchan.

7.
Vuelvo a los caminos
y cada gitano peregrino
me parece un verso andante.
Hablo con ellos
rimas anacrónicas
mientras mi hijo
con los otros niños
se acerca sonriente
a vernos
a los gitanos pasar.

Patchwork

1.
While I iron
a voice inside me
warns:
"The soul has need
of wrinkles,
need of pleats,
tucks and other
signs of age."

2.
As I dust the corners
A nameless lover
falls, disclaiming me:
"She was only the blue
waltzing of a word
I never knew her in myself."

3.
My house is full
of an old whispering
a flaking witchery
worn with repetition
that still ambushes unwary
ruffians at night.

4.
There are fragments of gold
and noon words
on the grass.
Fruits in season
and rock salt
in the wounds
left me
by the last ten years.

5.
Love
I am full of thorns
full of petals.
I carry the complicated
simplicity
of the word
between breast
and backbone.

6.
I filled up on roots
and laurel twigs
and yerbabuena and incense
and chatted with other bellies
that were gestating black walnuts
passionflowers and azaleas
but none could tell me
where the gypsies go
when they
leave town.

7.
I go back to the roads
and every gypsy on the way
seems like a walking verse.
I say anachronistic
rhymes with them
while my son comes up
with the other children, smiling
to watch us
the gypsies
passing by.

Carta a Arturo

Cariñito,
las hormigas han invadido
la alacena
y desfilan con un ataúd
de pan sobre los hombros.

Los petiazules se embriagan
de moras silvestres,
celebran la llegada del verano
todos en hilera sobre la barda.

Los caracoles cuán largos son
se resguardan del sol
bajo la microfronda
de las violetas.
Sabes? Las casas de
los caracoles no tienen
ventanas, sólo una puerta.

Me siento frente a la tarde
que lánguidamente
cuenta sus minutos
y escucho su vacío.

Apenas si te has ido
y ya extraño la suave
caricia de tus manos
sobre mis cabellos,
y tu risa y tu llanto,
y todas las preguntas
sobre mares,
lunas y desiertos.

Y todos los versos
se me van anudando
en la garganta.

79

Letter to Arturo

Darling,
the ants have invaded
the bread-box
and parade with a coffin
of bread on their shoulders.

The bluejays are getting drunk
on wild blackberries,
they're all in a row on the fence
celebrating the arrival of summer.

The snails are staying out of the sun
stretching like cats
under the microfronds
of the violets.
(Did you know that snails' houses
have no windows?—
Only a door.)

I sit down in front of an afternoon
that is languidly
counting its minutes
and listen to its emptiness.

You've hardly left
and already I miss the light
caress of your hands
on my hair,
and your laughter and your tears,
and all your questions
about seas,
moons and deserts.

And all my poems
are tying themselves together
in my throat.

Kilotons and Then Some

Bombs on hot and crowded Nagasaki
and Hiroshima.
Bombs on hated Hai-phong harbor and Hanoi.
Bombs on the Caribbean jewel Puerto Rico
for almost a century—
bombs on the presidential building
of socialist Chile in '73.

Bombs off Mexico's Veracruz
shot by U.S. Marines in 1914.
Bombs over the once many starfish
of now-radiated Pacific Isles.
Bombs over the Buddha's blood fields
in Cambodia.
Bombs over Christ's homeland of Palestine.

Bombs over the cactus and lizards
of the New Mexican desert.
Bombs over the Nevada oasis scattering
Las Vegas.
Bombs under the Utah Mormon paradise.
Bombs with no markings sold to
those with no future.

Bombs under the Mongolian Gobi desert.
Bombs under the Siberian rock ice.
Bombs on the heads of Afghanistan.
Bombs with Moslem moon and star
of Pakistan.

Bombs with designer shades from France.
Bombs with mantras and incense
reincarnates India.

Bombs from David's six-pointed star
into the oil rigs of Iraq.
Bombs with red stars over
rich rice fields of Asia.

Bombs with question marks
from South Africa's white elite.
Bombs with passages from the Koran
canned in Libya.
Bombs from the 14th century of lonely Iran.
Bombs from the ill-reputed saint
of North Korea Kim II Sung.

Bombs with no consideration
from his cousins in South Korea.
Bombs of the underdeveloped nations
just laying around.
Bombs of the SuperPowers leaving them dumb.
Bombs of the captive people getting louder,
bombs of the captors making them captives.

Bombs with names such as "TRINITY, 666,
LITTLE BOY, BLISTER BUSTER, HEAVY
METAL, BAR-B-QUED."
Bombs blessed by drunk church sinners
with sweaty palms.
Bombs with no chance of ever learning a trade.
Bombs four days old on the discount table.

Bombs the kind you'll never see.
Bombs the ones you only have to listen to
once—
and you'll never hear again.

Stupid America

stupid america, see that chicano
with a big knife
in his steady hand
he doesn't want to knife you
he wants to sit down on a bench
and carve christ figures
but you won't let him.
stupid america, hear that chicano
shouting curses on the street
he is a poet
without paper and pencil
and since he cannot write
he will explode.
stupid america, remember that chicanito
flunking math and english
he is the picasso
of your western states
but he will die
with one thousand masterpieces
hanging only from his mind.

Black Train through the Ancient
Empire of Chicago

Everywhere an ancient empire
is rained smooth and crumbling,
burned hollow, secrets broken open
and rows of windows plundered,
abandoned even by the homeless,
the monuments, catacombs
and temples of Chicago:

crusted foundries,
factories gutted with a frightening grin,
chemical companies' brickpaint signs dissolving,
smokestacks' thick white beard billowing in the glint,
tenements gaunt and arthritic without sleep,
confusion of warehouses sightless
at the disturbed mouth of underworld rivers,
remembering laborers' hands
in ghostly regimentation.

And now this black train screeches
like a nocturnal creature
escaped from the Chicago station,
leaving the centuried buildings
crutched between iron bridges,
amazed at the fear in their legs,
wary of vandals at night,
unemployed in the city.

Trumpets from the Islands of Their Eviction

At the bar two blocks away,
immigrants with Spanish mouths
hear trumpets
from the islands of their eviction.
The music swarms into the barrio
of a refugee's imagination,

along with predatory squad cars
and bullying handcuffs.

Their eviction:
like Mrs. Alfaro, evicted
when she trapped ten mice,
sealed them in plastic sandwich bags
and gifted them to the landlord;
like Daniel, the boy stockade
in the back of retarded classrooms
for having no English
to comfort third-grade teachers;
like my father years ago,
brown skin darker than the Air Force uniform
that could not save him, seven days county-jailed
for refusing the back of a Mississippi bus;
like the nameless Florida jíbaro
the grocery stores would not feed
in spite of the dollars he showed,
who returned with a machete,
collected cans from the shelves
and forced the money
into the clerk's reluctant staring hand.

We are the ones identified by case number,
summons in the wrong language,
judgment without stay of execution.
Mrs. Alfaro has ten days
to bundle the confusion of five children
down claustrophobic stairs
and away from the apartment.

And at the bar two blocks away,
immigrants with Spanish mouths
hear trumpets
from the islands of their eviction.
The sound scares away devils
like tropical fish
darting between the corals.

Niggerlips

Niggerlips was the high school name
for me.
So called by Douglas
the car mechanic, with green tattoos
on each forearm,
and the choir of round pink faces
that grinned deliciously
from the back row of classrooms,
droned over by teachers
checking attendance too slowly.

Douglas would brag
about cruising his car
near sidewalks of black children
to point an unloaded gun,
to scare niggers
like crows off a tree,
he'd say.

My great-grandfather Luis
was un negrito too,
a shoemaker in the coffee hills
of Puerto Rico, 1900

The family called him a secret
and kept no photograph.
My father remembers
the childhood white powder
that failed to bleach
his stubborn copper skin,
and the family says
he is still a fly in milk.
So Niggerlips has the mouth
of his great-grandfather,
the song he must have sung
as he pounded the leather and nails,
the heat that courses through copper,
the stubbornness of a fly in milk,
and all you have, Douglas,
is that unloaded gun.

The Given Account

—Puerto Rico, 1510

They said they were gods, and we believed—
they crossed uncrossable seas after all

in ships with sails like wings—but Salcedo
is dead. Pacing river shallows, turning rocks,

sifting sand for flecks of gold, he cut his foot
on stone or shell, sending braids of blood

downstream. Overhead, wind shook trees
so leaves and light spilled in, catching a school

of fish, a silver shimmer. I was there.
Kneeling on the bank, I dressed his wound

pressing strips of cloth to stop the flood
but red spots seeped through the weave,

my fingers wet with blood, his blood,
no different from mine. He winced, his face

paled by pain, but nothing, nothing changed,
no dove, no cloud, no beam of light, and he

a god or son of god? I, who came to drink,
struck dumb by one thought—they bleed, they die—

led him back into the pool and pushed
his head below. His arms thrashed, legs kicked,

lungs inhaled mouths of water. He stopped.
Three days I stayed to see him stir, but he,

not strongest, weakest or cruelest of them,
did not move. I pulled him out. He hung

wet and limp and heavy in my arms—
this man, this man, almost too much to bear.

Hubble's Law

Before dawn, fishermen motor far into the open sea.
The bay long dead. Their lanterns lit.

Meanwhile, in the plaza, the manicured trees
strung with lights, the fountain and its expanding rings.
The steeple. The brown, plaster Christ.
Yellow mountains rise in the background,

and the houses are sleeping. I sit at the window
and think of a dock stretching in darkness,
my hands, a net cast: it opens and opens wider,
the weights never breaking the surface, never sinking.

Beyond the pier, the lights disperse,
each a star beneath the stars, a boat, a man drifting out.

The Battle of Nashville

Snow gives the sky a new dimension—depth,
a soft glow, as if the air lit the yard,
which slopes to the city, which shimmers.
The river is always moving, but the atrium
on Fifth, the Kress, where blacks locked arms
and would not budge. A plow takes the hill,
where cars line up in rows, and half-built lofts
replace the houses. The man who built our house
built diesel engines, and kept the trucks
he couldn't fix. His daughters sold it all,
except the how-to books, the shop fan
he left in the attic. We're not brave,
but we find one another in bed each night,
your hand or my hand reaching out.
In the morning, you take the trash, and I make
the coffee. Nearby, battles were fought,
and men, whose wives waited for them, died.
If soldiers held the highest ground, one stood
here. If there is one, there is at least
one more. Standing shoulder to shoulder,

they share a blanket, as snow settles in the trees.
I think they are afraid. I think this is love.

～ᘡ ᘡ～

A Warm Day in Winter

The leash looped around my wrist, we stop
to let the dog piss across a trunk—
the branches stark this late in winter,
though everyone is out, spreading blankets
on the grass, eating with plastic forks.
We amble across the park without purpose
or direction, our wheels pausing
at stick and stone before we jostle on,
your eyes attuned to every first, fixed
upon the few leaves above, withered
but holding. You flail your fists
at the small sky, the brief light it carries.
Tomorrow, the cold will rush back
into the city, and neither you nor the dog
will understand or remember, though
you might respond cheerfully, not knowing why,
when we return one day in spring. I try
to see as you, without likeness or memory,
as I did the night that you were born.
Before, I couldn't guess your complexion,
the color of your eyes, the mark that spread
across your back like a map of the world.
I told myself it was because you didn't come
from me, but Mother says it was the same
for her. At once, the thought became the form
as in the myth, the woman springs
from her father's head, your face determined
in its particulars, the forehead's frown
beneath lamps that kept you warm, the hoarse cry
as you expelled the first breaths of air,
so in my arms, at last, I didn't know you,
but looked in wonder all the same,
noting how little you weighed. You will not
recall any of this, of course, which seems
a shame, when you are older, how

I fed you through the late hours in a room,
sterile and cold, but for paintings of landscapes
much like this one or how we walked
along the row of trees avoiding roots
that surfaced, and stopped awhile
beneath an elm on a warm December day.

～‿‿⌐

Proof

This yard is sacred. My son
reaches into the sky and cups the moon to his mouth.
When I close my eyes, the color makes
me think of his blanket, the great cosmos.

Before the Big Bang, the void ate light,
matter, time—there was no limit to that hunger.
Turned under the streetlamp, the rock's bright specks
look infinite. In a multiverse, he is here,
holding his small hand to his face, and he

is not here. Beyond one edge, a new world
imagines itself expanding in air.
We lean back in the damp grass. The leap
is cold and dark. The lungs open and open again.

～‿‿⌐

Lighter,

the word that comes to mind after many nights.
As when a plane descends over a city
you call home, the body's rise against the belt
strung across your lap. Darkness and lampposts,
like gold and silver beads below, falling
into them. Or better yet, wading in
the bioluminescent bay and each kick
creates a soft glow, each stroke makes you think
light could come from the body, and not
a world disturbed into brilliance. Because
it captures what I mean—both the weight
and how you see what you could not. As when

90

I heard him cry and lumbered down the hall
to find you there, first, pacing the room, singing
softly in his ear. Through the window,
the city sparkled and seemed to have grown
though, by day, I never see more than two
or three men working at once, lifting
together, say, a plank of wood. Years ago,
my mother sat beside my bed, eager to bear
the fever with me. We pass him back
and forth between us till it breaks,
and I no longer want what I wanted
before. As when one day you look upon
the house you've built and can't recall the field.

After 21 Years, A Postcard from My Father

The first time Dad sent me
his love through the mail,
he wrote a letter
and a one-dollar check
for chocolates, he said.
I was six years old, coarse
brown braids, knees like petrified
breasts, granny glasses that darkened
in the sun. I wore shorts under my uniform
and went to Father-Daughter dinners
with my friend Cindy and her dad.
My abuelo picked me up from school.

And Tony (a.k.a. my father)
said in his letter: "Obedece
a tu abuela. No te cortes el pelo.
Aquí te mando dinero para dulces y chocolates."

I changed the one to a nine on the check
and never wrote back. Never cashed
in on Dad's long distance love.

Today, I skip down the stairs
with the knowledge: *my father wrote to me!*
I understand now that this is all
I need to know. I will never see
what has tormented the man
from the day I was born,
the day he called himself a father
for the first time.

This afternoon on the bus,
I watched a retarded boy slapping himself
on the back, a gesture that started
as a caress, his hand moving
over his shoulder as if a cat
or a parrot perched there.

And then the hand grew
wild, angry, tormented, a slapping
that hunched him down on the seat of the bus.

"What's on your back?" I asked him.
He looked at me with eyes that pitied
my lack of vision, my need to know

everything. How could I not see
what his torment was?

"Wings," he said quietly.
"They won't leave me alone," he said.
"They're too heavy," he said.

⌁⌁⌁

Sor Juana's Litany in the Subjunctive

> (Sor Juana Inés de la Cruz, seventeenth-century
> Mexican nun, scholar and poet, is hailed the world
> over as the first feminist and Tenth Muse of the Americas.)

if I could rub myself
along your calf,
feel your knee
break the waters of my shame;

if I could lay my cheek
against the tender sinews
of your thigh,
smell the damp
cotton that Athena
never wore, her blood
tracks steaming in the snow;

if I could forget
the devil and the priest
who guard my eyes
with pitchfork and with host;

if I could taste
the bread, the blood, the salt
between your legs
as I taste mine;

if I could turn myself
into a bee and free
this soul, those bars
webbed across your window
would be vain, that black
cloth, that rosary, that crucifix—
nothing could save you
from my sting.

Confessions

(For the survivors)

1.
Bless me, Father, for my sins
spill out of me
when I think of rape.
(You know what rape is, right?)
When I think of men
with egos softer than pimples,
so scared of lesbians
they rape us in alleys and cellars
stab us on beaches,
use rangefinders to jack off
before shooting holes
through our woman-love.
Tucking that tail
between their own legs
they claim provocation, emasculation,
Sodom and Gomorra as a last resort.
And you sitting here, Father,
listening to my blasphemy
your hard head swollen
with righteousness, meting out penance
like strokes on your dick.

I know what you're up to.
I've been to your trial.

2.
Father, I cross myself
when I think of you
remembering how you slipped
unannounced,
quiet as Gabriel,
into that virgin
place between
my eleven-year-old thighs,
how every night you rested there,
a saint in his hollow,
an angel on the wing
bursting haloes
through my prayers.

3.
My shell is pink and gray
like a clam or a vagina. The whole
place smells like salt.
Further in, it's dark
and moist; when I contract,
Father, how narrow
you make me smile.

You're curious, I know.

A long white beam filters up
the middle of my spine, lining
the back walls like a warm tongue.
You're looking for home,
but not even the pearl
you find is precious.

4.
I eat hearts
of artichoke and palm
I eat wax
that drips from the votive

wicks of prostitutes
and nuns
I eat shadows
I eat thorns
I eat the cinnamon
light of your eyes, taste
of your skin after
you come.

   Come, Father, eat
of this body, drink of this
blood, as if the only memory
left in our peckered history
were curled under
the tongue
green seed
sprouting planets.

Outline for a Cuban Folk-Dance

For the quiet marlins at dusk
there's no desire harboring in the dark.
Yet you left hurriedly aroused
by premonitions
read in the erratic pattern of the rainfall.
The tides that never reached us
swallow the child absorbed in pressing twigs
on the pink sand
and set her free on the other side.
I thought of ribbons
distant shadows
streamers and red kites against the wind.

There's no desire left beneath the skin.
No marlins hushed in the fresh sunset.
No voices in the rain
washing through the spiraling wisteria.
Nothing that I can truly hear
or smell or possibly
mysteriously remember. I go about
polishing copper pots and silver
candlesticks. I rearrange the lies.
Travel from place to place.
Cool chickpea stew as I await.

When you return I hear the muffled fall
of acorns.
You retrieve the unplayed, open accordion
from the chair
and let it fall unharmed on your deliberate
search. You have indeed forgotten
the vase so delicately traced
with early tamarind
from your patio in Havana.

I now know
we sat too long between the acts.
Your shoulder brushes against the arc

of my name. It whispers old Assyrian riddles.
In rising tones recites in an Ionian dialect.
But the meanings are all lost
in the staleness of dead tongues.
Are these papyrus scrolls, I wonder,
beneath the reddened sponges of mamey
inside your brain?
Do you ever lament for the loss of the land
as you sway to the beat of a native dance-step?

Rodolfo "Corky" Gonzales

I Am Joaquín: an Epic Poem

I am Joaquín
lost in a world of confusion,
caught up in a whirl of a
         gringo society,
confused by the rules,
scorned by attitudes,
suppressed by manipulations,
and destroyed by modern society.
My fathers
      have lost the economic battle
and won
      the struggle of cultural survival.
And now!
      I must choose

between the paradox of
victory of the spirit,
despite physical hunger
               or
      to exist in the grasp
of American social neurosis,
sterilization of the soul
      and a full stomach.

Yes,
I have come a long way to nowhere,
unwillingly dragged by that
      monstrous, technical
      industrial giant called
               Progress
and Anglo success . . .
   I look at myself.
      I watch my brothers.
            I shed tears of sorrow.

I sow seeds of hate.
    I withdraw to the safety within the
circle of life . . .
        MY OWN PEOPLE

I am Cuauhtémoc,
proud and Noble
    leader of men,
King of an empire,
civilized beyond the dreams
    of the Gachupín Cortez.
who is also the blood,
    the image of myself.
I am the Maya Prince.
I am Nezahualcóyotl,
great leader of the Chichimecas.
I am the sword and flame of Cortez
            the despot.
                    And
I am the Eagle and Serpent of
            the Aztec civilization.
I owned the land as far as the eye
could see under the crown of Spain,
and I toiled on my earth
and gave my Indian sweat and blood
    for the Spanish master,
who ruled with tyranny over man and
beast and all that he could trample
                    But . . .
        THE GROUND WAS MINE . . .
I was both tyrant and slave.

As Christian church took its place
    in God's good name,
to take and use my Virgin Strength and
                    trusting faith,
The priests
    both good and bad,
                took
But
    gave a lasting truth that
                Spaniard,

100

                              Indio,
                                     Mestizo
were all God's children
and
          from these words grew men
                              who prayed and fought
                                             for
          their own worth as human beings,
                                     for
                                     that
                              GOLDEN MOMENT
                                     of
                              FREEDOM.

I was part in blood and spirit
          of that
                    courageous village priest
                              Hidalgo
in the year eighteen hundred and ten
who rang the bell of independence
and gave out that lasting cry:

          "El Grito de Dolores, qué mueran
          los Guachupines y que viva
          la Virgen de Guadalupe . . ."

I sentenced him
                    who was me.
I excommunicated him my blood.
I drove him from the pulpit to lead
          a bloody revolution for him and me . . .
                              I killed him.
His head,
          which is mine and all of those
          who have come this way,
I placed on that fortress wall
          to wait for independence.
Morelos!
          Matamoros!
                    Guerrero!
All compañeros in the act,

STOOD AGAINST THAT WALL OF
                        INFAMY
        to feel the hot gouge of lead
                which my hands made.
I died with them . . .
I lived with them
I lived to see our country free.
Free
        from Spanish rule in
                eighteen-hundred-twenty-one.
                        Mexico was free ? ?
The crown was gone
                but
all his parasites remained
                        and ruled
                        and taught
        with gun and flame and mystic power.
I worked,
I sweated,
I bled,
I prayed
        and
waited silently for life to again
                        commence.

I fought and died
                for
                Don Benito Juárez
                guardian of the Constitution.
I was him
                on dusty roads
                                on barren land
as he protected his archives
        as Moses did his sacraments.
He held his Mexico
                in his hand
                        on
                the most desolate
                and remote ground
                which was his country,
And this giant
                Little Zapotec

                                        gave
            not one palm's breath
of his country to
            Kings or Monarchs or Presidents
of foreign powers.

I am Joaquín.
I rode with Pancho Villa,
            crude and warm.
A tornado at full strength,
nourished and inspired
            by the passion and the fire
            of all his earthy people.
I am Emiliano Zapata.
                    "This Land
                            this Earth
                                        is
                                    OURS"
The villages
        the mountains
                the streams
        belong to the Zapatistas.
                    Our life
                    or yours
is the only trade for soft brown earth
and maize.
All of which is our reward,
            a creed that formed a constitution
                        for all who dare live free!
"This land is ours . . .
        Father, I give it back to you.
                        Mexico must be free . . ."
I ride with Revolutionists
                        against myself.

I am rural
        coarse and brutal,
I am the mountain Indian,
        superior over all.
The thundering hoofbeats are my horses.
The chattering of machine guns
        are death to all of me:
            Yaqui

Tarahumara
Chamula
Zapotec
Mestizo
Español

I have been the Bloody Revolution,
the victor,
the vanquished,
I have killed
    and been killed.
                I am despots Díaz
                and Huerta
and the apostle of democracy
                Francisco Madero.

I am
the black-shawled
faithful women
who die with me
or live
depending on the time and place.
I am
    faithful,
    humble,
        Juan Diego
        the Virgin de Guadalupe
        Tonantzin, Aztec Goddess too.

I rode the mountains of San Joaquín.
I rode as far East and North
        as the Rocky Mountains
                and
all men feared the guns of
            Joaquín Murrieta.
I killed those men who dared
    to steal my mine,
        who raped and killed
                my love
                my wife
then
I killed to stay alive.

I was Alfego Baca,
      living my nine lives fully.
I was the Espinosa brothers
      of the Valle de San Luis.
All
were added to the number of heads that
      in the name of civilization
were placed on the wall of independence.
Heads of brave men
who died for cause and principle.
Good or bad.
                  Hidalgo! Zapata!
                  Murrieta! Espinosa!
are but a few.
They
dared to face
The force of tyranny
                  of men
                    who rule
                  by farce and hypocrisy
I stand here looking back,
and now I see
                  the present
and still
      I am the campesino
      I am the fat political coyote
                              I,
of the same name,
                  Joaquín.
In a country that has wiped out
all my history,
                  stifled all my pride.
In a country that has placed a
different weight of indignity upon
                  my
                  age
                  old
                        burdened back.
            Inferiority
is the new load . . .
      The Indian has endured and still
emerged the winner,

The Mestizo must yet overcome,
    And the Gauchupín we'll just ignore.
I look at myself
and see part of me
who rejects my father and my mother
and dissolves into the melting pot
    to disappear in shame.
I sometimes
sell my brother out
and reclaim him
for my own, when society gives me
    token leadership
        in society's own name.

I am Joaquín,
who bleeds in many ways.
The altars of Moctezuma
    I stained a bloody red.
    My back of Indian slavery
            was stripped crimson
    from the whips of masters
    who would lose their blood so pure
    when Revolution made them pay
Standing against the walls of
    Retribution.
            Blood . . .
        has flowed from
        me
on every battlefield
            between
campesino, hacendado
    slave and master
        and
    Revolution.

I jumped from the tower of Chapultepec
    into the sea of fame;

My country's flag
    my burial shroud;
with Los Niños,
    whose pride and courage

could not surrender
                with indignity
                their country's flag
To strangers . . . in their land.
Now
        I bleed in some smelly cell
        from club,
        or gun,
        or tyranny,
I bleed as the vicious gloves of hunger
        cut my face and eyes,
as I fight my way from stinking Barrios
        to the glamour of the ring
                and lights of fame
                        or mutilated sorrow.
My blood runs pure on the ice caked
hills of the Alaskan Isles,
on the corpse-strewn beach of Normandy,
the foreign land of Korea
        and now
                Vietnam.

Here I stand
                before the court of Justice
                        Guilty
for all the glory of my Raza
                        to be sentenced to despair.
Here I stand
        poor in money
        arrogant with pride
                        bold with Machismo
                        rich in courage
                                and
                        wealthy in spirit and faith.
My knees are caked with mud.
My hands calloused from the hoe.
I have made the Anglo rich
                        yet
        equality is but a word,
        the Treaty of Hidalgo has been broken
        and is but another treacherous promise.

My land is lost
                    and stolen,
My culture has been raped,
            I lengthen
            the line at the welfare door
and fill the jails with crime.
            These then
are the rewards
            this society has
for sons of chiefs
                    and kings
                    and bloody revolutionists.
Who
gave a foreign people
            all their skills and ingenuity
to pave the way with brains and blood
for
those hordes of gold-starved
                            strangers
who
changed our language
and plagiarized our deeds
                        as feats of valor
                        of their own.
They frowned upon our way of life
        and took what they could use.
                        our Art
                        our Literature
                        our Music, they ignored
so they left the real things of value
and grabbed at their own destruction
                    by their greed and avarice
They overlooked that cleansing fountain of
                    nature and brotherhood
Which is Joaquín.
        The art of our great señores
                                Diego Rivera
                                Siqueiros
                                Orozco is but
another act of revolution for
                    the salvation of mankind.
                    Mariachi music, the

heart and soul
of the people of the earth,
the life of child,
and the happiness of love.
The corridos tell the tales
of life and death,
        of tradition,
     legends old and new,
     of joy
     of passion and sorrow
     of the people . . . who I am.

I am in the eyes of woman,
      sheltered beneath
her shawl of black,
      deep and sorrowful
      eyes,
that bear the pain of sons long buried
      or dying,
      dead
on the battlefield or on the barbed wire
      of social strife.
Her rosary she prays and fingers
endlessly
   like the family
working down a row of beets
      to turn around
      and work
      and work
    There is no end.
Her eyes a mirror of all the warmth
      and all the love for me,
And I am her
And she is me.
      We face life together in sorrow,
      anger, joy, faith and wishful
      thoughts.

I shed tears of anguish
as I see my children disappear
behind a shroud of mediocrity
never to look back to remember me.

I am Joaquín.
                    I must fight
                              And win this struggle
                              for my sons, and they
                              must know from me
                              who I am.
Part of the blood that runs deep in me
could not be vanquished by the Moors.
I defeated them after five hundred years,
and I endured.
          The part of blood that is mine
          has labored endlessly five hundred
          years under the heel of lustful
                    Europeans
                    I am still here!
I have endured in the rugged mountains
          of our country.
I have survived the toils and slavery
          of the fields.
                    I have existed
in the barrios of the city,
in the suburbs of bigotry,
in the mines of social snobbery,
in the prisons of dejection,
in the muck of exploitation
and
in the fierce heat of racial hatred.

And now the trumpet sounds,
The music of the people stirs the
                    Revolution,
Like a sleeping giant it slowly
rears its head

to the sound of
                    tramping feet
               clamoring voices
             mariachi strains
           fiery tequila explosions
        the smell of chile verde and
     soft brown eyes of expectation for a
                              better life.

And in all the fertile farm lands,
                    the barren plains,
the mountain villages,
smoke-smeared cities
                    We start to MOVE.
     La Raza!
Mejicano!
   Español!
       Latino!
             Hispano!
                 Chicano!
or whatever I call myself,
                 I look the same
                 I feel the same
                 I cry
                          and
                 Sing the same
I am the masses of my people and
I refuse to be absorbed.
             I am Joaquín
The odds are great
but my spirit is strong
                 my faith unbreakable
                 my blood is pure
I am Aztec Prince and Christian Christ
        I SHALL ENDURE!
        I WILL ENDURE!

Memory of the Hand

The hand recalls what it has held,
the fist of truth wedged inside the knuckles,

fitting into the drum of things you cared about,
lifting its memory to allow you

to be alone when
you are not alone,

forcing you to reach out, take care
of that memory you made up with your hands,

the one about taking your father's arm
you have never held,

helping him cross the street
where you let him go

without waving goodbye or making
a fist at him in anger.

The band aches for what it has held,
mist washing its fingers like smoke

where you hid your knowledge
of a sign language, a movement of joints,

palms and fingers trying to spell
that silent moment when

you touched what moved out
of your reach—

a soft yearning, a bare back,
the tiny mountain range of spine rising

to remind you the hand holds onto little flesh,
knows nothing about the skin except lines

on its own palms, deep furrows where
the weight of remembrance is held.

Helen

How things have changed, Helena,
the anguished cry for a homeland
left behind
the first encounter with
the tall, uniform faded towers of the empire,
the wide avenues
buried under immense layers of snow,
the traffic signs,
one way, no parking anytime, quarters only.
The daily toils with a heater,
with feet bumping into sleeping rugs,
and the scar on your left knee,
sad reminder of an escalator's collapse.

No time fur letters home, Helena,
now you are enthralled with
the greatness of the Intrepid Museum,
the aircraft carrier inhabiting
New York's port and the Hudson's waters.
Taken aback only by its greatness
and its illustrious history of wartime deeds
—as the guide books remind us—
its sea voyages
its impressive record of nautical miles.
Take a good look at its walls.
Oh, taken aback only by its greatness
Its walls smartly decorated
cannot hide the victims of bygone years.

This immense ship once happened to pass by your island
just to see what was happening.

How things have changed, Helena,
your mother misses
the final A left out of your name
in your last letter home.
This is how things are now, you tell her,

because your American boyfriend calls you Helen,
and you tell your friends
how he beds you
how he stays in your room
how he is free with you
how he never goes out with you
but, of course, Helena,
what will his friends say of a dark-skinned Mama like you?
And his mother, picture her shame,
unable to understand your English,
much less your Spanish.
So what? you answer,
you find him nice,
better than those Latin machos,
and so he continues to bed you
while he dates a Northamerican blonde
No, never a Latin man, for
how are you to improve your lot?
Are you forgetting that when Latin are machos
the gringos are . . . Forgive this pause.

Ah, Helen,
I find it difficult to call you by that name
—the missing A.
You must understand my fondness for your folks.

Pedro—mi amigo—would have long called you
una puta
for confusing stupidity
with improving your lot.

How things have changed, Helena,
the radio cassette, remote control,
la washing machine, la dishwasher,
treasures beyond your finest dreams.
Comida, fiesta, letrina,
never again to be found in your conversation.
Now you speak of lunch, parties and toilet,
rock, tours of the U.S. of A
and other countries
and, of course, your mink coat,
inseparable companion even in your summer days.

How things have changed, Helena,
far away many are still dreaming
and awaiting your next trip
to Tokyo, Paris or Frankfurt.
Letters from the beloved homeland
tearfully left behind
are torn
before they are read
because you think that they will ask you for money
and your income for the next three years
has already been spent.

Oh, Helena,
impatiently awaiting
Thanksgiving and
Halloween.

One would never believe, Helena,
what your birth certificate states:
Cabimota,
a sector of Jimayaco
between much hunger and little land,
province of La Vega,
half a life away from civilization,
República Dominicana.

<hr />

Martha at the Edge of Desire*

Martha grew up watching the workers
refining petroleum at her father's plant
watching the way their arms
suited their bodies
and their bodies suited to life
without ever attaining
sizable arms
or length of life.

*Translated by Jane Robinett

Because of this
Martha could go to an auction of men
and pick out the biggest.
She thought that all big men
had huge hearts
and could love more than the rest.

Martha began loving and wanting.
She believed her surrender was little
to give for such a serious lover.

So it went for seven years
and the big man had already made seven sons
all born at the right time and
at inopportune moments.

Martha woke up one day,
her seven sons tied to her skirt,
more aware of the weight of the big man
the man whose heart she had believed immense
more immense than the endless clouds
shaped by the smokestacks
of her father's oil refinery.

That day Martha went back to the auction
and walked among all the men
big, small, and bigger still
and returned to her house alone
without anyone,
to comfort her sons, to look them over,
to scrub their chests, seal up their pores,
to keep their hearts and bodies
from beginning to grow.

Maria and the Others*

I like to see Maria every morning
when her pride goes our for a walk
like someone innocently walking
a little poodle.
I watch her when she goes window-shopping
and the windows are nothing to her.
When the neighborhood seems ridiculous
when in her imagination
she has travelled in all the countries of the world
when she tells her girlfriends they have no
presence, class, breeding.
When she asks for brandy or cognac
with names known only to connoiseurs.

I watch her when she catches a gypsy cab
or when she sneaks into the pawn shop.
I watch her when everything she uses is imported.

Especially
I watch her
when she dresses up like a lady
or better yet
like what she believes she has always been.

*Translated by Jane Robinett

Victor Hernández Cruz

Going Uptown to Visit Miriam

on the train
old ladies playing football
going for empty seats

very funny persons

the train riders
    are silly people
    i am a train rider

but no one knows where i am
going to take this train

to take this train
to take this train
are popular   they get off
at 42 to change for the
westside line   or off
59 for the department store

the train pulls in & out
the white walls   dark-
ness   white walls   dark-
ness

ladies looking up i
wonder where they going
the dentist   pick up
husband pick up wife
pick up kids
pick up? grass?
to library   to museum
to laundromat   to school

but no one knows where i am
going to take this train

to take this train

to visit miriam
to visit miriam

& to kiss her
on the cheek
& hope i don't
see sonia on the
street

But no one knows where i'm taking
this train
   taking this train
   to visit miriam.

～ᴗ ᴗ～

Three Days/out of Franklin

the soul is a beautiful thing
& i live by the soul
when i walk
it takes me
            today
i didn't go to school
i read
got high
ate
read
wrote
got high
spoke to carlos
saw the indians
on t.v.
& in my mind
& heart
they kick
the white man
in the ass
went down
got high

took a bus
honeychild
& claudia
giggled
about paul
homemade
chicken
& rice
found a dime
sticking
in the tar
jefferson park
the wind
talks
night
morning
no school
black coffee
corn muffin
read david's
felix
listened
to joe bataan
wrote
i learned
today
beautiful
soul
went down
spoke to some
children
& slowly
remembered

chino
singing
baby
O
baby
in the
hallway
at 12-17

i smiled
at the rain
when it fell
from the window
wrote
head
night
morning
no school
but the world
& my soul
& all the love
that wants to
blow up
like joe bataan's
trombones
night

three days
with myself
& the world
soul is beautiful
thing
the smell of
everything
ahead
the earth
& all the people/
     victor hernández cruz
     exiled from franklin
     december 14 to 19

The Physics of Ochun

A group of professional
scientists
from Columbia University
heard that in an old
tenement apartment
occupied by a family

named González
a plaster-of-Paris
statue made in Rome
of Caridad del Cobre
started crying
The scientists
curious as they are
took a ride across
town to investigate
After stating their purpose
and their amazement
they were led to the
room where the statue was
Sure enough it was wet
under the eyes
Overnight, Señora González
told them, it had cried so
much that they were able
to collect a jar full of tears
The scientist almost knocked his
gold-rim glasses off his face
May we have this as a specimen
to study in our laboratory?
She agreed, and they took a taxi
with the jar to Columbia
They went directly to the lab
to put the tears through a
series of tests
They put a good amount of
the liquid under their
Strong Microscope
Lo and behold!
What they saw made them loosen
their neckties What they saw made them loosen
their neckties
There inside the liquid
clearly made out through
the microscope was the
word: JEHOVA
No matter how much they
moved the water they
kept getting the word

They sent for a bottle of
scotch
They served themselves in test tubes
They called the González family
to see if they could explain
All the González family knew
was that it was the tears
of Caridad del Cobre
They explained to Señora González
what was happening
She said that weirder than that
was the fact that her
window had grown a staircase
that went up beyond the clouds
She said she and her daughter
had gone up there to check it
out
because, she told them, a
long white rope had come out
of their belly buttons and some-
thing was pulling them up
What happened? the enthusiastic
scientists from Columbia University
wanted to know
We went up there and were
massaged by the wind
We got hair permanents
and our nails manicured
looking a purple red
My daughter says she saw
a woodpecker designing the
air
The scientists put the phone down
and their eyes orbited the room
We have to get out there
Incredible things are happening
They rushed back out
and into the González residency
They entered
It's in the same
room with the statue
They rushed in and went to the

window
So amazed were they
they lost their speech
All their organs migrated an inch
Clearly in front of them
a 3-foot-wide marble stair
which went up into the sky
The scientists gathered themselves
to the point of verbalizing again
They each wanted to make sure
that the other was "cognizant"
of the *espectáculo*
Once they settled upon reality
they decided that the urge to
explore was stronger than their
fears
One decided to take a writing pad
to take notes
One decided to take a test tube
in case he ran into substances
One decided to take a thermometer
and an air bag to collect atmosphere
Señora González, would you please
come up with us?
They wanted to know if she would
lead them up
If you could see it you could touch
it, she told them
She went out first and they
followed
The marble steps were cold
They could have been teeth of
the moon
As they went up the breeze smiled
against their ears
The murmur of the streets dimmed
They were climbing and climbing
when they felt a whirlpool in
the air
For sure it was the hairdresser
Señora González sensed the odor of
many flowers in the breeze

The scientist with the test tube
saw it get full of a white liquid
The scientist with the air bag
felt it change into a chunk of metal
The scientist with the writing pad
saw a language appear on it backwards
printing faster than a computer
The paper got hot like a piece of
burning wood
and he dropped it down into the
buildings
It went through an open window
and fell into a pot of red beans
A woman by the name Concepción was
cooking
Frightened she took it to a doctor's
appointment she had the next day
She showed it to the physician
who examined it
He thought it was the imprint
of flower petals
so even and bold in lilac
ink
The dream Concepción had during
the night came back to her
I know what's going on, doctor
I'll see you in nine months
Walking she remembered forgetting
to put the *calabaza* into the beans
and rushed home sparkling in
her yellow dress

El Trópico

for H. and A.

The amateur riders exchange glances
from the Trojan horses
that have led them here.
They look down
at their lost destiny
to where the palms drift in the salty breeze
while the children run barefoot
at the river's edge
or hide in the hammock
pretending to be captains of some grand galleon.
Their legs surround
the ample strength of these horses
that pull them closer to the forest,
wanting to get lost among the branches.
But afraid of being betrayed once more
the riders take control of the reins.

Dear Tía

I do not write.
The years have frightened me away.
My life in a land so familiarly foreign,
a denial of your presence.
Your name is mine.
One black and white photograph of your youth,
all I hold on to.
One story of your past.

The pain comes not from nostalgia.
I do not miss your voice urging me in play,
your smiles,
or your pride when others called you my mother.
I cannot close my eyes and feel your soft skin;
listen to your laughter;
smell the sweetness of your bath.
I write because I cannot remember at all.

127

An Unexpected Conversion

Mother hid from us the blue and white beads
her nanny, Brigida,
had given her, and the plate of
pennies in honey under the Virgin's skirt.
She rarely spoke about the island,
never taught us to cook black beans.

Father played Stravinsky and Debussy on Sundays.
Once, he relented and taught us the guaguancó.
He swore, as she did, they would never go back.
He's thirty years in exile and
about to retire.

But today, mother and I sit in the garden.
She rests on the edge of an old rusted swing
and speaks of reconstruction,
of roads and houses; "I know they'll
need an experienced engineer," she says looking at dad.
Her hair blows gently in the breeze.

I've never seen her look so young.
I've never felt so old.

The Child of Exile

Only weeks ago he finally stopped
looking for the shadows of Havana
palm fronds outside his door.
But now, for the first time in
thirty years, he speculates
about a home that isn't his.
By night, he dreams of fogless mirrors
and migratory birds.
He writes poems about forgotten relatives,
tobacco pickers and sugar cane fields.

He has packed his bags with resurrected
images of tiled houses,
white dunes and baroque cathedrals.

The Hyphenated Man

Do you wake up each day
with an urge for a bagel
with café con leche?
Do you flip back and forth
through *The Miami Herald* comparing every word
to *El Nuevo Herald?*
Do you circle around back alleys
trying to decide between McDonalds and
Pollo Tropical?
Do you feel guilty buying Cuban bread
at Publix,
while getting a cheesecake at Sedanos?
At Thanksgiving, do you creep into the kitchen
to put mojito on the turkey,
and then complain at Christmas because
there's lechón instead of turkey?
Do you find yourself two-stepping
to salsa beat and dancing guaracha
to every other jazz beat?
Does your heart skip a beat for Sonia Braga
while longing wistfully for the days of Doris Day?
If so my friend,
then you are the hyphenated man.
Yes, H-Y-P-H-E-N.
The hyphenated man
lurks beneath that confident exterior,
and it's time you consider
Hyphens Anonymous,
where the confused straddlers find refuge
and solace.
They meet once a week,
talk Spanglish to their hearts' content,
eat mariquitas with hot dogs, and
cuban coffee with Dunkin Donuts,

without explanations or alienations.
Not the twelve step program,
but the three step dilemma.
Join today and
get off the see-saw,
jump off the fence,
slide down the hill,
cross the bridge,
get into the circle,
turn from the mirror.
Don't get off the wagon,
get on the hyphen.
Do not delay.
Hyphens Anonymous can help you forget
who you are
or better
who you wish you could be.

Sorting Miami

> *I pale my cheek against the pane*
> *as the runway jolt blurs us into our city.*
> —Ricardo Pau-Llosa

I watch them unnoticed
from the cement railing outside
the Jose Martí YMCA, its glass doors locked for the day.

Tomatoes, limes, onions
hang in cellophane bags
from the rusted van.

Crates of papayas and avocados
surround this old vendor still smiling
after 11 years on the same street corner.

Friends take turn in the shade
exchanging stories
from a distant canvas.

A middle-aged woman, fighting a lost battle,
protects herself
with her red umbrella.

A young woman struggles
to push the baby carriage
along the brick sidewalk.

A Jeep pulls up
to buy its share
of the tropics.

I understand their voices,
and the silhouette of the vendor
could easily be that of my uncle, dead in Havana.

But in minutes,
I drive across a deep fissure
in the asphalt.
I wonder, how long will I be able
to step into this mirror of a city
and return home in one piece?

Freedom

for Belkis Cuza Malé

For 20 years they hid your words
afraid of you,
a young girl from Guantánamo,
the daughter of a cement factory worker.

They silenced poems of
cinderellas and silver platters,
frightened by your beautiful people
and portraits of sad poets.

Now, far from your island and them,
your poems shout without restrictions.
But the words remain unheard.
*Here, a poem
doesn't upset anyone.*

Blake in the Tropics

We leave the Jaragua hotel
in our stocking feet and shaven faces
to stumble over these bodies
yet to reach puberty.

They have turned dust into blankets
and newspapers into pillows
on a street edged in refuse.
Warm waves break against the sea wall,

never touching their bodies.
We are not in Blake's London and
the black on these boys
will not wash off with the dawn.

Geography Jazz

Yes! We abandon
the pastel façades,
the curves,
the sculptured towers
on the Beach.
Those glass doors
edged with flamingos
take us
Yes!
to another city
we recall
through
secondhand
memories.
Yes!

Mongo's hands,
ecstatic pain,
he beats the conga

we rise
we beat the tables
he rises
we sweat
he shouts
we shout
Yes!
he succumbs.
His skin is gray
taut
like the old hide
on his drum.

But now I hear
him
Yes! Pérez Prado.
She wants a mambo.
Who?
Lupita.
What's wrong with Lupita?
What does she want?
To dance.
They won't let her dance.
No?
But now she can dance,
here she is dancing.
Yes, yes, yes!
She wants that mambo.
1 2 3 4 5 6 7 8
arms to the sky,
she wants a mambo, a delicious mambo.

A mambo in sax?
It's Chocolate,
a thief in the dark,
playing between chords,
stealing melodies.
Chocolate and synthesis,
syncreticism,
sin,
sin of the Caribbean, no
limits, no regrets.

One escalating fusion
as sweet as chocolate.

Yes!
I hear them.
Mongo
Dámaso
Chocolate
I hear them all.
It's a bright place
and water sets no boundaries,
and time poses no obstacles.

~ ⚮ ~

How the Cubans Stole Miami

The Cubans have stolen Miami.
("Will the last one to leave
bring the American flag?")
And from whom did we steal it?

From the Basque sailor who
gave Biscayne its name?
Or perhaps from the Spanish missionaries who lived
with the mosquitoes by the swampy bay?

In all fairness, we must admit
we stole it from the Tequesta or the Seminoles,
natives, driven north by
Andrew jackson or south into the sea.

No, perhaps we stole it from the Spaniards
sent back to Havana after 300 years
of calling Florida home.
(And we complain about still being
in exile after only forty-four.)

If we didn't steal it from the Indians or the Spaniards
it must have been the Conks,
Bahamians who built the railroads with hands of coal
while being told to be more Negro like their neighbors
to the north.

134

I know, we stole it from
Flagler, Tuttle, Merrick and Fisher
who catered to the rich but never to the jewish.
(Only in Miami is a jew an Anglo.)
If I see one more photo of Domino Park
I'll turn into a Jew.

Was it he, papi, who stole Miami?
He, who engineered from the Bacardi building to
One Biscayne Tower
and every school addition from Edison
to Homestead High?

No, it must have been my mother.
(What was it Joan Didion wrote,
"a mango with jewels"?
poor mother, so lean and trim.)
She spent 34 years volunteering
(Sacándole el kilo, my father would sneer.)

The Museum of Science,
Viscaya,
The Youth Center,
The Archdiocese,
Ballet Concerto,
La Liga Contra el Cáncer,
The Mailman Center.
(A tour of Miami, you ask?)

Enough! says my dad,
locking up his checkbook tight.
"We're retiring out of Miami."
A new phenomenon,
"Cuban Flight,"
not to be confused with "White Flight."

If the Cubans have stolen Miami
and it's time they paid their dues,
then . . .

If I see one more photograph of Domino Park
who knows what I might do.

Woman, Woman

climb up
that ladder
bring down
the moon
or she
will tattle

tattle falsehood
to the skies
(and who
can tell
the truth
from lies?)

that it
is you
forever Eve
who rules
mere man
without
reprieve

When Conventional Methods Fail

. . . bat your eyelashes!

ain't nothing wrong
with using wile

:Eve used an apple
:Cleopatra used a rug
:La Malinche? oh she

      used Cortez
      to create
      La Nueva Raza

there's something
to be said for a
gal who understands
humanity, and thereby
the secret to success

feminists,
take heed:

      no se compliquen
      la vida!!

you're going at it
the hard way.

Gabriela Jáuregui

Fresa

I.
I asked my mother:
"Why can't I eat one?"
Since my doll had a strawberry
hair, hat, dress, smell.
She said,
"You'll get typhoid fever
like I did
just after you were born.
I almost died.
Strawberries
are irrigated
with shit, and
no matter how much
you wash them,
it won't come out.
You can only eat them
if they are cooked, in a jam
or a pie."

Later I learned
that strawberry
also means
yuppie,
stuck-up,
boring,
status quo, rich and uptight.
What my friends called girls
who wouldn't:
hang out with them,
smoke pot in the park,
or were too demanding.
I wasn't *fresa*.
Not dangerous.
Not difficult.
Not a threat.

II.
I eat a strawberry,
unwashed,
at the farmer's market
in Hollywood.
A little dirt
never killed
anyone.
The woman tells me they're delicious:
freshly picked
in her farm up the coast.
It tastes like fine sugar,
like mint almost.
The deep red of fresh blood
—a pinprick—
more purpled:
it is a heart
between my fingertips.

III.
Strawberries are the only fruit.
Seeds on the outside.
Ready for the world.
Fresa: the first fruit—from the latin, *fragra.*
Varieties grow in different regions:
Diamante, largest of all, from Watsonville, Salinas and Santa
    Maria.
Camarosa, pink, with a good shelf-life, from Oxnard, San Joaquin
    and San Diego.
Aromas, large but not fragrant, it turns out, probably named by
    some Mexican farmer as a *choteo* and more recently intro-
    duced to the market.
What names!
Seascape, Selva, Pacific,
Oso Grande, Gaviota, Chandler,
Camino Real—
The Royal Way,
regal, real
dark and deep,
newly pioneered in Santa Maria—
and *Ventana*, the window (open/closed?)
its lighter-skinned sister.

Families in
shades of red
like the blood
harvesting,
the blood
swelling in fingers
and feet
with toes red
and bloated—
overripe strawberries.
Backs are too-long bent,
muscles strained
to not rip the green leaves
off the top of each fruit.

IV.
Fresas: uptight, demanding.
In Strawberry, CA
methyl bromide
covers hands
and pumps
into arteries,
into red, red fruit,
to make it strong.
Poison and dirt
and red blood.

No matter how much
you wash them,
it won't come out.

Havana Blues

Hey
old man
sitting there
rocking slowly
back and forth
front porch.
Puffing on your Havana.

Rocking Chair
singing the blues
against wooden floor.
Chewing on your Havana.

Freshly pressed
blue guayabera
exposing your white chest hairs
and red turkey gobbler.
Thinking of your Havana.

Behind you
runs Interstate 10
no palm trees
no mango trees
no swift flowing river
rising to your second story

Casa de campo
angered by Cyclone Flora.
Crying for your Havana.

So your monthly struggle
straightens your troubled body
and you check for Uncle Sam's
once a month visit.
Dying for your Havana.

Hey
old man
your Havana is about to burn your lips
just like the ones before
and all the others to come
and all the others to come.

It's been 35 years
and counting
old man.
Don't die for your Havana.

～ᴗᴗ～

Forgotten Memory

Abuelita
Dolores
rocks back
and forth
in a daze
and when she laughs
her tongue sneaks through
the front teeth missing.

Occasionally
she'll stand
and run about
like a child
opening and closing
her palms
claiming to catch the wind
playing with icecubes
amazed she's able to hold water
in her hands.

Abuelita Dolores'
hair is gray and unkempt
flattened on the back
from long pillow hours

and her nylon socks
have long ago
lost their elasticity.

In penumbra
her life is a
medicine cabinet
where dreams of
broken elevators
and strewn high heel
spikes
are snapped
by the cold
steel razor
which weekly scrapes
her face.

Once upon a time
flapper-spinster-dancehall girl
your flower beds
lie naked
with petals blown
trampled by
time
love
and unborn children
dying to get out.

jesús papote

It was untouched energy that reached
the shakings of his embryonic testicles
he moved eyes closed body crouched face
inside her body nobody knew his identity
not even his name he laid inside casket
corpse brethren woman strung out deep
cornered jungle streets eyes closed body
crouched face tucked pregnant belly sali-
vating umbilical cord peddling multi-
cut heroin sub-ghetto fortress chanting
early winter 25-degree cold-frío shivering
lacked attention lacked warmth born-to-be
embryo asphyxiated 25 dollars powers pene-
trating veins venas veins venas pouring
rivers pouring up mountain muscles brain's
tributaries.

She allowed herself to be touched old men
seeking last-minute enjoyment thrills
social security military retirement pensions
on the woman about to give birth body running
down 13th street looking desperately for the
fix the fix hope-esperanza fix satisfaction
she tripped pained herself bleeding internally
the water bag had broken she did not care her
jugular veins were asking for attention to be
fed intravenously that was her priority to
satisfy her veins pinpointed needle metal rape
open pores scar-burnt hands.

She reached 1980 lower east side's 9th street going
up down empty cellars abandoned building
drug hideouts sad desperation christmas eve
thighs scratching up down abandoned lot she
met the fix la cura the fix la cura cura cura
she escaped stars relaxation she dreamt opium
drug re-leaving her into fantasy world beyond
universe still body mind ecstasy diluted chem-

144

icals soothing pain in brain she felt no body
no-motion-body knocked by powerful earthly drug
heroin she wanted heroin yes yes she wished
she loved heroin slow motion ejaculations
exploding nervous system open-preyed flesh human
body not feeling dry winter air christmas eve
nochebuena 12 o'clock tranquility night of peace
no mangers night of hope heroin reaching embryo
about-to-be-born little child silent night feeding
tubes struggling to survive being born to die
pneumonia choking or overdosed body 12 o'clock
abandoned lot dying fire all by himself alone:

He was born star of peace church bells
he was born busting out loud cry church bells
he was born son grand son great grand son
he was born generations america puerto rico
he was born europe africa 7 generations before
he was born latest legacy family tree inheritor
he was born he was born 20th century
urban story greatest told abandonment
concrete land new york city story of stories
contemporary poets felt the spirit in the air
those who searched for lost souls new prophecies
celebrating jesus christ one thousand nine hun-
dred and eighty times seeking christ spirit
ritual midnight mass family dinners children
fast asleep santa claus is coming silent night
holy night he pushed an echo into death's eulogy
one speech one experience one smell one feeling
one moment one look one touch one breath one cry
one prayer "i am jesús i have no last name so call
me jesús papote" his first words unnoticed by bells
midnight bells christmas day alley cat licking
wombs she slept she never felt maternal instinct
ultimate pain released for only she could give birth
for only she could experience red-faced explosions
elevated to that sacrificial offering called life
vida life vida life vida death life death new birth
abraham sacrificed consciously she sacrificed sub-
consciously invisible ancestor of soledad he spoke:

My name is jesús papote i am born in oppression
my death a deeper martyrdom unknown to pain to
solitude to soledad to soledad's seven skins to
darkness to darkness' mystery to mystery's spirits.

My name is jesús papote i live nine months gut soul
i was addicted i was beaten i was kicked i was punched
i slept in empty cellars broken stairways i was infect-
ed i was injected spermed with many relations
i ran from police jails i was high every day of life
stabbing murders 1980 20th-century moon rockets micro-
magnetic computer operations 120-story edifices united
states instant replay future 21st-century advanced
new york the world lives in 1970 new york underdevel-
oped world in 1960 new york i am in 1980 new york
born around 18th-century abandoned structures
fighting to prevent broken scars from creating cancer
to my death.

My name is jesús papote born holy saturday easter
sunday march mother parading 3rd avenues' lower
streets car horns how much how long hotels
parking lots cellars men women elders new jersey
staten island connecticut long island all entered
my mother's secret veins 10 dollars 15 dollars i
was created ethnic sperm consortium's passionless
thrills social club more men entering more men en-
tering i was conceived easter sunday resurrection
pagan abuses 1980 modern times.

She awoke she felt strange she relaxed the fix
had been applied nodding dance completed she
visited grandmother daisy flowers she could be
normal for a while folkloric mountain music
i met grandmother on my first day what an omen
grandma abuelita can you see me grandmother i
was the answer to your prayers your many unan-
swered prayers grandma i am alive can you see me
abuelita insisted to stay easter sunday veins
were pumping they take no vacation she had to

make the streets she walked past gossip's stares
abuelita felt ashamed abuelita felt herself no-
body she had failed her daughter's baptism con-
firmation communion dignity pride virginity left
behind but she prayed even harder faith almighty
god not diminished candles the seven powers pro-
mises abuelita prayed her prayers made it easy
tonight . . . food rest spring walk she had to fight
the street she had refused the pimp's protection
she had to fight the corner she had no friends
she felt free tonight's crosscurrents open ethnic
music she felt something strange inside she walked
the glorious town central park rides broadway
nights bridges she looked across the waters ferry
evening lights statue of liberty's torch carrying
hand so strong wall street sunday silent newspaper
tonight tomorrow village open sexual society she
opinionated she knew new york's empty crevices
camera eyes recorded the instinct she felt strange
she felt something inside.

My name is jesús papote may month flowers she dis-
covered me making her green throwing up she wanted
abortion she took pill after pill she had to wait
syphilis infection i came between the habit she
needed more i was an obstruction constant pressure
wrinkled inside cars in out constant pounding those
men were paying they had a right to hurt the habit
stronger tricks longer she became oral more and more
the money was not there one night nobody wanted her
she decided to extricate me she pounded punch after
punch like those men punch after punch abortion at
all costs she tired herself i lost my voice i support-
ed her she was weak she could not move sitting
sidewalk cold cement she laid in bowery vagabonds
feeling her for nothing this was it she wanted no
more no more.

My name is jesús papote june cold turkey center cold
turkey her system must contain itself without chemi-
cals cold turkey naked unseasoned no taste unfeathered
cold turkey dry frozen human force battle begun fight

sweat shivers attacks in all directions cold turkey
intravenous coup d'etat demanding charging torturing
nuclear blasts invasions delirium opiate roots electric
shocks kidnapping she threw up the world she greened
she scratched-drew-blood nails on scars scabbing
pores blood vessels eruptions hands on blood she
painted open mental torture digging into wall's
electricity cabled concussion paralyzing currents
she wrote god let me die god let me die she fought
we fought i was not an added burden i kept quiet
i held if she survived detoxified normal life no
more deserted streets no more pains no more misery
she won grandma she won she smiled she ate she
beat the odds.

My name is jesús papote 4th of July celebration
plane ride across to puerto rico mountain house
utuado high up clear nights future dreams new
life breathings caribbean enchanted nation long
rides past guajataca splendored beaches arecibo's
indian caves dorado evenings she entered san juan
white cemetery patriots resting singing to la
perla pearled down old spanish architecture el
morro distanced open sea curving palm trees tick-
ling skies connecting sea-breezing moon san juan
song folklore painting after painting came alive
leo-mildness-august night tidal waves moving bells
quietly sunset lowering her thighs cooled refreshed
stimulated sauna touches moon-lit beauty mark smiled
sun met in ocean eclipse mistress round-up night
after night shimmering fresh air slow pace coastal
sand walk fresh fruit pineapple spicy fish coconut
nights kissing early morning mango blossoms new sun
octapusing rays orange rainbows the ox-cart was your
solution your final triumph how beautiful you look
inside the western sunset phosphorous bay shining
artesian ponce musically carved saints flamboyant
trees luquillo beach preparations into rain forest
deities once lived they greet us they talk loíza
carnaval blackness río grande julia de burgos phras-
ings oh mamita i was so afraid oh mamita stay in
taíno mountains caguana-shaped symbol of cemí oh

mamita don't go back give birth in island nativeness
tropical greetings nurturing don't go back don't go back.

My name is jesús papote september pregnant body new
york spells trouble once-again-racing-fast struggles
rapid fire pellets struggles pouring anxieties 18th-
century remnants immigrant struggles spanish second
third-class citizens struggles education non-existent
struggles companion song of destiny struggles spell
troubles.

My name is jesús papote she october tried training
program cellar jobs she vowed not to use it again
columbus was discovered he discovered gold discov-
ered competition discovered defeat discovered lack
of opportunity halloween witch creeping in she said
no she said no strong they came back she said no
strong ugly cursed evil she said no strong she felt
pains i was restless i was acting up i had relapsed
i was choking i needed it she said no she said no
strong i was in pain she said no yes no yes no no
urgings yes yes achings no no yes no yes no yes
stubbornly she said no she said no she said no
strong.

My name is jesús papote november all souls day
grandma knocked on door oh no the prayers fell
defeated once again pain killers sleeping face
hallway scrambling avenues putrid dope stumbles
nightsticks digging digging deep spinal corded
night 300 dollars pure divinity bombarded atomic
explosions final war coma death radiation pellets
death la muerte sneaking in no breath feelings
death la muerte coming after us moving fast
death la muerte assured us she was winning
death la muerte doctors priests last testament
death la muerte trying to save me over my mother
death la muerte she refused her strength engulfed
death la muerte doorbell of fear
death la muerte abusing us unfairly
death la muerte nothing could be done

death la muerte divine hope of all living things
death was spitting its steel claws earthquake
we attacked her we fought her we prevented her
from penetrating our testicles we pulled her
intestines her naked slimy body we switch-bladed
cuts across her face we rumbled into her adam's
apple biting into her senses we squeezed her
obnoxious overweight loose teeth cancer we cut her
breasts we raped her we mugged her we escaped her we
iced her thanksgiving fiesta carved with delight
we were eating seasoned turkey triumph champagne
toast to that ultimate desire to live live vivir.

My name is jesús papote december christmas new
york city my inner cycle 9 months completed what
a life what a life my mother's mouth once again
on elder's variety theatre 2 dollars 40 mouths
every day christmas eve day oh sweet sour destiny
ghetto sacrifice wounded limbs tears surfacing
loneliness soledad seven skins solitude underneath
sub-vulgate open concubines society condones it
society has not cured itself from it society cannot
outlaw such misery right there for future children
to see to watch to fear right there in front of
little angels in naked open spaces oh but sad lonely
night dear saviour's birth long lay the world in
sin 'til he appeared thrill of hope save him jesus
alleycats symphony save him jesus abandoned tenement
screaming save him jesus indians buried inside cement
chanting save him jesus she did not hear final cry:

Mami Mami push push i'm coming out celestial barkings
Mami Mami push i don't want to die she slept
Mami Mami push i want to live she slept cough
Mami Mami i have the ability to love cough cough
Mami Mami fight with me again she slept she slept
Mami Mami i'm coming out out out push push push push
Mami Mami can you feel me can you hear me push push
push push empuja empuja cough cough push push push
empuja empuja Mami cough cough push push i am fighting

i am fighting push push nature nature i have a will
to live to denounce you nature i am fighting by myself
your sweeping breasts your widowing backbone
yearnings your howling cemetery steps your
death-cold inhuman palms Mami Mami wake up
this is my birthday little mornings king
david sang cough cough cough push push
why do I have to eulogize myself
nobody is listening i am invisible
why tell me why do i have to be
the one the one to acclaim that:

    We, nosotros, compassionate caring people
    We, nosotros, respectful of spanish-english forms
    We, nosotros, peace in mind tranquility
    We, nosotros, inside triangle of contradictions
    We, nosotros, nation-feeling-total-pride
    We, nosotros, strong men powerful women loving children
    We, nosotros, hispanic hemispheric majority
    We, nosotros, latinos million bicultural humanists
    We, nosotros, folkloric mountain traditionalists
    We, nosotros, spanish tongue culture older than English
    We, nosotros, conceiving english newer visions
    We, nosotros, multi-ethnic black-brown-red in affirmations
    We, nosotros, ghetto brothers black americans indians
          italians irish jewish polish ukrainians
          russian german food and music lovers
    We, nosotros, mathematicians of the magical undocumented
          dollar architects of close-knit spaces
    We, nosotros, 5th largest foreign market we consumed
          all the goods 83 years association of
          goods we fought world wars decorated up
          front to meet the fresh-troop enemy
    We, nosotros, oral poets transcending 2 european forms
          spanish dominance when spanish was strong
          english dominance when english was strong
          we digested both we absorbed the pregnancies
          we stand at crossroads 21st-century new man
          great grandfathers chornos-spirits sing
          with me allow me this one last wish limbo
          baptism of faith this one last christmas
          moment to my mother who doesn't answer

with the permission of all the faiths of all beliefs
with the permission of this land
with the permission of the elders
with the permission of english
with the permission of my community
with the permission of god:

    allow this spanish word to be understood
    i ask for your silence for language is
    always understood in any sentiment
    with your permission Mami
    i ask for one gift one magi gift
    inside these heavy odds
    there is a spanish word
    spanish ultimate of words
    that will survive
    there is a puerto rican
    blessing universal to the world
    hear it it is only for you
    for i love you i don't blame you
    i am also responsible for state
    of being, so with this, my only
    breath, my last wind, my last
    supper sentiment, i tell you
    with pride that i am proud to
    have been your son, to have come
    from you, with the tenderness
    of my grandmother's prayers,
    with the silent love of all my
    people, with the final resolution
    of our nationhood, i am asking
    for my blessings BENDICIÓN
    BEN . . . DI . . . CI . . . ON

she woke up she saw she startled she warmed she
protected she cried she broke the umbilical cord
she got up to follow the bells the bells the bells
cats dogs vagabonds all followed the tinkle tinkle
of the bells christmas bells nativity flowing bells
faith hope and charity bells 1980 jesus christ and
jesús papote midnight ecstacy of bells church steps
door opens organ stops up the aisle she exclaimed

jesús papote human legacy god the son at the right
hand holy spirit candles flowers incense wine water
and finally the people grandmother she offered jesús
papote to the people miracle cherubims flautists
dancing and singing rejoice rejoice eternity smiles
oh night divine oh night divine she knelt she smiled
jesús papote's presence in the dignity of our lives.

tito madera smith

(for Dr. Juan Flores)

he claims he can translate palés matos'
black poetry faster than i can talk,
and that if i get too smart,
he will double translate pig latin
english right out of webster's
dictionary, do you know him?

he claims he can walk into east harlem
apartment where langston hughes gives
spanglish classes for newly arrived
immigrants seeking a bolitero-numbers
career and part-time vendors of cuchi-
fritters sunday afternoon in central
park, do you know him?

he claims to have a stronghold of the
only santería secret baptist sect in
west harlem, do you know him?

he claims he can talk spanish styled in
sunday dress eating crabmeat-jueyes
brought over on the morning eastern
plane deep fried by la negra costoso
joyfully singing puerto rican folklore:
"maría luisa no seas brava,
llevame contigo pa la cama," or
"oiga, capitán delgado, hey, captain delgaro,
mande a revisar la grama, please inspect
the grass, que dicen que un aeroplano,

153

they say that an airplane throws marijuana
seeds."

do you know him? yes, you do,
i know you know him, that's right,
madera smith, tito madera smith:
he blacks and prieto talks at the same time,
splitting his mother's santurce talk,
twisting his father's south carolina soul,
adding new york-scented blackest harlem
brown-eyes diddy bops, tú sabes mami,
that i can ski like a bomba soul salsa
mambo turns to aretha franklin stevie
wonder nicknamed patato guaguancó steps,
do you know him?

he puerto rican talks to las mamitas
outside the pentecostal church, and
he gets away with it, fast-paced i
understand-you-my-man, with clave
sticks coming out of his pockets hooked
to his stereophonic 15-speaker indispensable
disco sounds blasting away at cold reality
struggling to say estás buena, baby
as he walks out of tune and out of
step with alleluia cascabells,
puma sneakers,
pants rolled up,
shirt cut in middle chest,
santería chains,
madamo pantallas,
into the spanish social club,
to challenge elders in dominoes,
like the king of el diario's
budweiser tournament
drinking cerveza-beer
like a champ,
do you know him?
well, i sure don't,
and if i did, i'd
refer him to 1960
social scientists

for assimilation
acculturation
digging
autopsy
into
their
heart
attacks,
oh,
oh,
there
he
comes,
you can call him tito,
or you can call him madera,
or you can call him smitty,
or you can call him mr. t.,
or you can call him nuyorican,
or you can call him black,
or you can call him latino,
or you can call him mr. smith,
his sharp eyes of awareness,
greeting us in aristocratic harmony:
"you can call me many things, but
you gotta call me something."

AmeRícan

we gave birth to a new generation,
AmeRícan, broader than lost gold
never touched, hidden inside the
puerto rican mountains.

we gave birth to a new generation,
AmeRícan, it includes everything
imaginable you-name-it-we-got-it
society.

we gave birth to a new generation,
AmeRícan salutes all folklores,

european, indian, black, spanish,
and anything else compatible:

AmeRícan,   singing to composer pedro flores' palm
                      trees high up in the universal sky!

AmeRícan,   sweet soft spanish danzas gypsies
                      moving lyrics la española cascabelling
                      presence always singing at our side!

AmeRícan,   beating jíbaro modern troubadours
                      crying guitars romantic continental
                      bolero love songs!

AmeRícan,   across forth and across back
                      back across and forth back
                      forth across and back and forth
                      our trips are walking bridges!

                      it all dissolved into itself, the attempt
                      was truly made, the attempt was truly
                      absorbed, digested, we spit out
                      the poison, we spit out the malice,
                      we stand, affirmative in action,
                      to reproduce a broader answer to the
                      marginality that gobbled us up abruptly!

AmeRícan   walking plena-rhythms in new york,
                      strutting beautifully alert, alive,
                      many turning eyes wondering,
                      admiring!

AmeRícan,   defining myself my own way any way many
                      ways Am e Rícan, with the big R and the
                      accent on the í!

AmeRícan,   like the soul gliding talk of gospel
                      boogie music!

AmeRícan,   speaking new words in spanish tenements,
                      fast tongue moving street corner "que

corta" talk being invented at the insistence
of a smile!

AmeRícan,   abounding inside so many ethnic English
people, and out of humanity, we blend
and mix all that is good!

AmeRícan,   integrating in new york and defining our
own destino, our own way of life,

AmeRícan,   defining the new america, humane america,
admired america, loved america, harmonious
america, the world in peace, our energies
collectively invested to find other civili-
zations, to touch God, further and further,
to dwell in the spirit of divinity!

AmeRícan,   yes, for now, for i love this, my second
land, and i dream to take the accent from
the altercation, and be proud to call
myself AmeRícan, in the u.s. sense of the
word, AmeRícan, America!

lady liberty

for liberty, your day filled in splendor,
july fourth, new york harbor, nineteen eighty-six,
midnight sky, fireworks splashing,
heaven exploding
into radiant bouquets,
wall street a backdrop of centennial adulation,
computerized capital angling cameras
celebrating the international symbol of freedom
stretched across micro-chips,
awacs surveillance,
wall-to-wall people, sailing ships,
gliding armies ferried
in pursuit of happiness, constitution adoration,
packaged television channels for liberty,
immigrant illusions

celebrated in the name of democratic principles,
god bless america, land of the star
spangled banner
that we love.

but the symbol suffered
one hundred years of decay
climbing up to the spined crown,
the fractured torch hand,
the ruptured intestines,
palms blistered and calloused,
feet embroidered in rust,
centennial decay,
the lady's eyes,
cataract filled, exposed
to sun and snow, a salty wind,
discolored verses staining her robe.

she needed re-molding, re-designing,
the decomposed body
now melted down for souvenirs,
lungs and limbs jailed
in scaffolding of ugly cubicles
incarcerating the body
as she prepared to receive
her twentieth-century transplant
paid for by pitching pennies,
hometown chicken barbecues,
marathons on america's main streets.
she heard the speeches:
the president's
the french and american partners,
the nation believed in her, rooted for the queen,
and lady liberty decided to reflect
on lincoln's emancipatory resoluteness,
on washington's patriotism,
on jefferson's lucidity,
on william jennings bryan's socialism,
on woodrow wilson's league of nations,
on roosevelt's new deal,
on kennedy's ecumenical postures,
and on martin luther king's non-violence.

lady liberty decided to reflect
on lillian wald's settlements,
on helen keller's sixth sense,
on susan b. anthony's suffrage movement,
on mother cabrini's giving soul,
on harriet tubman's stubborn pursuit of freedom.

just before she was touched,
just before she was dismantled,
lady liberty spoke,
she spoke for the principles,
for the preamble,
for the bill of rights,
and thirty-nine peaceful
presidential transitions,
and, just before she was touched,
lady liberty wanted to convey
her own resolutions,
her own bi-centennial goals,
so that in twenty eighty-six,
she would be smiling and she would be proud.
and then, just before she was touched,
and then, while she was being re-constructed,
and then, while she was being celebrated,
she spoke.

if you touch me, touch ALL of my people
who need attention and societal repair,
give the tired and the poor
the same attention, AMERICA,
touch us ALL with liberty,
touch us ALL with liberty.

hunger abounds, our soil is plentiful,
our technology advanced enough
to feed the world,
to feed humanity's hunger . . .
but let's celebrate not our wealth,
not our sophisticated defense,
not our scientific advancements,
not our intellectual adventures.
let us concentrate on our weaknesses,

on our societal needs,
for we will never be free
if indeed freedom is subjugated
to trampling upon people's needs.

this is a warning,
my beloved america

so touch me,
and in touching me
touch all our people.
do not single me out,
touch all our people,
touch all our people,
all our people
    our people
        people.

and then i shall truly enjoy
my day, filled in splendor,
july fourth, new york harbor,
nineteen eighty-six, midnight sky,
fireworks splashing,
heaven exploding
into radiant bouquets,
celebrating in the name of equality,
in the pursuit of happiness,
god bless america,
land of star
spangled banner
that we love.

my graduation speech

i think in spanish
i write in english

i want to go back to puerto rico,
but i wonder if my kink could live
in ponce, mayagüez and Carolina

tengo las venas aculturadas
escribo en spanglish
abraham in español
abraham in english
tato in spanish
"taro" in english
tonto in both languages

how are you?
¿cómo estás?
i don't know if i'm coming
or si me fui ya

si me dicen barranquitas, yo reply,
"¿con qué se come eso?"
si me dicen caviar, i digo,
"a new pair of converse sneakers."

ahí supe que estoy jodío
ahí supe que estamos jodíos

english or spanish
spanish or english
spanenglish
now, dig this:

hablo lo inglés matao
hablo lo español matao
no sé leer ninguno bien

so it is, spanglish to matao
what i digo
          ¡ay, virgen, yo no sé hablar!

tesis de negreza

(canción de bobby capó)
(reseña del dr. víctor manuel vega)

"mataron al negro bembón"
negrito cocolo llamado prieto
alborazado blah blah blah

"mataron al negro bembón"
ambujo separación
indistinguida blah blah blah

"hoy se llora noche y día"
nos dicen que somos
calpa mulato iguales blah blah blah

"porque al negrito bembón"
cambujos somos unidos
en este hemisferio *chino*
no existe el racismo blah blah blah

"todo el mundo lo quería"
coartado burla insensitiva blah blah blah

"porque al negrito bembón"
chumbo pueblo antipatía blah blah blah

"todo el mundo lo quería"
churusco entonces pues:

"y llegó la policía"
cimarrón defensa raza alta bravía

"y arrestaron al matón"
sus labios *criollos* suculentos

"y uno de los policías"
moreno saboreando sus pupilas

"que también era bembón"
cocolo no la tengo escondida

"le tocó la mala suerte"
cuarterón está aquí mismita

"de hacer la investigación"
soy *emancipado* para que enrojezcas
con mis cachondos coloreados

"le tocó la mala suerte"
falucho sangre roja mezclada

"de hacer la investigación"
jíbaro de congoleses chupetes
labios de erección grandiosa

"y sabe la pregunta"
grifo montañas sutil dulzura

"que le hizo al matón"
ladino betunando emoción
borinqueñosos poros

"porque lo mató"
liberto temblor besos volcánicos
del cielo viniste y devolviste

"diga usted la razón"
manumiso internas calenturas

"y sabe la respuesta"
mestizo profundas entrañas

"que le dio el matón"
moreno rosando sus raíces:

"yo lo maté por ser tan BEMBÓN"
morisco le contesta
voy a sacar la lengua para limpiarte
de tus sutiles prejuicios

"el guardia escondió la lengua y le dijo"
soy *niche* para insultarte cuando me insultes
para confrontarte cuando tu ignorancia
desigualdad escupe estereotipos

soy *lobo* voy a sacar la bemba patriótica
colectiva humana cuando me respetes
amistosamente

    "ésa no es razón"
    soy *loro* voy a sacar la bemba
    la que nunca había escondido

"para matar al bembón"
soy *mulecón* bemba enmelezada
con cien millones de negros
continentales

    "ésa no es razón"
    soy *muleque* marca de hierro
    caliente lacerado marca de *carimbo*

        "huye huye"
        soy *moyeto* aquí la segunda áfrica
        dividida por yemayá

            "que ahí viene el matón"
            soy *negro pardo* que se
            aparezca el matón

                "ésa no es razón"
                soy *quinterón* lo confronto
                con bembazo indigno

                    "yo te digo que viene"
                    soy *retinto* valiente ciudadano

                        "cortando bembas"
                        soy *saltoatrás* arresto
                        al criminal canalla

"ya se la cortó"
soy *tente en el aire*
    investigo la letra de bobby capó
"al negrito bembón"
soy *torno atrás*
        analizo la grabación
           de rafael cortijo
                los soneos dulce creativos

de ismael rivera
    soy *zambaigo*
        critico mi-tato-pecado
            repito mil veces este folklore
                "ésa no es razón"
                    soy *zambo* bemba escopeta
                        sacude bemba gloriosa
                            "esconde la bemba" nunca
                                mas soy un majestuoso
                                BEMBÓN.

nideaquinideallá

dc qué I know yo sí sé
backnforth here soy de aquí
regreso dicen y qué what
aterricé o acá o allá

my first name is de aquí
my last name is de allá
my last name is nideaquinideallá
yet-to-be defined
evolucionario hybrid

backnforth here soy de aquí
cannot be defined
cannot be categorized
cannot be pasteurizao
cannot be homogenizao

what's my new name?
¿cómo me dicen?
regreso a mi tierra nativa
me llaman y qué what
les contesto somos
we are the children
immigrant/migrantes
our madres cutting
blood crowns entering
fronteras wired fences
nuestros padres wrinkled

foreheads peso of dollar-
an-hour miseria
our uncles and tías
flesh-skinned manos
see-through cemented
tenements hard-core trabajo
mis hermanos and sisters
open-preyed borders
societal disasters

de qué i know yo sí sé
in my yet-to-be defined
birthplace homeland
dual citizenship accusations
indignations differentiations
pesadillas de callos
intellectual displacements
transplanting raíces
aquí no allá yes aquí allá
backnforth no sé si maybe
in between schizophrenia
cultural ataques in all
directions hip-hopping
nightmares paralyzing
incertidumbres frenéticas

aterricé o acá o allá
child of western hemispheric
creations ancestral inheritors
not knowing past three
previous generations
my boricua sobrenombre
original by parent's birth
caribbean by folklore
hispanic by culture
nuyorican by geographic
migrational displacements
latino by mutual promotion
urban by modern necessity
offspring of indigenous dialectics
too many hats to wear
too little time to square
qué vida what a life

I'm in the usa of america
and in us of a, you suffer
insignias of apathy
prejuicio subtle racism
minority status
us of a, you suffer
watching our nation invading other nations without an
    invitation

My middle name is de allá
constant anti-nuyorican
anti-latino born wedlock
on u.s. soil bilingual
problemas not me anymore
we in all of us ustedes
siempre malnombrándonos
we fight not to be brainwashed
so se acabó el relajo
stop mental disenfranchisement
my last new latest name:

     nideaquinideallá
     impossible to blend
     impossible to categorize
     impossible to analyze
     impossible to synthesize
     our guerrilla cultural camouflage
     survival linguistic construction
     at emergency moment's notice
     complex afirmaciones parametric
     principles fermenting
     secretive universal
     garabatopandegato
     continental yearnings
     complex jeringonza
     de mi hablar

     nideaquinideallá
     escríbelo junto
     sin letra mayúscula
     gracias

Caridad de la Luz (La Bru-j-a)

Ahora y siempre

Con aspiraciones en las nubes
nostalgia vive en los tiempos de hoy
tan maravillosos con sus risas y abrazos
también los rebalazos
pero el amor tiene brazos
que te levantan
hasta las estrellas que cantan

La alegría
la mía
que siempre sabía
en la compañía de mi gente
con respeto y orgullo presente

Aquí viene mi gente
con poderío presente
tan buenos y tan decentes
aquí viene mi gente

Abuelita desgranando gandules
yo la amo y le di todo lo que pude
y hasta hoy yo le doy respeto
como mi Reina
que le den todo en lo que se empeña

Todas las veces que me cuidaba
me aconsejaba tan preocupada
por todos los daños del mundo
su amor tan profundo
como el mar hasta el hondo
sin fin como su espíritu
canciones del coquí canto
brillando con su cultura bonita

Aquí viene mi abuelita
la tristeza y dolor me quita
me limpiaba cuando niña chiquita
aquí viene mi abuelita

168

Triste estoy separada de mi patria
mi isla bellísima con sus palmas y playas
el dinero nos controla
con sus sueños de mentiras
el coquí casi no respira
porque camiones rompen
se llevan las montañas donde cantaba

Cuando chiquita
nunca me imaginaba
un tiempo sin el coquí
pero su canción vive en mí

Nuestra isla
empuja palante
este mundo no tiene bastante
guarda la tierra
ante que se muera
donde nació tu abuela

De donde viene tu gente
seas consciente
abre la mente
y quema los puentes
con la flama de resistencia
Purifica la isla de nuestra infancia

Madre isla
te quiero quitar tu dolor
mi isla de viejo primor
cultura de puro sabor
aquí tienes mi amor
ahora y siempre

Mi madre

Mi madre desde pequeña
tenía la cara de una reina
con su corona de pelo oro
y sabiduría en sus ojos
con capacidad de mente fuerte
e inteligencia transparente
Chiquita, finita con ropas que no le cabían
y una boquita color rosita
que guardaba todo lo que sabía
esperaba ser una bailarina
Su sueño de rosas tenía espinas
los bailes antiguos
la tocaron con tanto brillo
bailando con su tío
ella era una estrella
Con sus movimientos de campesina
en su tarima de marquesina
y fuertecita se quedó
cuando a América llegó
con un hermanito y madre encinta.
Porque su padre se murió
en Puerto Rico lo dejó
fuertecita se quedó
y nadie la cargó
No lloró, no calló
derechita se marchó
hasta la cara de Nueva York
Mi madre bella flor
mi madre puro amor
la vi crecer como Madre y Mujer
y no lo creo cuando veo su sagrado poder
¡Ay, buena Madre!
¡Tanto diste y tanto das!
tú eres mi mundo entero
mi estrella y tanto más

Te adoro

Nuyorico

The Palm trees are tall like the skyscrapers
the entrance says Welcome over the gate and
Margarita lost a shoe bailando Salsa
she threw away the other to dance descalza
Such a hard life she's after
but she smiles like a fool at
Pablo in his yellow Malibu
singing Babalu
after winning Capicu
Who knew that the
spirits dance Mambo to Hip Hop
Eating snowflakes at tropical pit stops
this place we forgot, the puddles of
our hearts flood out
in large amounts
Come drink for all the natives
look around we are all related
Peace and Love is so underrated
Qué bueno que
you made it
to the best place in town
from Puerto Rico
all the way to the Boogie down
Check the smells and sounds
of the underground
that you've found here

Check out the sabor
in every flavor
as the owner Pedro
counts his pesos
Giving besos
is a common custom

The bus boys you can trust them
with your life, tranquilo
it's safe at night
and if you're in the mood

to view the city lights of paradise
you don't even have to go to Paris
you can go out on the Rosie Perez Terrace

Where tropical sounds can be found
you can sit or just lounge or
get Boricua down
mi casa, su casa
qué pasa
spoken here
mi raza, su raza
love is in the air
nothing compares to Nuyorico
it'll make you fall in love
bésame mucho
and all the above
You'll be greeted with kisses and hugs
la comida, la musica y la cultura
eso es la droga
dancing feet will rip the rug up

At night the windows are covered with sudor
every cabana is a smoky humidor
you can recognize the scent from the door
contraband provides the music and more

And out on the veranda
the hostess Cassandra
guarantees all your needs will be served
the entertainment is superb
el vacilón
is the secret password
Ay yo, you never heard
about the coquito
served by Enrique
who only espeakeh
el inglés un poquito

While Angelina cooks and cleans for a fee
nothing here is free
but to pay is to be
so the patrons and me

we get along
singing songs of
la isla bonita
Here we are all Boricua
and if you no comprendo
mi lengua sokay
I'll espeak eslow en
acento nuyorico

S. P. I. C.

S. P. I. C.-S. P. I. C.-it doesn't mean the same thing to me
S. P. I. C.-S. P. I. C.-I define my dictionary
S. P. I. C.-S. P. I. C.-Ten cuidao como llamarme a mi
S. P. I. C.-S. P. I. C.-con mi e.s.p. I see what I see

Spanish People In Crisis
Speak Politely I'm Crazy
Spain Probably Isn't Caring
Statehood Probably Isn't Coming
Separated People Inevitably Crumble
Start Participating In Culture
Strong Pro-Independence Community
Society prefers indifference collectively
Speaking Powerfully Involves Commitment
Similar Patterns In Chimps
Slander Purposely Impairs Confidence
Surviving Peoples Insensitive Comments
Socio Political Insanity Continues
Speaking Purposefully Is Constitutional

Still Placed In Cadenas
Seize Puerto Ricans In Chancletas
Spiritualists Praying Ignite Candles
Some Propaganda Is Comedy
Stop Praising Ignorant Celebrities
Sharing Perspectives Is Cleansing
Solidarity Provides Immense Connection
Stepping Passed Indignant Critics
Selling Poison In Clinics

Staying Poised Inside Conflict
Slavery Practiced In Caribbean
Spaniards Pummeled Indigenous Caciques
Seeing Persecution Is Crushing
Shoe Points Impale Cockroaches
Stop Parades Including Columbus

Soy Perfecta Inventando Caridades
Seeking Past Inner Conquistador
Speak Properly In Code
Some Poetry Is Censored
Sexy Pero Inteligente, Coño

Gracias, Thank you very mucho!
Buenos nachos!

Nativity: For Two Salvadoran Women, 1986–1987

Your eyes, large as Canada, welcome
this stranger.
We meet in a Juárez train station
where you sat hours,
your offspring blooming in you
like cactus fruit,
dresses stained where breasts leak,
panties in purses tagged
"Hecho en El Salvador,"
your belts, like equators,
mark north from south,
borders I cannot cross,
for I am a North American reporter,
pen and notebook, the tools
of my tribe, distance us
though in any other era I might
press a stethoscope to your wombs,
hear the symphony of the unborn,
finger forth infants to light,
wipe afterbirth, cut cords.

"It is impossible to raise a child
in that country."

Sisters, I am no saint. Just a woman
who happens to be a reporter,
a reporter who happens
to be a woman,
squat in a forest, peeing
on pine needles,
Watching you vomit morning sickness,
a sickness infinite as the war in El Salvador,
a sickness my pen and notebook will not ease,
tell me, ¿por qué están aquí?,
how did you cross over?
In my country we sing of a baby in a manger,
finance death squads,

175

how to write of this shame,
of the children you chose to save?

"It is impossible to raise a child
in that country."

A North American reporter,
I smile, you tell me you are due
in December, we nod,
knowing what women know,
I shut my notebook,
watch your car rock
through the Gila,
a canoe hangs over the windshield
like the beak of an eagle,
babies tum in your wombs,
summoned to Belén to be born.

Hit and Run

Had you raped me my hate
would be radiant, sure of itself,
a memory in bruises
I could despise.
Instead we loved and sighed
from one new moon to the next . . .
then you left.

If I am pregnant I will abort,
expel you as readily as you did me,
plastic-lined can of limbs
and crushed skulls,
I, the doped-up murderess, exiting
the clinic, my insides bleached
clean, clean, what a coup,
even the gateway car awaits me.

Or, if I am pregnant, heavy with you,
a mountain, a cow, indifferent to all
but the clouds and this love

doubling inside me,
is it a girl? A head, pink and bruised,
bobs up between my thighs,
your lips and eyes,
but see how she loves me,
I am the victor here, leaving
the clinic with a pink bundle
of your best features,
your violence washed down the sinkhole
with the placenta.
Saintly, abstract:
loving you in her,
touch us and I'll
sink a knife into you, sir.

Julio Marzán ───────────────────────────

The Translator at the Reception for
Latin American Writers

Air-conditioned introductions,
then breezy Spanish conversation
fan his curiosity to know
what country I come from.
"Puerto Rico and the Bronx."

Spectacled downward eyes
translate disappointment
like a poison mushroom
puffed in his thoughts as if,
after investing a sizable
intellectual budget, transporting
a huge cast and camera crew
to film on location
Mayan pyramid grandeur,
indigenes whose ancient gods
and comet-tail plumage
inspire a glorious epic
of revolution across a continent,
he received a lurid script
for a social documentary
rife with dreary streets
and pathetic human interest,
meager in the profits of high culture.

Understandably he turns,
catches up with the hostess,
praising the uncommon quality
of her offerings of cheese.

⌒⌒⌒

Arresting Beauty

This unlicensed Mexican sells flowers
from plastic buckets in a supermarket cart.
He commits this crime on my corner,
trafficking fragrance and bunched beauty
on crowds returning from church
or cresting rushed from subway stops.
I will testify, officer, I have witnessed
colors he has spread over this street,
have seen the passing victim's eyes
after they inhaled the petalous freshness
and changed the course of their day,
veered by the power of his merchandise.
And who knows what confused delight
aromatically invades those homes
his mums, lilacs and roses have remodeled,
what drastic life consequences proceed
from the peace of his potent, soft flowers.

Ethnic Poetry

The ethnic poet said: "The earth is maybe
a huge maraca/ and the sun a trombone/
and life/ is to move your ass/ to slow beats."
The ethnic audience roasted a suckling pig.

The ethnic poet said: "Oh thank Goddy, Goddy/
I be me, my toenails curled downward/
deep, deep, deep into Mama earth."
The ethnic audience shook strands of sea shells.

The ethnic poet said: "The sun was created black/
so we should imagine light/ and also dream/
a walrus emerging from the broken ice."
The ethnic audience beat on sealskin drums.

The ethnic poet said: "Reproductive organs/
Eagles nesting California redwoods/
Shut up and listen to my ancestors."
The ethnic audience ate fried bread and honey.

The ethnic poet said: "Something there is that
doesn't love a wall/That sends
the frozen-ground-swell under it."
The ethnic audience deeply understood humanity.

The Old Man

After the Crash,
no God spoke but money,
money the highest art
decorated his world,
now dented and tarnished,

whose brass surface
only murkily reflects
second-deck cabins,
muffled trumpet solos
as faded tuxedos lead
dully sequined gowns,
crossing the Atlantic
in lost younger lives,
heralds of an old deity
as unreliable as TV,
library novels,
even the latest news of ancient deceits,
so he tunes out
to shuffle from room
to identical room
in remolded slippers,

amenable to death's
preliminary offers
because the bald world's
tired somersaults
he knows by heart.

Calle de la Amargura

In Havana there is a street called Calle
de la Amargura or Street of Bitterness.

On the Street of Bitterness
a man runs from the rain
arms raised into the next imagination.

A woman sits head down
on the stoop of a house
where her indiscretions
fly about like butterflies.

All songs end,
memories soar over rooftops,
an eyelid swells with desire.

On the Street of Bitterness,
Calle de la Amargura, there are boys
scratching their tongues,
they dare not speak, they wait
their tum in the line of understanding.

On that street
a daughter is dying.
Her father searches for a cure
and finds instead the pillar of his wife,
covered with lizard scales,
melting with the rain.

On the Street of Bitterness,
Calle de la Amargura, no one is surprised
at the awful taste of Paradise.

Philadelphia

The coffee has redeemed itself by now.
I am awake enough to see you walking
down the street to your apartment
exhausted like a sparrow
after long work in the tenements.

You linger in my memory hunched a little,
tragic, hurt by men. The afternoon haze
is *café con leche* in the city,
the block busy with unemployed
latinos, sipping beer, playing
dominos, whispering deals at the corner.

Across the street the huge Lithuanian
church has become ridiculous.
Hardly anyone enters. Rhythm and form
fly away with the pigeons
and the river is a slab of dirty wood.
You turn the corner, disappear.
Philadelphia is awash in loss.
This is the dream the coffee drowned.

The Floating Island

> *. . . brillando contra el sol y contra los poetas . . .*
> Heberto Padilla

There it is, the long prow
of the Caribbean, charging to break
the map's complexion.
It is a key, a crocodile, a hook,
an uncoiling question,
a stretch of sinews catching
dribbles from the continent
under which it will, forever, float.

The island mouth is smiling
or frowning, who can tell,
stuffed with waning intentions,
sugarcane and sand.

Such a little place,
such an island listing against sorrow
in the middle of the ocean's gut,
playing make believe
queen of brine, dressing up in green
and calling forth its poets for praise,
its leaders for chesty boasts,
inventing for itself a pantheon
of tropical saints, a vast
and profound literature,
an epic history to rival Rome's.

There it is, pretending it shimmers
over the heads of its people,
denying the terror it feels
when no one listens, denying
that it is always almost drowning,
that it cannot help anyone, least
of all itself, that it is only
a strip of dirt between morning and night,
between what will be and what was,
between the birth of hope
and the death of desire.

Cómo desnudar a una mujer con un saxofón

No es fácil.

El aire que sale del estómago
debe traer
la sal del mar.
Las yemas de los dedos
deben hablar
de palmeras
de membrana a surco
o de soles que trabajan
de noche.
Los sonidos,
agua y metal,
casi vena,
deben confundir
oído y hombro,
y descender
hasta las rodillas
con la misma suavidad
de quien maneja
un chevrolet 53
a 30 millas por hora,
en un freeway de Los Ángeles.
Los ojos deben permanecer
cerrados
hasta que la noche
tenga 24 horas,
la semana más de siete días
y no exista Ia palabra
desempleo.
Y entonces,
abres los ojos,
y quizá
encuentres la sonrisa
de ella.

Pero esto no significa
más que un categórico
saludo de hola,
quihúbole,
What's going on, ése,
porque también
en la plusvalía
hay
pasión.

In My Perfect Puerto Rico

My gray mother would be
combing her mother's white hair
on their turquoise-painted porch
under mango trees
among hummingbirds

My black grandfather
in the next rocking chair
happily looking on

My four-foot-eight cousin Sonia
would be out back
in a wooden shack
washing clothes
or running in the garden
tending to her dogs
She wouldn't walk with a limp
wouldn't be sick
She'd have working kidneys
she'd live past thirty

My father would be hunting
all over this side of the island
with his best friend Angel Rodríguez
for reusable items
dumped on the lush countryside
they would be recycling pioneers

I would have a choice
of which cousin to visit
We would still be young
and beautiful
Yolanda
Lili
Wanda
Evelyn
Ivelise

Hilly
We would still be together
and not just old scattered pieces
of what we once were

Homemade Hot Sauce

for mom

Mother goes out on the hunt
in search of prime specimens
little red peppers
some green
Her market of choice
a vegetable post by the side of the road
Year after year you can find
the old man there
under a perennial baking sun
his makeshift market in the wind
Mother slowly stalks the produce
scrutinizes the baby bananas
pores over the *vianda*
pauses to ask if I'd like her
to cook some for dinner
then analyzes the *aguacates*
turing them over
squeezing them lightly as they rest
in the palm of her wrinkled hand
finally she comes up on them
chubby as plum tomatoes
their skins shiny
smooth as plastic
their fiery nature screaming
from inside glad sandwich bags
where they hang on a tree

Back home mother
patiently washes each one
grinds up spices with her
wooden mortar and pestle
Pounds with such force

the hanging pictures
over the dinner table
all dance to her cooking drum
And when her concert has ended
she packs them into
an old vinegar bottle
adds a fresh splash of vinegar to the mix
then promptly places
her concoction outdoors to ferment
under a Puerto Rican sun

El Coto Laurel

Dinner with mom
and with *tía* Carmín
consists of a heavy soup
we call *sancocho*
It consists of stories
about the exquisiteness
of grandmother's cooking
how she stretched a sliver of onion
and little garlic cloves
during the Second World War
enough to cook a pot
of beans for two nights
How the taste of those beans
could never be duplicated

Dinner with mom
and with *tía* Carmín
consists of a warm sunset
white curtains flowing
in the kitchen
annoying mosquitoes
under the table
and highball glasses
filled with passion juice

From the Moment You Died

September 12th, 1999

From the moment you died
until it was time to bury you
it poured wind-swept torrential rains
Lightning and thunder
shacking the coffin your wife chose
from a full-color glossy catalogue

It rained ceaselessly day and night
Gray permeated the meals we ate in the kitchen
while you lay just a glance away in the living room
clutching a set of black rosary beads
your hands folded under a dainty white veil

Our little cement house saturated
as the family stayed up all night
keeping you company
joking about you from time to time
crying from time to time

It was someone else's dream my rummaging
through tin cans of crackers
to eat with cheese at 4:30 a.m.
my sweeping and mopping around you
arranging the folding chairs your morning guests
would sit in to visit with you
assuring myself they'd be color coordinated
just as you'd wish
blues with blues
grays with grays

It had to be someone else's dream
as daylight shown through the front door
that never closed all night
revealing the white water crashing into the land
the sky wide open and crying

I stood in your kitchen
watching the procession of shadowy figures
under dark umbrellas one by one

189

they came to verify it was you
it was really you Salomon Mercado Torres
clutching those black rosary beads
dressed in your brown polyester suit
lying in that box your wife picked out
from a color catalogue
Toñita the mortician provided

The Dead

Where I lay the dream of
following myself in your soul
—Julia De Burgos

I face the universe
when I speak to the dead
I lay as they do
in their coffins
My body upright
revealed to the wide expanse
of the firmament

There I speak with mother
in some brightly lit hallway

She says she is going
to sleep with father
His voice resonating from inside
a black room she enters

I often speak to the dead
They share their days with me
provide advice
They have no wings
no halos
no emitting light from within
They're people just like you and like me

Silence

Who could detain me with useless illusions
when my soul begins to complete its work?
—Julia De Burgos

When the joker appears
with mouthfuls of shadows and smoke
crazily waving his self-import in my face
like flags waving front suburban homes
as if to cover the hate crimes of this country

When he yells to idle my mind
spewing out vortexes in tongues
filled with false virtues
like commercials that mask
the plunder of impoverished lives
the enslavement of darker skin
the raping of female years

I know the joker is oblivious
that his time steadily dwindles
like any man's life
That a pine box
a crematorium await him
just as they await me
That he does not know
my silence is an impenetrable shield

New York at 17

Stepping into the Waldorf Astoria lobby
for the first time feels like
stepping into the Million-Dollar Movie
Breathless I stand staring
at graceful chandeliers
at wine-colored Persian rugs
the finest comforters
beneath my feet

I am an explorer walking with trepidation
discovering what is unknown
my mother's daughter
afraid of doing something wrong

But no one says anything
no one interrupts my expedition
As I enter the powder room
the one bigger than
our Atlantic City train-row apt
the powder room where
like Natalie Wood
I recline on a chaise lounge
That stunning cushioned place
dressed in pinks and mauve
and shiny brass fixtures
That beautiful room
with velvet running water

New York at 26

Arriving in the City
I land at the base
of the World Trade Center
There climb on mammoth escalators
toward the sky
I'm swept-up by the current
of a thousand people
Everyone here is important
Everyone a personality
Everyone part of New York City's life

Not far from those tall towers
Chinatown spins with activity
Chinese heard in the wind
sidewalk carts
from corner to corner
seafood for sale
aromas permeate

the south end of the city
sesame chicken aromas
moo-shoo-pork
garlic-eggplant aromas
people line up for a good meal

Squeezing through the crowds
I cross Canal Street
into Little Italy
there waiters wear
long white aprons
there the smell of espresso
snaps me to attention
there I see diners
sitting in street cafés
sipping red wine

They are lovers in my dreams

~~~

Milla

Mi abuela, Puerto Rico

Milla lived eons ago
when sandals pounded dirt roads
blazing hot under palm tree-lined skies.
Milla's long dark hair flowed side to side,
glistened in the noon light.
Mahogany skinned, she shopped;
plátanos, yucas, a bark of soap.
Milla worked,
striking clothes against wooden boards,
gathering wood for evening meals,
feeding chickens, hogs, dogs,
and roosters at dawn.
Milla traveled only once
to Chicago.
A color-faded photograph serves as document.
Smiles and thousands of hugs
for the grandchildren on a park bench.

Milla's a century old
and still remembers every one of us
even those left over in the U.S.
She still carries a stick
certain of her authority
over four generations.
Milla outlived two world wars,
saw the first television,
the first electric bulb in her town,
Hitler, segregation,
the Vietnam War,
and Gorbachev.
Milla can speak of
the turn of the century land reforms,
of the blinded enthusiasm
for a man called Marín
and the mass migration of the 1950s.
Milla can speak of her beloved husband,
sugar cane cutter for life.
She can speak of the love of a people,
of the pain of separation.
Milla can speak of the Caribbean Ocean,
the history of the sun and sand
and the mystery of the stars.
Milla maintains an eternal candle lit
just for me.
Milla will live for all time.

~ ~ ~

Juanita

Mi tía, Puerto Rico

Juanita between sugar canes
peeking through a wonderful face,
splendid eyes,
beautifully shaped nose & lips
to speak melodies with.
Beaming bronze skin,
perfection of an earthly figure
strolling through the plaza square.

Juanita
breathing life into the dead,
medium of light that makes us all so happy.
Materializing miracles from impossibilities,
providing food from soil,
creating homes from ashes,
teaching tolerance by living.

Juanita
the eye against harm,
keeper of the key
kneading dough for fried patties,
tending to crippled children,
to the salt of the earth
beneath a warm sea breeze in the evening.

Juanita
mending broken souls all her worldly days,
providing smiles at every end,
lending breasts for pillows to the brokenhearted.

Juanita
hummingbirds at her feet.

Mango Juice

Eating mangoes
on a stick
is laughing
as gold juice
slides down
your chin
melting manners,
as mangoes slip
through your lips
sweet but biting

is hitting piñatas
blindfolded and spinning
away from the blues
and grays

is tossing
fragile *cascarones*
on your love's hair,
confetti teasing him
to remove his shoes
his mouth open
and laughing
as you glide
more mango in,
cool rich flesh
of México
music teasing
you to strew
streamers on trees
and cactus

teasing the wind
to stream through
your hair blooming
with confetti
and butterflies

your toes warm
in the sand.

The Desert Is My Mother

I say feed me.
She serves red prickly pear on a spiked cactus.

I say tease me.
She sprinkles raindrops in my face on a sunny day.

I say frighten me.
She shouts thunder, flashes lightning.

I say hold me.
She whispers, "Lie in my arms."

I say heal me.
She gives me chamomile, oregano, peppermint.

I say caress me.
She strokes my skin with her warm breath.

I say make me beautiful.
She offers turquoise for my fingers,
    a pink blossom for my hair.

I say sing to me.
She chants her windy songs.

I say teach me.
She blooms in the sun's glare,
    the snow's silence,
    the driest sand.

The desert is my mother.
El desierto es mi madre.
The desert is my strong mother.

El desierto es mi madre

Le digo, dame de comer.
Me sirve rojas tunas en nopal espinoso.

Le digo, juguetea conmigo.
Me salpica la cara con gotitas de lluvia en día asoleado.

Le digo, asústame.
Me grita con truenos y me tira relámpagos.

Le digo, abrázame.
Me susurra, "Acuéstate aquí".

Le digo, cúrame.
Me da manzanilla, orégano, hierbabuena.

Le digo, acaríciame.
Me roza la cara con su cálido aliento.

Le digo, hazme bella.
Me ofrece turquesa para mis dedos,
  una flor rosada para mi cabello.

Le digo, cántame.
Me arrulla con sus canciones de viento.

Le digo, enséñame.
Y florece en el brillo del sol,
  en el silencio de la nieve,
  en las arenas más secas.

El desierto es mi madre.

El desierto es mi madre poderosa.

Graduation Morning

for Anthony

She called him Lucero, morning star,
snared him with sweet coffee, pennies,
Mexican milk candy, brown bony hugs.

Through the years she'd cross the Río
Grande to clean his mother's home. *"Lucero,*
mi lucero," she'd cry, when she'd see him
running toward her in the morning,
when she pulled stubborn cactus thorns
from his small hands, when she found him
hiding in the creosote.

Though she's small and thin,
black sweater, black scarf,
the boy in the white graduation robe
easily finds her at the back of the cathedral,
finds her amid the swirl of sparkling clothes,
finds her eyes.

Tears slide down her wrinkled cheeks.
Her eyes, *luceros*, stroke his face.

University Avenue

We are the first
of our people to walk this path.
We move cautiously
unfamiliar with the sounds,
guides for those who follow.
Our people prepared us
with gifts from the land,
       fire
              herbs and song
hierbabuena soothes us into morning
rhythms hum in our blood
abrazos linger round our bodies
cuentos whisper lessons *en español*.

199

We do not travel alone.
Our people burn deep within us.

⁓ ⌣ ⌣ ⌒

1910

In Mexico they bowed
  their heads when she passed.
   Timid villagers stepped aside
    for the Judge's mother, Doña Luz,
who wore her black shawl, black
  gloves whenever she left her home—
   at the church, the *mercado* and the *plaza*
    in the cool evenings when she strolled
     barely touching her son's wrist
      with her fingertips,
who wore her black shawl, black
  gloves in the carriage that took her
   and her family to Juárez, border town, away
    from Villa laughing at their terror when
     he rode through the village shouting,
      spitting dust,
who wore her black shawl, black
  gloves when she crossed the Río Grande to
   El Paso, her back straight, chin high
    never watching her feet,
who wore her black shawl, black
  gloves into Upton's Five-and-Dime,
   who walked out, back straight, lips quivering,
    and slowly removed her shawl and gloves,
     placed them on the sidewalk with the other
      shawls and shopping bags
       "You Mexicans can't hide
       things from me," Upton would say.
       "Thieves. All thieves.
       Let me see those hands."
who wore a black shawl, black
  gloves the day she walked, chin high,
   never watching her feet, on the black
    beams and boards, still smoking
     that had been Upton's Five-and-Dime.

Two Worlds

Bi-lingual, Bi-cultural
able to slip from "How's life"
to *"M'están volviendo loca,"*
able to sit in a paneled office
drafting memos in smooth English,
able to order in fluent Spanish
at a Mexican restaurant,
American but hyphenated,
viewed by anglos as perhaps exotic,
perhaps inferior, definitely different,
viewed by Mexicans as alien
(their eyes say, "You may speak
Spanish but you're not like me")
an American to Mexicans
a Mexican to Americans
a handy token
sliding back and forth
between the fringes of both worlds
by smiling
by masking the discomfort
of being pre-judged
Bi-laterally.

Now and Then, America

Who wants to rot
beneath dry, winter grass
in a numbered grave
in a numbered row
in a section labeled Eternal Peace
with neighbors plagued
by limp, plastic roses

springing from their toes?
Grant me a little life now and then, America.

Who wants to rot
as she marches through life
in a pin-striped suit
neck chained in a soft, silk bow
in step, in style, insane.
Let me in
to boardrooms wearing hot
colors, my hair long and free,
maybe speaking Spanish.
Risk my difference, my surprises.
Grant me a little life, America.

And when I die, plant *zempasúchitl*,
flowers of the dead, and at my head
plant organ cactus, green fleshy
fingers sprouting, like in Oaxaca.
Let desert creatures hide
in the orange blooms.
Let birds nest in the cactus stems.
Let me go knowing life
      flower and song
will continue right above my bones.

Desert Women

Desert women know
about survival.
Fierce heat and cold
have burned and thickened
our skin. Like cactus
we've learned to hoard,
to sprout deep roots,
to seem asleep, yet wake
at the scent of softness
in the air, to hide
pain and loss by silence,
no branches wail

or whisper our sad songs
safe behind our thorns.

Don't be deceived.
When we bloom, we stun.

～～～

The Grateful Minority

Why the smile, Ofelia?

Ofelia who?

Why the smile at lysol days
scrubbing washbowls, mop—
mopping bathrooms for people
who don't even know your name.

Ofelia who?

Dirty work you'll do again tomorrow,
mirrors you've polished twenty-five years.

Some days I want to shake you
brown women who whistle while
you shine toilets, who smile gratefully
at dry rubber gloves, new uniforms,
steady paychecks, cleaning
content in your soapy solitude.

Ofelia who?

Like desert flowers you bloom
namelessly in harsh countries
I want to shake your secret
from you.   Why?   How?

～～～

Bribe

I hear Indian women
    chanting, chanting
I see them long ago bribing
the desert with turquoise threads,
in the silent morning coolness,
kneeling, digging, burying
their offering in the Land

chanting, changing
        Guide my hands, Mother,
        to weave singing birds
        flowers rocking in the wind, to trap
        them on my cloth with a web of thin threads.

Secretly I scratch a hole in the desert
by my home, I bury a ballpoint pen
and lined yellow paper. Like the Indians
I ask the Land to smile on me, to croon
softly, to help me catch her music with words.

Elías Miguel Muñoz

Repetitions

One doesn't have to be
eighty
to write about endings.
There are autumns of all ages.
This one I'm going through
is only thirtysomething.

I'd love to be cynical.
I'd love to make fun
of my Cuban American angst,
of my ethnic tragicomedy.
Baby Boomer and Yuca,
Cubiche, Yuckie *con mojo*.
But I can't
this situation is
a serious situation.
Although there's nothing new
about my plight:
I've laughed so many times
at this gray sky and these
dying trees.
And yet today those trees
and that sky are my companions,
not my invention.
As real as death.

Como la misma muerte.

One doesn't have to be
eighty
to write about repetitions

Repetitions happen at any age.
And they are always painful.
It hurts to have to wait
for spring. Again.
It hurts to describe
an autumn day without you,

these same old leaves.
This new repetition.
Again.

⌒‿‿⌒

Summer of the Body

When the Filipino doctor,
soft-spoken and fatherly,
inquires,
Are you close to your grandfather?
(Or did he say *were* you close?)
And he tells me of the necessary end.
(Perhaps he said "inevitable.")
The NO CODE.
The usual resuscitation that
the almost-dead man will not receive.
There's no point, says the doctor.
Because sooner or later
(any second now)
we all must endure
the summer of the body.
No one is exempt.

We are prepared,
I guess.
We have already bought
the burial plot and
we have chosen the lettering
for his tombstone.
(We were so pleased
to see the graveyard;
the tombs were hidden
under welcoming grass.)
We'll offer him a wake,
his *velorio*.
And we will dress him in a guayabera.
I guess we'll do
what has to be done.

Abuelo's hands,
his massive fingers,
still warm.
His skin cannot bear another shot.
That's why we have this perfumed cream,
clean sheets and feather pillows,
this cool air,
for him.

Summers of the body can be merciless.

Mariano, the Air

I believe today is Friday.
On this train headed for Madrid,
I'm thinking of Mariano.
Driven mad by the memory,
I remember Mariano.
He took care of me.
He worried about me.
"Cuánto te quiero," we said.

On this train headed for Madrid
I'm reliving our fantasy:
We were childhood friends.
(Mariano in Segovia
with his *amiguito*;
both leaning against
the front door of a church,
reluctant to enter,
freezing to death,
kept barely alive
by their desire.)

I realize this now:
It was Mariano who made
the first move.
I didn't seek him out.
(I never look for them.)

What do I do now, on this train,
to get Mariano out of me?
Breathe again. Deeply.
Or maybe this is life:
running, desperate
for oxygen.

Mariano, the air.

Sugarcane

can't cut
cut the cane
azúca' in chicago
dig it down to the
roots sprouting spray paint on the
walls on the hard cold
stone of the great gritty city
slums in chicago
with the mansions in the hole
in the head of
the old rich left behind
from other times lopsided
gangster walls overgrown taken
over by the dark
and poor overgrown with no
sugarcane but you
can't can't cut
cut the water
bro'
from the flow and
you can't can't cut
cut the blood
lines from this island
train one by one throwing off
the chains siguaraya
no no
no se pue'e cortar
pan con ajo quisqueya
cuba y borinquen no
se pue'en parar

I saw it
saw black a-frica
down in the city
walking in chicago y
la cuba cuba

gritando en el solar
I saw it
saw quisqueya
brown
uptown in the city
cryin' in chicago
y borinquen
bro'
sin un
chavo igual but
you can't can't cut
cut the water
bro'
from the flow and
you can't can't cut
cut the blood
lines from this island
train one by one throwing off
the chains siguaraya
no no
no se pue'e cortar
pan con ajo quisqueya
cuba y borinquen no
se pue'en parar

¡azúca'!

Judith Ortiz Cofer

Lessons of the Past

For my daughter

I was born the year my father learned to march in step
with other men, to hit bull's eyes, to pose for sepia photos
in dress uniform outside Panamanian nightspots—pictures
he would send home to his pregnant teenage bride inscribed:
To my best girl.

My birth made her a madonna, a husbandless young woman
with a legitimate child, envied by all the tired women
of the pueblo as she strolled my carriage down dirt roads,
both of us dressed in fine clothes bought with army checks.

                    When he came home,
he bore gifts: silk pajamas from the orient for her; a pink
iron crib for me. People filled our house to welcome him.
He played Elvis loud and sang along in his new English.
She sat on his lap and laughed at everything.
They roasted a suckling pig out on the patio. Later,
no one could explain how I had climbed over the iron bars
and into the fire. Hands lifted me up quickly, but not before
the tongues had licked my curls.

                    There is a picture of me
taken soon after: my hair clipped close to my head,
my eyes enormous—about to overflow with fear.
I look like a miniature of one of those women
in Paris after World War II, hair shorn,
being paraded down the streets in shame,
for having loved the enemy.

                    But then things changed,
and some nights he didn't come home. I remember
hearing her cry in the kitchen. I sat on the rocking chair
waiting for my cocoa, learning how to count, *uno, dos, tres,*
cuatro, cinco, on my toes. So that when he came in,
smelling strong and sweet as sugarcane syrup,
I could surprise my *Papasito*—
who liked his girls smart, who didn't like crybabies—

with a new lesson, learned well.

The Idea of Islands

The place where I was born,
that mote in a cartographer's eye,
interests you?
Today Atlanta is like a port city
enveloped in mist. The temperature
is plunging with the abandon
of a woman rushing to a rendezvous.
Since you ask, things were simpler
on the island. Food and shelter
were never the problem. Most days,
a hat and a watchful eye were all
one needed for protection, the climate being
rarely inclement. Fruit could be plucked
from trees languishing under the weight
of their own fecundity. The thick sea
spewed out fish that crawled into the pots
of women whose main occupation was to dress
each other's manes with the scarlet hibiscus,
which as you may know, blooms
without restraint in the tropics.
I was always the ambitious one, overdressed
by my neighbors' standards, and unwilling
to eat mangoes three times a day.
In truth, I confess to spending my youth
guarding the fire by the beach, waiting
to be rescued from the futile round
of paradisiacal life.
How do I like the big city?
City lights are just as bright
as the stars that enticed me then;
the traffic ebbs and rises like the tides,
and in a crowd,
everyone is an island.

They Never Grew Old

I am speaking of that hollow-eyed race
of bone-embraced tubercular women and men,
the last of whom I caught a glimpse of
in the final days of my childhood.

Every family had one
hidden away in a sanitarium—
a word whispered when certain names
came up in conversation. And when I asked
my mother what it meant, she said,
a very clean place.

Once, I saw one; a rare
appearance by a distant cousin
our family tried to keep invisible.
From a neighbor's house across the road,
I looked upon the visitor in a white dress
that seemed to hang upon her skeletal frame
like a starched garment on a wire hanger.
She held a handkerchief to her mouth
the entire time. The circle of polite relatives
sat back in the chairs around her.
The coffee cup at her side would later
be discarded, the chair she floated on—she seemed
to have no volume or weight—would be scrubbed
with something so strong, it made one cry; the whole house
sanitized and disinfected after her brief stay.

Though these sad, thin cousins were rarely seen
in our living rooms, they were a presence in the attics
and closets where we kept all our unwanted kin.

And they too had their heroes and myths.

As a girl I heard the story of two young people,
put away to die and forgotten,
who met in the cool, pine-scented corridors
of their hospital prison, and fell in love.
Desperate to be together, they escaped
into the night. It was a young woman

who found them under an embankment bridge,
a damp place where a creek one could step over ran.
Lying in each others' arms, their bodies were marbleized
with fever and morning dew. They were a frieze
in a Roman catacomb: Eros and Psyche in repose.

Moved by their plight, the girl brought them food
and a blanket. But dying creatures are easy to track,
and they were soon found by townspeople scandalized
that the ill should want to make love. A priest
was called in before a doctor. I surmise
that they died in separate beds.

        Back then, I was convinced
the story of the dying lovers clinging to each other
in the dark cave, was the most romantic thing I would ever hear,
the spot on their lungs that killed them, I imagined
as a privileged place on the body's ordinary geography.

I too wanted to live in *a very clean place*,
where fragile as a pale pink rosebud I would sit
among my many satin pillows and wait for the man with whom
I would never grow old, to rescue me from a dull life.
Death and love once again confused
by one too young to see the difference.

                            ～⁓⁓↷

The Lesson of the Sugarcane

My mother opened her eyes wide
at the edge of the field
ready for cutting.
"Take a deep breath,"
            she whispered,
"There is nothing as sweet:
Nada más dulce."
       Overhearing,
Father left the flat he was changing
in the road-warping sun,
and grabbing my arm, broke my sprint
toward a stalk:

"Cane can choke a little girl: snakes hide
where it grows over your head."

And he led us back to the crippled car
where we sweated out our penitence,
for having craved more sweetness
than we were allowed,
more than we could handle.

The Latin Deli: An Ars Poetica

Presiding over a formica counter,
plastic Mother and Child magnetized
to the top of an ancient register,
the heady mix of smells from the open bins
of dried codfish, the green plantains
hanging in stalks like votive offerings,
she is the Patroness of Exiles,
a women of no-age who was never pretty,
who spends her days selling canned memories
while listening to the Puerto Ricans complain
that it would be cheaper to fly to San Juan
than to buy a pound of Bustelo coffee here,
and to Cubans perfecting their speech
of a "glorious return" to Havana—where no one
has been allowed to die and nothing to change until then;
to Mexicans who pass through, talking lyrically
of *dólares* to be made in El Norte—
                                    all wanting the comfort
of spoken Spanish, to gaze upon the family portrait
of her plain wide face, her ample bosom
resting on her plump arms, her look of maternal interest
as they speak to her and each other
of their dreams and their disillusions—
how she smiles understanding
when they walk down the narrow aisles of her store
reading the labels of packages aloud, as if
they were the names of lost lovers: *Suspiros*,
Merengues, the stale candy of everyone's childhood.

She spends her days
slicing *jamón y queso* and wrapping it in wax paper
tied with string: plain ham and cheese
that would cost less at the A&P, but it would not satisfy
the hunger of the fragile old man lost in the folds
of his winter coat, who brings her lists of items
that he reads to her like poetry, or the others,
whose needs she must divine, conjuring up products
from places that now exist only in their hearts—
closed ports she must trade with.

So Much for Mañana

After twenty years on the mainland
Mother's gone back to the Island
to let her skin
melt from her bones
under her native sun.
She no longer wears stockings,
girdles or tight clothing.
Brown as a coconut,
she takes siestas in a hammock,
and writes me letters that say:
"Stop chasing your own shadow, *niña,*
come down here and taste the *piña,*
put away those heavy books,
don't you worry about your shape,
here on the Island men look
for women who can carry a little weight.
On every holy day,
I burn candles and I pray
that your brain won't split
like an avocado pit
from all that studying.
What do you say?
Abrazos from your Mami and a blessing
from that saint, Don Antonio, *el cura.*"
I write back: "Someday I will go back
to your Island and get fat,
but not now, Mamá, maybe *mañana.*"

216

The Hollow

For years we scavenged among the dark sands
and ate the moist findings we called bread,
fallen to this ground to teach us
the vertical rules of the spirit.
Above was light and below was hunger.
Even when the wind blew around the few thick trees,
nothing but sand-plated trunks, they could not mark
with what undulations they should the blowing.

And finally we pleased ourselves with a few grunts,
agreeing this meant that, and that meant this.
Soon we learned to sing foreboding.
Because of this and that, a colossus was
on its way because we noticed the shadows
the cliffs threw our way could not be drunk
by the cracked land. So we lived
in those shades and concluded
that our relief from the heat
was love of simple darkness.

It is of no use to disguise our love of shadows.
The colossus will stare mutely
and we will learn to not run from him, we averred.
It turned out to be a horse someone had dreamt.
Our grunts by then had become beliefs.
The dreamer throws images to the horizon
and they fall to the ground as things among beings
who must decipher them. We knocked against its belly,
harder after we were no longer timid.
Nothing. How could we know
it was looking for a wall and memory?

We drew back, took another look
at the sand, the shadows, and we said,
the horse is simply another cliff
even if we cannot live under it.
Who knows why we invented the sacred,
but our punishment came. Forgetting. Swallowing.

Sleeping under the stars, we wanted to call
Night the great shadow.
No one has adored language more than we did then.

~⟨⟩~

Progress

They are the flood's fingerprints—the lizard
scurrying across a wall, the fly's buzz gelled
in hover, the spider's hairline drift,
the vulture and the albatross and all
the kited wings, all the living things
that bring the sea's unleaden habits
to air and land. Their floated
masteries would a normal practice be
had the rains endured and the whirling
arks never keeled. It is no accident
that when men fled the dense quotidian
to rub the empty stars, they wombed
their weight in freedoms
of untroubled space. Suit bubbled,
tubed to air and duty, they bowed
to the mosquito lighting on a pond,
the mantis and the jay. They homaged
the bat's pendulum and the ant's intact dive
from canopies where serpent and monkey
mirror each other's coil and hold.
The flood, maligned in murderous tales,
was not at all about a hated world.
It was and is a call to disregard the plumb,
as do the dancer's silken veil, the flag
folding like kelp in the just breeze,
the balloons of heat and helium.
Behold the hummingbird who will not forget
water's freedom in a falling world.
It did not have to lift toward emptiness
a moon away from its kind,
and ponder continent and season
in spun blurs eclipsed by a gloved thumb
to understand the stillness of journey.

For the Cuban Dead

Once they were men fully because they belonged,
and everywhere they looked and chatted and sipped
a bit of coffee, whisked away a fly with a wrist
or jolted a newspaper readably straight,
or flirted, or worried about the world and where
the damn country was going as a trolley rolled
and curtains dipped and bulged breast-like
and hid again in the proper window. They were
home and citizens of it and dared and loved
and were decent and stole and killed and loved again.
They were home. How like the root in the earth,
the crease in the linen, the wind rending the cloud,
the growl in the hunger, the pavement sprayed
with waves crashing against the sea wall.
How like all right things in the mind of place,
they jostled and failed, learned and betrayed.
Like coins in pockets made for them
they cried stridently or simply tinkled in murmurs,
and it didn't matter if talk or life had substance.
Right of place was substance.

There is no enough in exile. Not enough anger,
and the blanket of safety always leaves the feet bare.
And it is here, no matter how clean and golden,
that one learns how different the wrist and the fly
and the shot of wave, how it never stops
calling although the law of distance deafens.
Memory is the heart's gravity.
The accent of their children
becomes unbearably alien, a dampness
from the sidewalk creeping past the thin sole
and into the ignored sock. Now nothing
escapes notice and the balance is always against.

And it hits them, these never again composed,
that the time to see and hear was then,
when rightness held even the stormy evils

219

of the quotidian in the same palm
with the trash of years of seconds
and the kissed joys.
Then, as we have come to know, was
the proper place to gaze at the dust
of butterfly panoplies, ponder
the calligraphic crud on china,
relinquish decorous ears to taut goatskins,
wash in the lace of Sunday clouds,
and otherwise pay attention
with one's whole life to shadows
knitting five centuries of incomparable capital,
field's antique jewel and the cradling shore.
God it was who let them die
filled with late understanding,
so who dares say we the innocent lurk
unpunished in the works and days?

Winter Landscape with a Bird Trap

After Bruegel
Not all the birds think the kernels
above the stick-propped board
are the gift of heaven. Some spy
and dawdle on the barren twigs
the season has knitted.
Like melted cages, the branches cannot hold
yet the ambition is there.
As in the ice that so wants to burst
into warmth and drown
the paunchy mother with her wrapped child,
the skaters swinging sticks, the ambling villagers—
all caught in the hungers, minutes and pennies.

And the bundling snow too wants its kill,
to take these talky mammals down
like the thin wolf or the late-born fawn.
All the forces of the wild will not shear
the species that hides in skins and houses.
Indeed, they've brunt down

nature's clock and storage
and war on borrowed soil. By mine
and net they balance the world
into purpose. And now a clever one

props a board up, drops corn and waits
for the birds to lose the fear
that brought them through the sun
green talon and claw. To fall
now under blight's sagacious shadow
in this parody of shelter, this house
the kind master must have built just for them—
the artless few who stayed the acrid season.

Was it wrong to hope for dropped petals of food
and a slice of roof to warm the ground?
And wrong to take the string that arcs
in the bitten gusts for the summer rope
a blur of children jump through?
Who but the safe dark starling
staring at the loose finches and sparrows
cradling into the trap could damn
their needs? Did he not scoff
at the scarecrow to crown his beak with corn
when all the harvester could do was hope
he'd had his fill? Starling's kin holds the string,
the brother featherless wing that shuts the trap.
The grim window is nature, too.

Ibises, Miami

They are too large for the tangling city scene,
the dusty roar, the trash, blares and edges
of its speeds. And yet they alight serene

on median strips and bank lawns, the richest
beast in view. Asian ballerina balanced
to strike a lizard in the reeds. Just

to feed the tight white frame and dance
in that slow motion garners praise,
but ibis also aims to startle remembrance.

with simple feats. Behold the art by which they raise
their necks to pluck then loop to preen
and how, while gardeners mow and yawn, they poise

their fan wings on a hedge and weave their lean
legs and talons like tendrils on a branch.
They watch the ruckus of world with an eye as keen

as any other bird's, but when they launch
to flight it is not in fear but sadly sure
their act has not a single sigh procured.
Art's awkward duty is to ask too much.

Ten-Pound Draw

On my first trip to London
I learned that the best way to
see the city is from the top
of a red double-decker bus
If you want to be loved on the
first night in more than one
position you have to help with
the cooking

On my second trip to London
I learned that the best way to
get your smoke on was to first
find out where the dark faces live
I rode the Tube to Brixton Station
and found them all over the world
living at the end of the line

At the top of the escalator
a brother selling oils and incense
sends orders into his cell phone
You think righteousness must be
a booming market

The black girls the blahk girls
The black girls on the block
smile and insist that I am Pakistani
when I tell them that I'm Nuyorikistani
so I talk como like this y como like
that y como like kikireeboo tan linda
no doubt it's all good
I am all of that if you want me to be
but do you know where I can find
a ten-pound draw

No luck finding the parliament funk
and Roger in Reading said I can't
ask for a dime bag so I buy ten
bottles of Egyptian musk and show

Brotherman the thirst in my eyes
He leads me to the smoke
for a small finders fee

I am willing to take these chances
in spite of the suspicious glances
but just in case I buy a Big Ben postcard
address it to The Crazy Bunch
c/o El Barrio and write:
"Yo, if I don't make it back home
I was thinking about y'all
when I went to this place called Brixton
looking for a ten-pound draw"

Black Boots

title for a jazz
riff a catwalk
strut Fifth Avenue
stroll black
boot leather
bass fashion
mama look
good as

hell

Forty-One Bullets Off-Broadway

It's not like you were looking at a
vase filled with plastic white roses
while pissing in your mother's bathroom
and hoped that today was not the day
you bumped into four cops who
happened to wake up with a bad
case of contagious shooting

From the Bronx to El Barrio
we heard you fall face first into
the lobby of your equal opportunity
forty-one bullets like silver push pins
holding up a connect-the-dots picture of Africa
forty-one bullets not giving you enough time
to hit the floor with dignity and
justice for all forty-one bullet shells
trickling onto a bubble gum-stained mosaic
where your body is mapped out

Before your mother kissed you goodbye
she forgot to tell you that American kids
get massacred in gym class
and shot during Sunday sermon
They are mourned for a whole year while
people like you go away quietly

Before you could show your
I.D. and say, "Officer—"
four regulation Glock clips went achoo
and smoked you into spirit and by the
time a special street unit decided what was
enough another dream submitted
an application for deferral

It was la vida te da sorpresas/sorpresas
te da la vida/ay dios and you probably thought
I was singing from living la vida loca
but be you prince/be you pauper
the skin on your drum makes you
the usual suspect around here

By the time you hit the floor
protest poets came to your rescue
legal eagles got on their cell phones
and booked red eyes to New York
File folders were filled with dream team
pitches for your mother who was on TV
looking suspicious at your defense

knowing that Justice has been known
to keep one eye open for the right price

By the time you hit the floor
the special unit forgot everything they
learned at the academy
The mayor told them to take a few
days off and when they came back he
sent them to go beat up a million young
black men while your blood seeped through
the tile in the lobby of your equal
opportunity from the Bronx to El Barrio
there were enough shots to go around

Nobody Knows My Name

I'm tired
dead anonymous tired
of getting mail addressed
to all those people I never was:

Gustazo	Perez
Gustavio	Penley
Gary	Porris
Gus	Perry
Gustaf Pirey.	

Nobody here knows my name.
This would never have happened in Havana.

Ghost Writing

I live with ghosts.
Laggard ghosts who wear their fatigue like a sheet
Petulant, unrepentant ghosts who never sleep
Ghosts like mouth sores
Ghosts that look me in the eye at midday
and buzz in my ears in the dead of night
Chinese laundry ghosts
Ghosts that tap and tease and taunt
Politically correct ghosts
Feminist ghosts
Holy ghosts
Ghosts of a chance
Gustavo-come-lately ghosts
Mami and *Papi* ghosts
The ghosts of all my Nochebuenas past.

My ghosts and I,
we have what you'd call this complicated relationship.
At this very moment, they tap tap tap tap tap
on the back of my head,

227

just behind my ears.
They know I'm listening, I pretend that I'm not.
But with every ghostly tap my spine vibrates
like a tuning fork.
If I could, I would leap to grab the greatest ghost
of them all and wring his neck like a wet towel.
But my life offers no such satisfactions.
The ghosts extract their pound of flesh
gram by gram, day by day.
You cannot sneeze them away.
They do not respond to treatment or medication
(my therapist is a ghost).

By now, the ghosts are more me than me.
One of them wrote this poem.

Velorio

I didn't look at him.
I said I wanted to remember
him as he was
when he was
alive.
It wasn't true.
I refused to look
because I don't
want to remember him,
dead or alive.
I want to forget him
as he forgot us.
Say it
because it hurts.

What I Used to Know

The number of the house where I was born and how get to the park. I used to know how old my parents were the year I was born and when they were married. (But they never said why they lived apart after the wedding, or what they saw in each other.)

I used to know the smell of my father's warehouse, how it felt to stand on top of the stacks of rice and beans (*arroz* El Sabio, *frijoles* Bola Roja). I used to know the name of the black truck driver who put me up on his shoulders and carried me around.

I used to know where my mother kept her sewing machine, which of the beds was mine and which my brother's, the combination to the piggy bank—actually a miniature metal safe—and how much money, in dollars and *pesos*, was in it.

I used to know Tessie's last name, my first crush. I remember Alina (or was it Alicia?), my second crush, not as beautiful as Tessie, if it was Tessie. I never knew whether either one of them liked me. If they did, I would remember it.

All this was fifty years and more ago, in another country and another language, one in which *saber*, to know, also means to taste. Today I know this: Not knowing what I used to know *sabe mal*. Tastes like hell.

The First Rock and Roll Song of 1970

The unemployed sky above the clouds
that have replaced the hair on the buildings
whose tenants live and look forward
to the last supper on the lost calendar
They swallowed years before they were born
and tormented by the consolidated edison grass
who never took dancing lessons from the sun

The wind hits the clothing lines
secondhand underwear take off into eternity
The owner panics and jumps out the window
to look for them because he will not be able
to face his friends again if he gets buried
without those underwears he has not finished
paying for yet. Last night a teenage mother

put an airmail stamp on the forehead
of her illegitimate son and threw him out
the window to make it on his own in this
cruel world. The woman pleaded insane
To the authorities when she was arrested
and was sentenced to night school to finish
High School and become a full time waitress

When the war is over and the motion
picture industry shows how america won again
there will be nobody in the audience.
Little boys and girls shout at each other:
"My father's coffin makes your father's coffin
look like a box of matches." The fee to pee
will be discontinued. Shaved head morticians
dance with their favorite dead politicians
and the next president of the united states
will learn how to read the help wanted ads

Nighttime Sunshine Mind Game

did she tell you
as she read the cards
that your heart is
a foreign country
without borders to impede
love at first sight
on the last day of the universe?

did she tell you
that a secret overt admirer
who prefers to remain anonymous
all the nights of his illusions
detects eternity in eyes
that wear your delicate body?

did she tell you
he is constantly thinking
about constantly telling you
he constantly thinks about you
when he's pretending to sleep
after doubting another vision
of how he ended up lost
in the desert of his thoughts?

did she tell you
about an endless daydreamer
who spends all his spare time
fantasizing about your after-life
indicating that you will never
be absent from his inner conflict
long after you cease being fine
to then become fantastic!

did she tell you
he is capable of necrophilia
should you sleep late
the following morning
after finally meeting yourself
over the somewhere else rainbow

within walking distance from
a satisfaction that never comes

did she mention
a familiar undiscovered garden
where the flowers at all hours
are incredible and impossible
& the sublime season shines
in an everlasting summertime
inside of mirrors the night stares into

where the living stays easy
& ghost stories are fascinating
& the wine is victoriously red
& the history of eternal miseries
continues to repeat itself slowly?

did she tell you this?
did your finger tips tremble
as you suddenly remember meeting
in the perfumed valley of shadows
where the moon stays full forever
in a slow dream of fast dancing
& eternal romancing before dawn?

Miguel Piñero

A Lower East Side Poem

Just once before I die
I want to climb up on a
tenement sky
to dream my lungs out till
I cry
then scatter my ashes thru
the Lower East Side.

So let me sing my song tonight
let me feel out of sight
and let all eyes be dry
when they scatter my ashes thru
the Lower East Side.

From Houston to 14th Street
from Second Avenue to the mighty D
here the hustlers & suckers meet
the faggots & freaks will all get
high
on the ashes that have been scattered
thru the Lower East Side.

There's no other place for me to be
there's no other place that I can see
there's no other town around that
brings you up or keeps you down
no food little heat sweeps by
fancy cars & pimps' bars & juke saloons
& greasy spoons make my spirits fly
with my ashes scattered thru
the Lower East Side . . .

A thief, a junkie I've been
committed every known sin
Jews and Gentiles . . . bums and men
of style . . . runaway child
police shooting wild . . .
mothers' futile wails . . . pushers

making sales . . . dope wheelers
& cocaine dealers . . . smoking pot
streets are hot & feed off those who bleed to death . . .

all that's true
all that's true
all that is true
but this ain't no lie
when I ask that my ashes be scattered thru
the Lower East Side.

So here I am, look at me
I stand proud as you can see
pleased to be from the Lower East
a street-fighting man
a problem of this land
I am the Philosopher of the Criminal Mind
a dweller of prison time
a cancer of Rockefeller's ghettocide
this concrete tomb is my home
to belong to survive you gotta be strong
you can't be shy less without request
someone will scatter your ashes thru
the Lower East Side.

I don't wanna be buried in Puerto Rico
I don't wanna rest in long island cemetery
I wanna be near the stabbing shooting
gambling fighting & unnatural dying
& new birth crying
so please when I die . . .
don't take me far away
keep me nearby
take my ashes and scatter them throughout
the Lower East Side . . .

The Book of Genesis According to St. Miguelito

Before the beginning
God created God
In the beginning
God created the ghettos & slums
and God saw this was good.
So God said,
"Let there be more ghettos & slums"
and there were more ghettos & slums.
But God saw this was plain
so
to decorate it
God created lead-base paint
and then
God commanded the rivers of garbage & filth
to flow gracefully through the ghettos.
On the third day
because on the second day God was out of town.
On the third day
God's nose was running
& his jones was coming down and God
in his all knowing wisdom
knew he was sick
he needed a fix
so God
created the backyards of the ghettos
& the alleys of the slums
in heroin & cocaine
and
with his divine wisdom & grace
God created hepatitis
who begat lockjaw
who begat malaria
who begat degradation
who begat
   GENOCIDE
and God knew this was good
in fact God knew things couldn't get better
but he decided to try anyway.
On the fourth day
God was riding around Harlem in a gypsy cab

when he created the people
and he created these beings in ethnic proportion
but he saw the people lonely & hungry
and from his eminent rectum
he created a companion for these people
and he called this companion
capitalism
who begat racism
who begat exploitation
who begat male chauvinism
who begat machismo
who begat imperialism
who begat colonialism
who begat wall street
who begat foreign wars
and God knew
and God saw
and God felt this was extra good
and God said
VAYAAAAAAA.
On the fifth day
the people kneeled
the people prayed
the people begged
and this manifested itself in a petition
a letter to the editor
to know why? WHY? WHY? Qué pasa, babyyyyy?????
and God said,
"My fellow subjects
let me make one thing perfectly clear
by saying this about that:
    NO . . . COMMENT!"
But on the sixth day God spoke to the people
he said . . . "PEOPLE!!!
the ghettos & the slums
& all the other great things I've created
will have dominion over thee"
and then
he commanded the ghettos & slums
and all the other great things he created
to multiply
and they multiplied.

On the seventh day God was tired
so he called in sick
collected his overtime pay
a paid vacation included.
But before God got on that t.w.a.
for the sunny beaches of Puerto Rico
He noticed his main man Satan
planting the learning trees of consciousness
around his ghetto edens
so God called a news conference
on a state of the heavens address
on a coast to coast national t.v. hook up
and God told the people to be
COOL
and the people were cool
and the people kept cool
and the people are cool
and the people stay cool
and God said
Vaya. . . .

This Is Not the Place Where I Was Born

puerto rico, 1974
this is not the place where i was born
remember—as a child the fantasizing images my mother planted
within my head —
the shadows of her childhood recounted to me many times
over welfare loan on crédito food from el bodeguero
i tasted mango many years before the skin of the fruit
ever reached my teeth
i was born on an island about 35 miles wide 100 miles long
a small island with a rainforest somewhere in the central
regions of itself
where spanish was a dominant word
& signs read by themselves
i was born in a village of that island where the police
who frequented your place of business, hangout or home came as
servant or friend & not as a terror in slogan clothing
i was born in a barrio of the village on the island

where people left their doors open at night
where respect for elders was exhibited with pride
where courting for loved ones was not treated over confidentially
where children's laughter did not sound empty & savagely alive
with self destruction . . .
i was born on an island where to be puerto rican meant to be
part of the land & soul & puertorriqueños were not the
minority
puerto ricans were first, none were second
no, i was not born here . . .
no, i was not born in the attitude & time of this place
this sun-drenched soil
this green-faced piece of earth
this slave-blessed land
where the caribbean seas pound angrily on the shores
of pre-fabricated house/hotel redcap hustling people gypsy taxi cab
fighters for fares to fajardo
& the hot wind is broken by fiberglass palmtrees
& highrise plátanos maríano on leave & color t.v.
looney tune cartoon comic-book characters with badges
in their jockstraps
& foreigners scream that puertorriqueños are foreigners
& have no right to claim any benefit on the birthport
this sun-drenched soil
this green-faced piece of earth
this slave-blessed land
where nuyoricans come in search of spiritual identity
are greeted with profanity
this is insanity that americanos are showered
with shoe-shine kisses
police in stocking caps cover carry out john wayne
television cowboy law road models of new york city detective
french connection/deathwish instigation ku-klux-klan mind
panorama screen seems
in modern medicine is in confusion needs a transfusion quantity
treatment if you're not on the plan the new stand
of blue cross blue shield blue uniform master charge
what religion you are
blood fills the waiting room of death
stale air & qué pasa stares are nowhere
in sight & night neon light shines bright
in el condado area puerto rican under cover cop

stop & arrest on the spot puerto ricans who shop for the flag
that waves on the left-in souvenir stores—
  puertorriqueños cannot assemble displaying the emblem
nuyoricans are fighting & dying for in newark, lower east side
south bronx where the fervor of being
puertorriqueños is not just rafael hernández
viet vet protest with rifle shots that dig into four pigs
& sociable friday professional persons rush to the
golf course & martini glasses work for the masses
& the island is left unattended because the middle-class
bureaucratic cuban has arrived spitting blue-eyed justice
at brown-skinned boys in military khaki
compromise to survive is hairline length
moustache-trimmed face looking grim like a soldier
on furlough further cannot exhibit contempt for what is
not cacique-born this poem will receive a burning
stomach turning scorn nullified classified racist
from this pan am eastern first national chase manhattan
puerto rico . . .

Los caudillos

written from aztlán de leavenworth

Stifling
    Crystal City
          heat
rouses Texas sleepers
    the long siesta finally over
at last, at long, long last
    politics wrested from
tyrannical usurpers' clutches
    fires are stoked
flames are fanned . . .

    conflagrating flames
of socio-political awareness.

    In rich Delano vineyards
        Chávez does his pacifist thing
"lift that crate
    & pick them grapes"
stoop labor's awright—with God on your side.

Small wonder David Sánchez
    impatient & enraged in East L.A.
dons a beret, its color symbolizing
    Urgent Brown.

    Voices raised in unison
        in Northern New Mexico hills
"¡esta tierra es nuestra!"
        cached clutter: invalid grants/unrecognized treaties
their tongues are forked,
        Tijerina;
Indo-Hispano
    you're our man.

Denver's Corky boxing lackeys' ears back
    let them live in the bottoms for awhile
see how they like a garbage dump
    for a next door neighbor.

José Angel Gutiérrez: MAYO's fiery vocal cat
    the world does not like energetic noisemakers
or so says papa henry b. (the savior of San Anto)
    who only saved himself.

In Eastern Spanish Ghettos
    Portorro street gangs do
Humanity.

        Young Lords: (Cha-Cha, Fi & Yoruba)
                burglarize rich folks' antibiotics
        rip off x-ray units/hospital
                —become medics of the poor—
        ghetto children must not die
                of lead poisoning & T.B.

Latin Kings: (Watusi Valez & the rest)
    if you're doing social service
how can you be on
    terrorizing sprees (with priest accompanist)
in near Northside Chicago?

        Ubiquitous? We're everywhere!

Arise! Bronze People,
    the wagon-wheels gather momentum.

Kid Hielero

He had a couple of fights
but they didn't add up.
Kid Hielero became a name for the bars,

A name for a laugh
as if who could believe it
looking at him now,

or it was just a name to remember
the way one talked about radio shows,
The Shadow, and who could remember

the man's real name, Lamont Cranston—
as if a radio guy could have a real name—
but it's what we said anyway,

and didn't think about it.

Anyone from Nogales in the Fifties
would remember it—
well they'd remember it but maybe not him:

Kid Hielero took his name
from the old ice house
right on Grand Avenue coming in,

the *hielero*, where he worked for a while
the way everyone worked for a while
at some point in life.

Small towns work like this.

The ice chutes used to pass over
the road through town
and ice water dripped like rain

on the cars underneath.
It could have been a car wash
and everybody could have been rich

but it wasn't, and they weren't.
These were the days when the railroad
needed ice

for the cabbages and the lettuce,
the masses of sugar beets.
It was in the days when small towns,

these small towns,
you know what I mean,
needed themselves.

Kid Hielero died
in another time altogether,
suffering the invention of cancer.

When it happened
all he wanted was watermelon.
It was a fancy hospital

and the nurses got some
even though it was winter, September.
I remember they said they were ready

for this. They said
somebody who's dying,
they always want watermelon.

It's the women from Mexico
in the kitchen, they knew
right from the beginning

this would happen.
Not for him, of course, not specifically,
just for people like him.

So they freeze a little in the summer.
They said the women in the kitchen said
it's from another time

and it's all I could say, too,
yes, I said.
I think that's true,

it's from another time.
I think that's what you say,
and I think it helps.

Kid Hielero watched the World Series
and ate the watermelon
and died,

and he left me his daughter
for a wife.
It happened quick

So that everyone forgot
about the watermelon,
just like The Shadow's real name.

But there it is
and I don't know what you do with it,
this knowing about what the dying

want to eat.
You remember it sometimes
but not everyone else does.

You just remember it
because there you are with it
every time you eat watermelon.

Combing My Hair in the Hall

Each time the doors to her room were opened
a little of the gathered light left
and the small room became blacker
moving somewhere in a twilight toward night.
And then a little of the light left
not her room, but her falling face
as each time she opened the smaller doors
that were her wooden eyes.
She talked only with her mouth then
no longer with the force of her wild eyes
and that, too, made her less,
each word leaving her now
as the way her firm bones had abandoned her.
Then she spoke with her woman's hands
only, no words left, then only with her smell
which once had been warm, tortillitas,
or like sugar breads just made.
In the half-words of our other language,
in the language of the new world
of which she had had time to show me
only half, I tried to speak to her,
to fill her up, to tell her the jokes
of the day, and fill her too much
with laughing, fill her fat like she had been,
and my brother Tomas tried too, we
touched her, were made to touch her,
we kissed her even, lips trying
to quickly press back the something
as children even we could feel
but whose name she had not told us,
and as we kissed her, bent and kissed her,
we could smell her, I shivered, and we both
breathed out hard when we had to
put our lips there, like later we would learn
to drink pulque and be men, trying even that
to push her back into herself.
But she was impatient with us, or smarter,
or quicker, so that we did smell her,
she made us, and taste the insides of her,
and take her in small parts with us

but not like drink, not like men—instead,
like the smell of bread taken by the heart
into the next day, or into dreams.
Every night she wanted to be young again
as she slept there on her bed
and in the night, in the minute she could
no longer talk, and did not smell, or wake,
she was, again, young: we
opened our mouths
and asked words about her, cried
bits of ourselves out through our eyes,
each sigh expelled, each tear,
each word said now making us,
us less, not her, each word gone
making room in ourselves for her,
so that one day, again, she laughs hard,
a Thursday, four voices stronger, five,
laughs at something none of us understands,
standing there, comb in hand, laughs
at something silly, or vain, or the story
of the six sisters of mercy, perhaps, she
just laughs looking at all of her new faces
full in the mirror at the end of the hall.

We Didn't Bury Him

We didn't bury him, they did.
They didn't know
that he had a ring with an M nor did they know
that he always brought pan dulce home.
That he never went to church but believed in God.
That he loved mother but had a mistress.
That he loved us but never touched us.
That he gave and worked but was avaricious.
That he cursed in English but not in Spanish.
That he drank and smoked once.

They didn't know that he kicked me once when I lost 10 cents.
And that he cried when his father died.

They didn't know that he taught me to cry.
And that he told me I was stupid when I cut my foot.

They didn't know that he baked the turkey at the wedding.
And that he winked his eye when we left on our honeymoon.
Nor did they know that he kissed our little girl when we
were not looking.

They didn't know him, they buried him when he died.

We didn't. (I, my mother and brothers.)

The Blast Furnace

A Foundry's stench, the rolling mill's clamor,
the jackhammer's concerto leaving traces
between worn ears. Oh sing me a bucket shop blues
under an accordion's spell
with blood notes cutting through the black air
for the working life, for the rotating shifts,
for the day's diminishment and rebirth.
The lead seeps into your skin like rainwater
along stucco walls; it blends into the fabric of cells,
the chemistry of bone, like a poisoned paintbrush
coloring skies of smoke, devouring like a worm
that never dies, a fire that's never quenched.
The blast furnace bellows out a merciless melody
as molten metal runs red down your back,
as assembly lines continue rumbling
into your brain, into forever,
while rolls of pipes crash onto brick floors.
The blast furnace spews a lava of insipid dreams,
a deathly swirl of screams; of late night wars
with a woman, a child's book of fear,
a hunger of touch, a hunger of poetry,
a daughter's hunger for laughter.
It is the sweat of running, of making love,
a penitence pouring into ladles of slag.
It is falling through the eyes of a whore,
a red-core bowel of rot,
a red-eyed train of refugees,
a red-scarred hand of unforgiveness,
a red-smeared face of spit.
It is blasting a bullet through your brain,
the last dying echo of one who enters
the volcano's mouth to melt.

They Come to Dance

An aged, hondo-scarred Buick
pushes dust around its wheels
as it slithers up Brooklyn Avenue
toward La Tormenta, bar and dance club.

The Buick pulls up to clutter
along a cracked sidewalk
beneath a street lamp's yellow luminance.
A man and a woman, in their late 30s,
pour out of a crushed side door.

They come to dance.

The man wears an unpressed suit and baggy pants:
K-Mart specials.
She is overweight
in a tight blue dress.
The slits up the side
reveal lace and pantyhose.

They come with passion-filled bodies,
factory-torn like *ropa vieja*.
They come to dance the workweek away
as a soft rain begins to buffet
the club's steamed windows.

Women in sharp silk dresses and harsh,
painted-on make-up crowd the entrance.
Winos stare at the women's flight across
upturned streets
and up wooden stairs.

Men in slacks and cowboy shirts
or cheap polyester threads
walk alone or in pairs.

"¿Oye, compa, qué pues?
Aquí, nomás, de oquis . . ."

Outside La Tormenta's doors
patrons line up to a van dispensing tacos
while a slightly opened curtain
reveals figures gyrating
to a beat bouncing off strobe-lit walls.

They come to dance
and remember
the way flesh feels flush
against a cheek
and how a hand opens slightly,
shaped like a seashell,
in the small
of a back.

They come to dance
and forget
the pounding hum
of an assembly line,
while the boss' grating throat
tells everyone to go back to work
over the moans of a woman
whose finger dangles
in a glove.

They come to dance:
Former peasants. Village kings.
City squatters. High-heeled princesses.

The man and woman lock the car doors
and go through La Tormenta's weather-stained
curtain leading into
curling smoke.

Inside the Buick are four children.
They press their faces
against the water-streaked glass
and cry through large eyes;
mirrors of a distant ocean.

Deathwatch

1.

There is a room in the old house
where the dead sleep,
not dead like without life,
dead like winter,
breathing the moments in
but decay everywhere.

In spring, blossoms burn with color
but each wrinkle, every new invasion
of gray over black on your head
is only a fraction step
in your lifelong demise.

Living with you, Pop,
was like being on a deathwatch.
A slow dying of day, a candle flickering.
What of the man who taught high school
in Ciudad Juárez, wrote biology books
and stormed the rigid government-
controlled system there—
the one who dared new life?

Where have you been, my father?
You were always escaping,
always a faint memory of fire,
a rumor of ardor;
sentenced to leaving
but never gone.

2.

He will never understand
the silence that drove me to the alley,
that kept me tied
to the gravel of deadly play;
why I wanted to die, just to know him.

One day I got drunk with a work crew
and everyone talked about their
imprisoned dads, their junkie dads, their no-dads
and I said I had a dad, but I never heard him
say love, never heard him say son,
and how I wished he wasn't my dad,
but the others yelled back:
How can you judge?
How do you know what he had to do
to be there! Could I do better?
Could I walk in his shoes
and pretend a presence?

3.

He wasn't always there.
Lisa died as an infant
after accidentally eating *chicharrones*
he sold on cobblestoned streets in Mexico.
Seni was abandoned and left with his mom.
A story tells of a young Seni who answered the door
to a stranger, wet from a storm.
She called out, "Mama Piri"—
she always called her grandmother mama—
who rushed into the room and told her,
"Don't worry . . . it's only your father."

Alberto and Mario, born of different women,
one of whom died giving birth,
stayed in Mexico when Dad left.
By then he had married Mama. She was 11 years younger
and he was almost 40 and still running.
Three more children were born across the border
to become U.S. citizens.
Then a long drive to Watts
where another daughter came.
These were the children he came home to,
the ones who did not get away.
How can I judge?

4.

An Indian-shawled woman trekked across
mountains and desert on an old burro,
just outside the village of Coahuayutla
In her arms was a baby in weavings,
whimpering in spurts, as the heat
bore down harder with each step
and snakes dangled close to them
from gnarled trees.

Bandits emerged from out of the cactus groves.
"Give us your money, if your life has any value."
The woman pleaded mercy, saying her husband
was with Pancho Villa
and she had to leave because *federales*
were going to raid her town.
"We don't care about no revolution,"
a bandit said. "Nobody cares for us,
but us . . . give us what you got."
She held close the tied wrappings filled with infant.
Another bandit saw the baby and said:
"This is your child, mother?"
"And of a revolutionary," she replied.
"Then go . . . your mother-love
has won you a life."
My grandmother continued on her way;
Dad had crossed his first *frontera*.

5.

Trust was a tree that never stayed rooted;
never to trust a hope of family
never to nurture the branches of a child
awake with ripening fruit.
He trusted less the love we gave
as he mistrusted doctors.
He seldom went to doctors.

One time doctors put him in a hospital
for tests. He had a cough that wouldn't

go away. They had him splayed and tied with tubes
to monitors and plastic bottles.
After a few days, he called my brother and me
to take his car and wait in front of the hospital
steps. When we got there my dad
ran from the front door and into the car.
He had removed all the attachments,
put on his clothes,
sneaked past the nurse's station,
and waited by a phone booth for our arrival.
He claimed the hospital was holding
him hostage for the insurance money.
Doctors called and demanded
his return. Dad said never.
He had his own remedies.

6.

He was the one who braved the world's
most heavily guarded border,
the one who sold pots, pans and insurance,
and worked construction sites,
the one who endured
the degradations of school administrators,
who refused his credentials,
forced to be a janitor—
what they called a "laboratory technician"—
cleaning up animal cages and classrooms;
the closest he would get to a profession.

Every so often, Dad hauled home
hamsters, tarantulas, king snakes
and fossiled rocks.
My father, the "biologist," named
all the trees and plants
in our yard, gave them stickers
with unpronounceable syllables.
He even named us:
I was *Grillo*—cricket;
my brother became *Rano*, the frog;
Ana was *La Pata*, the duck;

And Gloria, he transformed into *La Cucaracha*:
    Cockroach.
By renaming things, he reclaimed them.

7.

All around the room are mounds of papers:
Junk mail, coupons, envelopes (unopened & empty),
much of this sticking out of drawers,
on floor piles—in a shapeless heap
in the comer. On the wooden end
of a bed is a ball made up of thousands
of rubber bands. Cereal boxes
are thrown about everywhere,
some half full. There are writing
tablets piled on one side, filled
with numbers, numbers without pattern,
that you write over and over:
obsessed.

For years your silence
was greeting and departure,
a vocal disengagement.
I see you now walking around in rags,
your eyes glued to Spanish-language *novelas*,
keen to every nuance of voice and movement,
what you rarely gave to me.
This silence is now comfort.
We almost made it, eh Pop?
From the times when you came home late
and gathered up children in both arms
as wide as a gentle wind
to this old guy, visited by police and social workers,
talking to air, accused of lunacy.
I never knew you.
Losing you was all there was.

Running to America

They are night shadows
violating borders;
fingers curled through chain-link fences,
hiding from infra-red eyes,
dodging 30-30 bullets.
They leave familiar smells,
warmth and sounds
as ancient
as the trampled stones.

Running to America.

There is a woman
in her finest
border-crossing wear:
A purple blouse from
an older sister, a pair of worn
shoes from a church bazaar.
A tattered coat
from a former lover.

There is a child
dressed in black,
fear sparkling from
dark Indian eyes,
clinging to
a beheaded Barbie doll.

And the men,
some hardened, quiet,
others young and loud—
You see something like this
in prisons.

Soon they will cross
on their bellies,
kissing black earth,

then run to America.

Strange voices
whisper behind garbage cans,
beneath freeway passes,
next to broken bottles.
The spatter of words,
textured and multi-colored,
invoke demons.

They must run to America.

Their skin,
color of earth,
is a brand
for all the great ranchers,
for the killing floors
on Soto Street,
and as slaughter
for the garment row.
Still they come:
a hungry people
have no country.

Their tears
are the grease
of the bobbing machines
that rip into cloth,
that make clothes,
that keep you warm.

To the Desert

I came to you one rainless August night.
You taught me how to live without the rain.
You are thirst and thirst is all I know.
You are sand, wind, sun and burning sky,
the hottest blue. You blow a breeze and brand
your breath into my mouth. You reach—then *bend
your force, to break, blow, burn and make me new.*
You wrap your name tight around my ribs
and keep me warm. I was born for you.
Above, below, by you, by you surrounded.
I wake to you at dawn. Never break your
knot. Reach, rise, blow, *Sálvame, mi dios,
Trágame, mi tierra. Salva, traga*, Break me,
I am bread. I will be the water for your thirst.

The Ninth Dream: War (in the City in Which I Live)

All my life—let me say this so you understand—all my life
I have heard stories of the river and how people were willing
to die to cross it. To die just to get to other side. The other
side was the side I lived on. "And people die to get here?"
My mother nodded at my question in that way that told me
she was too busy to discuss the matter and went back
to her ritual of rolling out tortillas for her seven children, some
of whom asked questions she had no answers for. We were
poor as a summer without rain; we had an outhouse and a pipe
bringing in cold water from a well that was unreliable
as the white man's treaties with the Indians, unreliable
as my drunk uncles, unreliable as my father's Studebaker
truck. I was six. It was impossible for me to fathom
why anyone would risk death for the chance to live like us.

Confessions: My Father, Hummingbirds
and Frantz Fanon

Every effort is made to bring the colonised person to admit the
inferiority of his culture . . .
—Frantz Fanon

And there are days when storms hover
over my house, their brooding just this side of rage,
an open hand about to slap a face. You won't believe me

when I tell you it is *not* personal. *It isn't.* It only feels
that way *because the face is yours.* So what if it is the only
face you've got? Listen, a storm will grab the first thing
in its path, a Persian cat, a sixth-grade boy on his way home
from school, an old woman watering her roses, a black
man running down a street (late to a dinner with his wife),
a white guy buying cigarettes at the corner store. A storm
will grab a young woman trying to escape her boyfriend,
a garbage can, a Mexican busboy with no papers, *you.*
We are all collateral damage for someone's beautiful
ideology, all of us inanimate in the face of the onslaught.
My father had the biggest hands I've ever seen. He never
wore a wedding ring. Somehow, it would have looked lost,
misplaced on his thick worker's hands that were, to me,
as large as Africa. There have been a good many storms
in Africa over the centuries. One was called *colonialism*
(Though I confess to loving Tarzan as a boy).

Death in Vietnam

the ears of strangers
                    listen
fighting men tarnish the ground
            death has whispered
                            tales to the young
and now choir boys are ringing
                            bells
            another sacrifice for America
                    a Mexican

            comes home
his beloved country
                gives homage
and mothers sleep
                    in cardboard houses

            let all anguish be futile
tomorrow it will rain
and the hills of Vietnam
resume
            the sacrifice is not over

My Father Is a Simple Man

for my father Alfredo

I walk to town with my father
to buy a newspaper. He walks slower
than I do so I must slow up.
The street is filled with children
we argue about the price
of pomegranates, I convince
him it is the fruit of scholars.
He has taken me on this journey
and it's been lifelong.
He's sure I'll be healthy
so long as I eat more oranges,

and tells me the orange
has seeds and so is perpetual;
and we too will come back
like the orange trees.
I ask him what he thinks
about death and he says
he will gladly face it when
it comes but won't jump
out in front of a car.
I'd gladly give my life
for this man with a sixth-
grade education, whose kindness
and patience are true . . .
The truth of it is, he's the scholar,
and when the bitter-hard reality
comes at me like a punishing
evil stranger, I can always
remember that here was a man
who was a worker and provider,
who learned the simple facts
in life and lived by them,
who held no pretense.
And when he leaves without
benefit of fanfare or applause
I shall have learned what little
there is about greatness.

Barrios of the World

barrios of the world,
where we live and strive,
where rich and poor separate
       their worlds
into different realities;
barrios of the world,
paradoxes
seething with rage/unsanity

a new world cometh,
world of awareness,
plagueless world,
spectral world,
love struck world,
composite of man's humanity,
cauldron of sister/brother-hood.

el chuco, los, alburque, denver,
san anto, el valle, laredo,
the midwest, boricua harlem,
change is coming to you
bird-like, vibrant, vehemently virile.

la voz del Chicano proclaims
hermandad-carnalismo-humanidad,
like bumper stickers cauterizing
gods of all dimensions.

god is chicano, mexican, hispano
   cholo, pocho, mexican-american,
   american of spanish surname (ASS!)
   boricua, puertorro and a host
   multihued
   proclamando divinity, dignity,
   humankind moving forth . . .
   for us, there is our reality,
   it is real and virile/fertile,

simplicity unadorned
scorched by sun and drenched in love,

chicano destiny being created
carnales one and all, we do not fear
the providence others claim,
we just seek our own horizons;
peaceful people that we are,
we'll defend our right to live.
somos la raza, hogar/jacal creators,
pyramid builders, cathedral makers,
living en el diablo, siete infiernos,
coronado, la lorna y kern place,
creators of our destinies
desde bareles a maravilla.

Thanksgiving

On Thanksgiving afternoon
I sat on a green couch
sedated and thinking
of much of my life
which I could not recall
but in cinematographic
capsulized vignettes:
The stench of grass in April
cows looking over us as my cousin ties
his shoe.
An old crone peering out of a church door
hands spread out toward heaven.
A stream of soft water running
from a sink in a hotel
in Madrid.
Rain seeping into nylon stockings
a pair of black pumps clacking
on cobblestone.
A Christmas tree stuck
in the middle of an attic
in Jersey City, U.S.A.

Sitting on the couch
totally incapable of writing
a preamble to my own death:
nobody would read it and besides
it would ramble.

Elizabeth, New Jersey

This, my beautiful city
remains the same.
There is always
a young, blonde matron
with her four-month belly
searching for bargains
needing new sandals;
there's the sweet
would-be whore
ogling at the $1.67 nail polish
sold at C,H, Martin's;
and the five happy, unlucky bums
sprawled out on the benches
in front of the old, landmark graveyard.
There is always
a fourteen-year-old Adenis
jumping the railroad tracks
regaling his babe;
and some ancient woman
atop a third-floor walkup
nursing her cancerous cat.
At la Palmita
the Cuban workmen
never stop dreaming or swearing.

Daybreak

In this moment when the light starts up
in the east and rubs
the horizon until it catches fire,

we enter the fields to hoe,
row after row, among the small flags of onion,
waving off the dragonflies
that ladder the air.

And tears the onions raise
do not begin in your eyes but in ours,
in the salt blown
from one blister into another;

they begin in knowing
you will never weaken to bear
the hour timed to a heart beat,
the wind pressing us closer to the ground.

When the season ends,
and the onions are unplugged from their sleep,
we won't forget what you failed to see,
and nothing will heal
under the rain's broken fingers.

Marked

Never write with pencil,
m'ija.
It is for those
who would
erase.
Make your mark proud
        and open,
Brave,
            beauty folded into
    its imperfection,
Like a piece of turquoise
        marked.

Never write
with pencil,
m'ija.
Write with ink
        or mud,
or berries grown in
gardens never owned,
     or, sometimes,
        if necessary,
        blood.

Compliments

They say I don't look thirty
They also say
I don't look Mexican.
They mean them, I guess,
as compliments.

If that is so,
then it must be
complimentary
to not be

thirty
or
Mexican.

Therefore,
I guess,
they don't
(as much)
like people
who are over
thirty
or too
Mexican.

But now they know
and therefore, I guess
it means
that now
they don't
(as much)
like me.

⌒ᶺᵕᶺ⌒

Sweet Remember

Sweet remember
when you ask our little girls to be
so sweet,
sit neat,
cry easy,
and be oh so pretty on a shelf

When our young women who are decent
are to always be
in company
of strong young men
who can
protect them

When parents breathe
a sigh of relief

to see their daughters married
and now safe
and someone else's
responsibility

When girls and women
are expected
to play at home, which others should protect,
to always breathe in innocence
and be shielded from heavy news, and death,
to sing and paint
and, when appropriate,
to scream and faint

Sweet Remember
that Marta Díaz de C.
had her legs spread
on an electric bed
as someone probed with great delight
to see her scream
till dead.

Sweet Remember
that Cristina R.L.O.
was taken in the night
from her parents' home
and husband's bed
and forced to talk with massive rape,
incontinence, indecency,
and forced to faint while hanging by her knees,
wrists tied to feet, till circulation ceased

Sweet Remember
Elsa B.
whose naked 3-year daughter
was immersed
in ice-cold water,
as the Sergeant pulled her tits and whispered in her ear,
"Whore, come sleep with me
and do it sweetly
or we will not let
the child's head up

until she kicks no more."
And when she did,
they threatened a
Portrait in Two:
Whore and Child Whore—
side by side in bed—
with plenty of volunteers
to tear them both
right through the core
mass party rape in
stereo
and screams
galore
"and then we'll know
where we can find
and kill
your husband."
And sad and sick,
to save her child,
she spoke.

And Sweet Remember
young Anita S.
who was raised to think her womanhood
was in her breasts
and inside panties and to be covered
in a dress
and then,
because the village teacher was
a critic
of the government,
and a family friend,
she was "detained,"
and called a Marxist,
had her breasts
slashed at with knives
and bit by soldiers eager
for their flesh
and had then "Communist"
burnt with electric pen
and shocks
into her upper thigh

and her vagina
run by mice,
and live to know
her womanhood
was in her soul.

And Tina V., María J., Encarnación,
Viola N., Jesusa I. and Asunción
who screamed first and did not think to strike
who'd never fired a gun or learned to fight
who lost their husbands, parents, children and own lives
and oft times dignity or body parts or eyes
and some whose pregnant nipples tied with string
were yanked toward opposing walls
and back
till babes were lost
and blood was running black.

Sweet Remember
this is why
I do not ask
my child to cry
to sit sweet helpless and be cute
to always need a male escort
to think that only he protects,
not she, herself, and not she, him
to think herself so delicate
so weak,
to hold as inborn right a man's protection
or his pity for a tear on pretty cheek

But I will teach her
quite instead
that she is her own brave life
till dead
and that there are no guarantees in life
nor rights
but those that we invent
and that the bravest thing of all
to think, to feel, to care and to recall
is to be human
and to be complete

and face life straight
and stand on solid feet
and feel respect for her own being
temple, soul and head
and
that she owns her strong brave life
till dead

Gloria Vando————————————————————————

New York City Mira Mira Blues

From the freeway you can almost
hear them screaming in their
red brick coops (no hyphen, please)
      HELP ME, HELP ME
through glass grids silhouetted
like chicken wire against the
skyscrapers of Madison, Fifth,
Park and lately Third Avenue,
where the old el used to shield
the homeless, now homes the shielded.
¡Ay, bendito! What did they do
to this city in their urgent need
to sprinkle liberalism like holy water
on the heads of the oppressors?
They should have played fair, *hombre*:
they should have left the *jíbaros*
in the mountains of their Isla Bonita,
perched like birds of paradise
on Cerro Maravilla observing
the rise and fall of the earth's curve
as it slumbers beneath the sea;
left them in El Fanguito, squatting
on the squatters squatting on the land
that once was theirs; left them
in Borinquen, where there was no cool
assessment of who owned what,
no color line splitting families
in two or three, where everyone,
todo el mundo, was tinted
with *la mancha de plátano*—but no,
they needed votes. Sure votes.
Had to buy them, fly them in by
planeloads, skies darkening thickly
with visions of barrios to come.
Since it was so easy getting in,
you'd think it would be easy getting out,
but where to go, and who'll take you in?
Take you in, yes; but give you shelter?

273

The Triborough Bridge, 50 years old
in gold cloth 50 feet high spanning
its towers, waves greetings to us as
we cross the East River, where I swam
as a child, running home as fast as
I could to stash my sopping clothes
in the hamper before Abuelita found
out and exiled me to my island bed.
Now dressed in punk colors, FDR Drive
shouts SAVE EARTH: GIVE A SHIT and
raises a SHAKER-KLASS-AMERICA fist
to the inmates on Welfare Island
whose view ah the view of the
newyorkcityskyline is optimum,
while the Old Rich on tree-lined
Sutton Place only get to see slums.
Welfare Island whose one aesthetic
function is to spew enough smoke
and soot into the air to obscure
Queens and itself, if the wind
is right, in a merciful eclipse.
Welfare Island, where our poet
Julia de Burgos was confined, forgotten,
all her protest silenced with yet
another 2 cc's of thorazine.

On 110th Street, my concrete manger
overlooking Central Park, only Spanish
signs remain to remind us of the second-
to-the-last immigration wave: Cubanos
seeking refuge when class status takes
a backseat to red slogans, red tape.
The Bay of Pigs non-invasion spurs
them on to invade us, Miami first, then
slowly up the coast like a spreading
thrombosis that ruptures in Nueva York,
where all Hispanics blend into one
faceless thug, one nameless spic.

The cab cuts like a switchblade
across the park; I try to hear Ives'
marching bands meeting in noisy combat

on Sheeps Meadow, but later sounds
intrude, reintroduce themselves
like forgotten kin—midnight, a baby
carriage, my mother crossing the park
from her sitter's on the eastside
to her husband's on the west. And she,
loving the leaves' black dance against
the night, recalls her mother's warning
that she not try to blot out the sky
with one hand, but oh! there beneath
the trees, the immensity of space is
palpable—she feels safe. And, lacing
the earth, a fragrance she cannot discern
causes her to yearn for home. She hums

half expecting the *coquís* to sing along.
It is that time of night when muggers
are out—even then before the word
was out—blending into shadows, bushes,
trees, like preview footage of Vietnam,
waiting to assault whatever moves,
whatever breathes. She breathes hard
but moves so fast they cannot keep up—
Westside Story before they learned
that death set to music could make
a killing at the boxoffice. With one
Robbins-like leap up a steep incline,
we escape; I sleep through it. Now
I'm wide awake watching every leaf quake
in the wind as her young limbs in flight
must have then, fifty years ago
on that moonless night in Central Park
where fifty years before that
sheep grazed and innocence prevailed.

We exit on 86th Street, head down
Central Park West, past the Dakota
to our safe harbor in the heart
of Culture and Good Manners with
Lincoln Center only steps away.

Next door a flop house. Old people
with swollen legs sunning themselves
on folding chairs, used shopping
bags with someone's trash,
their treasure, at their feet.
The buzzards of the human race
cleaning up other people's droppings.
We walk around them, as though
proximity could contaminate. Nearby
those less prosperous prop themselves
up against their own destruction.
I see my children stepping carefully
between them, handing out coins
like Henry Ford. I see them losing
faith, losing hope, losing ground.

But I am home, *home*, I tell myself.
Home from the wheat and the corn
of Middle America, where whole-
someness grows so tall you cannot
see the poverty around you, grows
so dense the hunger cannot touch you.
Home to the familiar, the past; my
high school moved comfortably closer,
renamed LaGuardia for the Little Flower
who captured our hearts with
Pow! Wham! and *Shazam!* on newsless
Sunday mornings during the war.
Home to my Westside condo with free
delivery from columns A to Z,
a xenophobic's dream come true.
Home to the city's long shadows
casting tiers up, across and down
skyless streets and buildings,
an Escher paradox turning a simple
journey to the corner into a fantasy
in chiaroscuro. Yes, I'm home,
home, where my grandmother's aura
settles softly and white like
a shroud of down, stilling, if only
for a moment, the island's screams.

Swallows of Salangan

Morton Feldman Dies at 61;
An Experimental Composer
——The New York Times

Sixty-one? I thought you were that back
then when you first lumbered into our
lives "like a bear," my daughter said,
clutching hers and giving up her bed
without an argument. An owl, I thought,
observing two tufts of slick, brown hair
hanging free like weary horns; eyes intense,
intimidating, behind the thickest lenses
I had ever seen, then suddenly small,
glasses raised, scanning the inch-close
page with laser speed. It was summer
that March in Corpus Christi. A scent
of jasmine and moist tweed slipped past
you into the kitchen mingling at random
with the bacon and the coffee. Crumbs
from your lips added an aleatory voice
to the graph paper score you hummed:
you were making history at my breakfast
table and I, Clio, was feeding you honey.
Only your music was minimal. I was

impressed. Not only by your presence
but what you left with me, what stayed,
permeating the bones of memory until today
when I play your records at the library,
huge headphones holding pieces of the past
together in a vise of sound—sound, Morty,
your sound—disquieting, "getting
under the seat" as you had warned, yet
reverential, hushed, as if in mourning
for itself. Once, in Houston—remember?—
washes of that sound, a voix celeste
like a swell of keening swallows filled

the Rothko Chapel you honored, hallowing
the art, the chapel and all therein. Now
a scant two decades later, you are dead
and much is made of disillusion. But
it wasn't you or your music or the media
hype—perhaps the hype—that led
to disillusion, what my father maintained
is the worst thing that could happen.
Something sinister shortened America's
attention span to 30 screaming minutes,
the reading line to 19 picas, hemlines
to the crotch. This is a time of expedience,
of shrink-wrapped identical portions. No
foreplay. No afterthought. Get on with it.
And you, freed from "the intrinsic morality
of the medium," creating your own morality
with a four-and-one-half-hour string quartet
that ended to an almost empty hall—Ah,

where to preserve your innocence, Morty,
in a cage, under glass, the wolf at the door?
Had you forgotten that *4' 33"* of silence
was more than our culture could endure?
Even then, back then, my friend, when
you were Schubert to a flower generation.

Perspectives*

One looks around and sees
Eudocia hard-working and convinced
that for herself, Reginaldo and their children
Alfonso and Rita there is no way back.

One looks around and discovers
Rosa with her faith in the lottery
"these dreams are better than the movies,
they cost one dollar and last a whole week."

One watches Maria Luisa sighing over
the soap operas that uplift her,
one hears her repeat as an excuse:
"in this loneliness they are my happiness."

One watches the working women in the subway
hiding their mistreated hands,
untended nails, hiding behind glasses
the circles under the eyes, dark, permanent.

One watches blue-collar workers
during rush hour gradually deafened by
a noise similar to, as the Daily News has stated,
the sound made by a jet's landing.

One watches the young latinos
"loose joints," "acid" and "loose cigarettes"
boys of few years who lost
their original humanity on these streets

And one watches the girls too,
an adolescence brief, fragile, going:
stripped of illusion at twenty,
brought to childbed by Mondays and diapers.

*Translated by Jane Robinett

One looks at the garbage, the trash
on 103rd Street, at the drunks;
at the people hunting for "specials"
in the second-hand clothing stores.

And one begins to feel differently
this bad air; to walk over the dead
fighting against death itself
to try to make a new life.

Wo/Men*

Wo/men draped in black
multicolor socks and strong arms
hair and moustaches, hairy legs
hormones and hairs . . . patchy with suffering.

Sad women, who never smile
lacking teeth, lacking dreams
women/earth, dirt farm and hoes
women/cabbage, tomatoes and wool
women/man, child and tenderness
iron women, rock women.

*Translated by Daisy Cocco de Filippis

Haiti*

I imagine you a virgin
before forerunning pirates
had removed your mohagony dress
to leave you thus
with your bare, round breasts
and your torn grass-skirt
barely green,
timidly brown.

Haiti,
I imagine you an adolescent
fragrant vertivert, tender with dew
without the numerous scars
displayed in the traffickers' maps
and multicolor banners sold
on the sidewalks of Port Prince,
Jaimel, St. Mark and Artibonite
in a dramatic tin plate bargain.

Haiti,
traveller who eagerly smiles at me
interrupting the quiet of paths,
softening stones, paving dust
with your sweaty, bare feet
Haiti who can give art a thousand shapes
and who paints the stars with your hands
I found out that love and hate
share your name.

*Translated by Daisy Cocco de Filippis

Reports

> *"With so much sunlight to remember how could
> he bet in favor of a lack of feelings?"*
> —Camus

"It's five o'clock and you still haven't given me the report"
. . . he will be arriving now
he will see first the turquoise and then the blue
turning to dark blue
. . . the deep water is always dark . . .
"You promised to get me the reports today"
. . . Will there still be daylight?
Will the dusk be as long as those here?
As resistant to the night?
"Did you hear me?"
. . . he will see his wife there in the crowd
and tenderness will become infinite

. . . nothing like the light at the end of the labyrinth
"I'm leaving at 5:30. You have half an hour"
then the light,
the sun will be like an airport after a long flight
and we will love the little things of a daily life rediscovered
. . . revaluing them even though they choke us sometimes
"The half hour is almost up"
. . . she will have put flowers in the house . . .
everything will be clean and orderly . . .
the table set . . . her rice
. . . after a journey the house always seems
like a sweetheart we haven't seen for a long time.
"The report?"
. . . And he will think how stupid it was to travel into the dark
. . . holding so much sunlight in his present . . .
"I didn't do it."
"Good night."

me caes sura, ése, descuéntate

eres el tipo
de motherfucker
bien chingón
who likes to throw the weight around
y aventar empujones
y tirar chingazos
and break through doors
bien sangrón
saying con el hocico
"that's tough shit!"
bien pesao
el cabrón

y precisamente por esa razón
whereas ordinarily
out of common courtesy or stubbornness
the ground I'd stand and argue principles—
esta vez que no
porque esa clase de pendejadas
mi tiempo fino no merece
y mucho menos mi energía
sólo que ahí se acaba el pinche pedo

y no creas tú que es que yo a ti te tengo miedo
si el complejo ese es el tuyo
¿porque sabes qué, ése?
out of pure self-interest
I like to wear only shoes that fit
me gusta andar comfortable

La loca

han visto
a esa viejita
que todos los días
pasa bien a prisa
por la calle san fernando
hablando sola
a veces rezando
a veces echando
con un tono de voz
pues que convence:

"you good for nothin'
sonavabitches. son un
montón de putos y putas
chapetes relajes."

y los perros guatosos
ladriladre
pero de lejitos
aunque la gente
sí se asoma
por entre cortinas
y a sus portales
otros salen
encantados de la vida
provocando unas cuantas cochinadas:

"viejo puto desgraciao. se
te va a caer la verga, cabrón.
y tú también vieja
perra caliente."

con bolsa antigua
sobre un hombro
y con paño desteñido
sobre canas despeinadas
se pasea por el barrio
arreglando sus asuntos

persignándose al pasar
por en frente de la iglesia
y tirándoles el dedo
a relajes y chapetes

⌒‿⌣‿⌒

was fun running 'round descalza

barefoot is how I always used to be
running barefoot
like on that hot summer
in the San Juan Projects
they spray-painted all the buildings
pastel pink, blue, green, pale yellow, gray
and in cauldrons tar bubbling, steaming
(time to repair the roofs)
its white smoke filling summer air with aromas of nostalgia
for the future
and you, barefoot,
tender feet jumping with precision
careful not to land on nest of burrs or stickers
careful not to tread too long on sidewalks
converted by the scorching sun into comales
"¡se puede freír hasta un huevo en esas banquetas!"
exclamaba la gente
ese verano tan caliente
no sooner than had the building wall/canvasses been painted clean
did barrio kids take to carving new inspirations
and chuco hieroglyphics
and new figure drawings of naked women
and their parts
and messages for all
"la Diana es puta"
"el Lalo es joto"
y que "la Chelo se deja"
decorated by hearts and crosses
and war communications
among rivaling gangs
El Circle
La India

pretty soon kids took to just plain peeling plastic pastel paint
to unveil historical murals
of immediate past well-remembered:
más monas encueradas
and "Lupe loves Tony"
"always and forever"
"Con Safos"
y "Sin Safos"
y que "El Chuy es relaje"
and other innocent desmadres de la juventud
secret fear in every child
que su nombre apareciera allí
y la música de los radios
animando

    "Do you wanna dance under the moonlight?
    Kiss me, Baby, all through the night
    Oh, Baby, do you wanna dance?"

was fun running 'round descalza
playing hopscotch
correr sin pisar la líneas—
te vas con el Diablo

was fun running 'round descalza
shiny brown legs leaping with precision
to avoid nido de cadillos crowned with tiny blossoms pink
to tread but ever so lightly on scorching cement
to cut across street glistening with freshly laid tar
its steam creating a horizon of mirages
rubber thongs sticking, smelting
to land on cool dark clover carpet green
in your child's joyful mind
"Got to get to la tiendita, buy us
some popsicles and Momma's Tuesday Light!"

was fun running 'round descalza

transference

i.

with a dashing smile
a handsome Black busdriver welcomes you on board
you and the Salvadorean lady that you met at the stop
she had hurriedly splashed Oil of Olay on her face
suddenly, self-conscious, uttering
"Ay, disculpe, señorita. Es que . . ."
proceeding to explain that in this country
people are always in a hurry
even when there's no need!
she exclaimed,
tightening the cap on the bottle

you take a seat by the window
as the bus advances to the next stop
where, on hops
a young Puerto Rican
sporting a white starched shirt and tie
overcoat, umbrella and lunchbag in hand
he walks down the aisle
smiling flirtatiously at the ladies
and nodding a courtly good morning
to an old white gent
seated towards the rear of the bus
who must remember this old neighborhood
in those thriving years
quaint post-war red-brick houses
neatly trimmed patches of green
shade trees abounding
a legacy of hard times
and hard work
inspired by the American Dream
now transformed
to meet the future
on equal grounds

and the bus advances
the heads of passengers bopping
their postures swaying to the motion of the bus

as it glides over bumps and dips
their eyes gazing through dark glass windows
STOP
says the sign
in red and white
the bus stops, perpendicular to the freeway
where traffic rolls at the erratic pace of 8 o'clockers
running late
some didn't find the time to pack a lunch
another junk food excursion expected at noon, no doubt
a preoccupation that must be dismissed
the traffic demands it
metallic bodies
glistening in the eastern sunlight
meandering down curving lanes
brake lights flashing
on and off
in sequential delay
"Put your blinker on, dumbass!"
some are surely thinking
while others might be conjuring their tardy excuses
as they race with time
"What time does that read?
Sixty-four degrees.
Darn, I missed it!"
some surely are fretting over their forgetfulness
as the radio weatherman issues the forecast
a few, likely, are prepared
"Sure am glad I wore my space helmet—
looks like acid rain in the horizon."

the bus proceeds alongside the freeway
bound toward the concrete skyline
at the threshold of downtown
billboards captivate the eye with every glance
a montage of seductresses
"Es tan suave"
beckons the sophisticated lady
in black satin
her moist, red lips enticing you
to taste that whiskey *importado*
adjacent, a glamorous model poses

her elegant fingers balancing a cigarette
filtering smoke
her ebony face is frozen in a smile
of lasting satisfaction

the next stop is Viet-Town
its landmark, an oversized rectangular sign
stark, one-dimensional red letters
on a bright flat yellow background
V I E T N A M P L A Z A
around here, not many wait on buses
they walk it
or ride bikes
or some cruise in their Mercedes Benz's
but the derelicts
they love to ride the bus
gives them somewhere to go
"Oh, no," a passenger cringes
in reluctant anticipation
as a bum climbs on board
his stench instantly mingling
with the fragrances of Polo
Estee Lauder
and Oil of Olay
"What a relief!"
the passenger sighs
as the bum mumbles something to the driver
and is let off at the next stop
where on hops another
grumbling to himself
and everybody holds their breath
as he staggers to the rear
holding on to the support railing

and the bus advances
cutting through dark morning shadows
cast by pastel skyscrapers
the hues of sand, sea and skies
"Gimme a transfer"
the decrepit skid utters to the driver
"Ah don' wn' go ov' th' bridge."
and the driver tears the slip

and hands it to him
and one common act
alters the course of a half-man's destiny
the price, a free strip of recycled paper
bearing meaningless schedules, transfer points
and destinations
one wretched soul's documentation
of transference

ii.

click-click clock-clock
high heels conquering concrete
sidewalks with their familiar cracks
and unpredictable dips

from the parking lot you approach the order of the day
from the corner of one eye you discern
silhouettes emerging from the banks of the bayou
you step up your pace,
catching up with a woman in a business suit
"Pretty bad, huh?"
"'Morning" she responds
and the urgency of the 8 o'clock hour
averts further contemplation
a man walks hurriedly ahead of you
his hand clutching tightly
a leather briefcase
at the doors of the courthouse
you catch up with him
"Morning" you nod
his face remains expressionless
as he enters before you

as the elevator ascends
your thoughts descend
to the banks of the bayou
you marvel at the adaptive abilities of these human creatures
but suddenly, with a start
further thought is dismissed
why ponder the grotesque aspects of the greater metropolis?
much more pleasureable

savoring a cup of coffee
gazing out a ninth-floor window
viewing the vastness of the heavens
an immensity of blue
holding one's perceptions of aesthetics
intact:

the earth in timely motion
the sun illuminating man's creations
futuristic structures lending eyeful form
at once, concrete and abstract
testimony to the capacity of the human mind
that can imagine
beyond
a horizon

There Were Times

there were times
you and I
were hungry
in the middle of a city of
full bellies
    and we ate bread with
syrup on top and we joked
and said we ate dessert morning
noon & night, but
we were hungry—
so I took some bottles to the
store and got milk and
stole deviled ham because
it had a picture of the devil
on it and I didn't care—
    my favorite place
        to climb
           and sit was
                Devil's Rock,
          no one else
             would sit there, but
                it was the
                    highest place
                    around—
taking care
of each other,
an old lady and a child
being careful
not to need
more than can be
given.
    we sometimes went to the
place where the nuns lived and
on certain days they would
give us a bag of food, you
and the old Mexican nun talking,
you were always gracious;
and yet their smell of dead
flowers and the rustle of their robes

always made me feel
shame: I would rather
steal.
         and when you held my bleeding nose
for hours, when I'd become
afraid, you'd tell me
                         —Todo se pasa—.
after you died I learned
to ride my bike to the ocean
         I remember the night
              we took the '5 McCallister
                   to the ocean and it was
                        storming and frightening
                   but we bought frozen chocolate bananas
                        on a stick and ate them
                             standing, just you and I
                                  in the warm, wet night—
and sometimes I'd wonder why
things had to pass and I'd
have to run as fast as I could
till my breath wouldn't let me
or climb a building scaffold to the
end of its steel or
climb Rocky Mountain and
sit on Devil's Rock
and dare the devil
to show his face
or ride my bike till the
end of the streets hit
sand and became ocean
and I knew
the answer, mamacita, but
I wouldn't even say it to
myself.

grandmother to mother to
daughter to my daughter,
the only thing that truly
does not pass is
love—
and you
knew it.

Biographies

Jack Agüeros (1934-), an award-winning poet, author of plays and screenplays as well as a community activist, was born and raised in East Harlem to parents from Puerto Rico. Although he initially studied engineering at Brooklyn College on the G.I. Bill after serving in the United States Air Force, he became inspired to write plays and poems, and later graduated with a degree in English literature. It was during this time as a college student that he began to receive his first literary awards, and continued writing and publishing essays, television scripts and plays, all the while working as an activist and advocate for the Puerto Rican community in New York; among many notable roles for the community, Agüeros was appointed at one time as deputy director of the Puerto Rican Community Development Project (PRCDP), the nation's first Puerto Rican anti-poverty organization. His publications include a short story collection, *Correspondence Between Stonehaulers* (1991), and collections of poetry, including *Lord, Is This a Psalm?* (2002), *Sonnets from the Puerto Rican* (1996) and *Dominoes & Other Stories from the Puerto Rican* (1993). Agüeros was most recently the recipient of the Asan World Prize for Poetry (2012).

Miguel Algarín (1941-) is a renowned poet and the founder of the Nuyorican Poets Café on the Lower East Side of Manhattan. A native of Santurce, Puerto Rico, Algarín moved with his working-class parents to New York City in the early 1950s. Algarín became a spokesman for the Nuyorican literary movement in the late 1960s and founded a center in which its poets and playwrights could perform their works in a setting reminiscent of the coffee houses of the beat generation. Algarín played an important leadership role in the definition of Nuyorican literature by compiling, with Miguel Piñero, its first and only anthology, *Nuyorican Poetry: An Anthology of Puerto Rican Words and Feelings* (1975). In 1979, he took part in the launching of Arte Público Press, which became the leading publisher of Nuyorican literature, as well as the leading publisher of Chicano and Cuban American literature. Algarín has written plays, screenplays and short stories, but is principally known as a poet. One of the foremost experimenters with English-Spanish bilingualism, his books include *Mongo Affair, On Call* (1980), *Body Bee Calling from the 21st Century* (1982), *Time's Now / Ya es tiempo* (1985) and *Love Is Hard Work: Memorias de Loisaida / Poems* (1997, Lower East Side Memories/Poemas). Algarín is a graduate in English of the University of Wisconsin and Pennsylvania State University. After teaching English at Brooklyn College and New York University, Algarín went on to teach at Rutgers University until his retirement in 2001.

Alurista (Alberto Baltazar Urista, 1947-) is considered one of the pioneers of Chicano literature. At age thirteen he immigrated to the United States with his family, settling in San Diego, California, and began writing poetry. He went on to obtain an M.A. from San Diego State University and a Ph.D. in literature from the University of California-San Diego. In the late 1960s, he began writing poetry seriously for publication and he assumed the pen name of Alurista, which is virtually the only name he uses to this date. A prolific and talented poet as well as a pioneer of bilingualism in Chicano poetry, Alurista was one of the first poets to support the Chicano Movement through his poetry: he was the writer and signer of important manifestoes of the movement, a founder of the Movimiento Estudiantil de Aztlán (MECHA, Chicano Student Movement of Aztlán) in 1967, and one of the first to establish the concept of Aztlán in literature. His publications include the following books of poetry: *Floricanto en Aztlán* (1971, Flowersong in Aztlán), *Nationchild Plumaroja, 1967-1972* (1972, Nationchild Redfeather), *Timespace Huracán: Poems, 1972-1975* (1976), *A'nque* (1979, Although), *Spik in Glyph?* (1981), *Return: Poems Collected and New* (1982); *Z Eros* (1995); *Et Tu . . . Raza* (1997) and *As Our Barrio Turns . . . Who the Yoke Be On?* (2000).

Novelist and poet, **Julia Alvarez** (1950-) was born in the Dominican Republic to politically connected parents, who had to take the family into exile in New York City when she was ten years old. Alvarez graduated summa cum laude as an English major from Middlebury College in 1971, and in 1975 she earned a Master's degree in Creative Writing from Syracuse University. As a creative writer, she has received grants from the National Endowment for the Arts and the Ingram Merrill Foundation. After publishing poems and stories in literary magazines, she published a book of verse, *Homecoming* (1984) and her first novel, *How the García Girls Lost Their Accents* (1991); in so doing, she joined a wave of Hispanic writers breaking into mainstream presses with their tales of immigration and growing up within the United States. In 1994, she published the novel *In the Time of the Butterflies*, which was later made into a feature film, and, in 1995, another collection of poems, *The Other Side / El Otro Lado*. In 1995, Alvarez published a collection of autobiographical essays, *Something to Declare: Essays*. Among Alvarez's other novels are *In the Name of Salomé* (2001), *Before We Were Free* (2002) and *Saving the World* (2006).

Born on the Jesús María ranch settlement in South Texas, **Gloria Anzaldúa** (1942-2006) has become a leading figure in Latina feminism and lesbian literature. Anzaldúa grew up doing agricultural field work on large farms and ranches; she continued supporting herself in this manner until she graduated from Pan American University with a B.A. in 1969. In 1972, she received an M.A. in English from the University of Texas at Austin, after which she worked as a teacher, often for migrant children. During the late 1970s and early 1980s, Anzaldúa began teaching at colleges in California and studying for a while in the Ph.D. program at the University of California at Santa Cruz, where she concentrated on feminist theory and cultural studies. Anzaldúa's first book, the highly influential *Borderlands / La Frontera: The New Mestiza* (1987), blends literary genres and the English and Spanish languages as well as memoir and feminist analysis. She was also the editor of *Making Face, Making Soul / Haciendo Caras: Creative and Critical Perpsectives by Feminists of Color* (1990), which won the Lambda Literary Best Small Press Award. Anzaldúa also wrote several children's books, including *Prietita Has a Friend* (1991), *Friends from the Other Side / Amigos del otro lado* (1993) and *Prietita y La Llorona* (1996). Among several honors in her lifetime, Anzaldúa was the recipient of a National Endowment for the Arts Fellowship, the 1991 Lesbian Rights Award and the 1992 Sappho Award of Distinction.

Naomi Ayala (1964-), a native of Puerto Rico, is an accomplished poet who writes in both English and Spanish, as well as an educational teaching consultant and arts administrator focused on environmental causes. After moving to New York in her teens, she later graduated from the Bennington College of Writing Seminars with an MFA. The award-winning author of two poetry collections, *Wild Animals on the Moon* (1997) and *This Side of Early* (2008), her poems also appear in various anthologies, including *First Flight: 24 Latino Poets* (2006) and *Puerto Rican Poetry from Aboriginal Times to the New Millennium* (2007). Honors for writing include awards such as the 2001 Larry Neal Writers Award for Poetry from the DC Commission on the Arts and Humanities. Ayala has also participated at various levels in humanities work, most notably co-founding the New Haven Alliance for Arts and Cultures.

Jimmy Santiago Baca (1952-) is one of the most successful Chicano poets to come out of the oral tradition, tempered by prison experiences and the Chicano Movement. Baca was born in Santa Fe, New Mexico, in 1952 to Mexican and Apache-Yaqui parents who abandoned him to be raised by his Indian grandparents; he was later raised in an orphanage. In 1973, Baca was sentenced to five years imprisonment for narcotics possession. In a maximum security prison in Arizona, Baca taught himself to read and write and he passed his G.E.D. exam. In prison, Baca discovered poetry and began penning his first compositions. While still serving time, *Mother Jones Immigrants in Our Own Land* (1979) had been accepted for publication by Louisiana State University Press. The accolades from mainstream critics expanded with his next books: *What's Happening* (1982), *Martin and Meditations on the South Valley* (1987) and *Black Mesa Poems* (1989). In 1993, Baca also published a book of autobiographical essays, *Working in the Dark: Reflections of a Poet in the Barrio* in 1993, wrote a screenplay for a film, *Bound by Honor*, which was released by Disney's Hollywood Pictures, and in 2001 released his award-winning memoir, *A Place to Stand: The Making of a Poet*. Baca continued to produce volumes of well-received poetry, including *Healing Earthquakes: A Love Story in Poems* (2001), *Winter Poems along the Rio Grande* (2004), *C-Train and Thirteen Mexicans: Dream Boy's Story* and *The Importance of a Piece of Paper* (2004). For *Black Mesa Poems*, Baca became the first Hispanic poet to win the Wallace Stevens Poetry Award. He is also winner of the Pushcart Prize, the Before Columbus American Book Award, a National Endowment for the Arts Fellowship and other honors. Baca has served as a poet in residence at Yale University and the University of California-Berkeley and has received an honorary doctorate from the University of New Mexico.

Ruth Behar (1956-) was born in Cuba in 1956. After Castro's rise to power in 1959, she and her family left Cuba, along with the majority of the Jewish people on the island. She is a noted anthropologist, documentary film-maker and the author of several books, essays, collections of poetry and short fiction. Behar holds an M.A. as well as a Ph.D. in Anthropology and is the author of *Translated Woman: Crossing the Border with Esperanza's Story (1993), The Vulnerable Observer: Anthropology That Breaks Your Heart* (1996), *An Island Called Home* (2007), as well as the forthcoming *Traveling Heavy: A Memoir In-between Journeys* (2013). The editor of *Bridges to Cuba / Puentes a Cuba* (1995) and co-editor of *Women Writing Culture* (1995) and *The Portable Island: Cubans At Home in the World* (2008), Behar has been the recipient of several honors, including fellowships from the MacArthur Foundation and the John Simon Guggenheim Memorial Foundation. She is currently Professor of Anthropology at the University of Michigan.

Bárbara Benson Curiel (1956-) is a Mexican-American writer and poet who writes in both English and Spanish, as well as a professor and feminist scholar. Benson Curiel holds an M.A. in Spanish from Stanford University and a Ph.D. in literature from the University of California-Santa Cruz. Her published work includes short stories, poetry collections such as *Speak to Me in Dreams* (1989), as well as scholarly articles on Latino/a literature featured in several anthologies. Currently, Benson Curiel is a professor at California State University at Humboldt.

A poet of broad vision, perhaps because of his grounding in science and engineering, **Richard Blanco** (1960) was born in Madrid almost immediately after his parents took refuge there from the Cuban Revolution. Shortly after his birth, his family resettled in Miami, where he grew up. Along the way, he studied literature, architecture and design, but earned a B.S. in Civil Engineering (1991) and an M.A. in Creative Writing (1997) from Florida International University. He has since taught Creative Writing at universities and published poetry widely in some of the major magazines and anthologies, including *The Best American Poetry* 2000, *The Breadloaf Anthology of New American Poets*, *The Nation*, *Ploughshares*, *American Poetry* and many others. His first book, *City of a Hundred Fires* (1998), which explores his biculturalism as a Cuban American, won the Agnes Starrett Poetry Prize from the University of Pittsburgh Press. *Directions to the Beach of the Dead* (2005) also develops themes of home, place and identity. Blanco's most recent honor was as the United States inaugural poet for Barack Obama's second inauguration. Only the fifth poet in history to read at an inaugural ceremony, he was the first immigrant, the first Latino, the first openly gay person and the youngest person to receive this honor.

José Antonio Burciaga (1940-1996) was a Chicano poet, as well as a writer, humorist and muralist. He began writing as part of his position in the U.S. Air Force, later contributing to local newspapers and journals in California. His published work, written in both English, Spanish and sometimes a combination of the two, includes several short stories such as *Río Grande, Río Bravo* (1978), *El Corrido de Pablo Ramírez* (1980) and *La Sentencia* (1984); poems such as *La verdad es que me canso* (1976) and *The Care Package* (1980); and the essay collections *Weedee Peepo* (1988), *Drink Cultura* (1993) and *Spilling the Beans* (1995). Burciaga was honored in his lifetime with awards such as the National Hispanic Heritage Award for Literature and the American Book Award from the Before Columbus Foundation for his collection of poetry and drawings *Undocumented Love* (1992).

The most recognized and respected female poet in Puerto Rican history, **Julia de Burgos** (1914-1953) was born in Santa Cruz, Puerto Rico, into an economically disadvantaged family that, despite its poverty, encouraged and supported Julia's education. In 1935, she received her degree in education from the University of Puerto Rico and became a teacher in rural Puerto Rico, where her love of nature influenced her writing. Here and later in San Juan, she wrote many of the memorable poems that celebrate the Puerto Rican countryside. Inspired by the movement for independence of Puerto Rico, she published her first book, *Poemas exactos a mí misma* (Exact Poems to Myself), in 1937, and wrote children's plays while living and working in San Juan. Also in San Juan in 1938 she published one of her most successful books, *Poemas en veinte surcos* (Poems in Twenty Rows). In 1939, she was awarded the Institute of Puerto Rican Culture poetry prize for *Canción de la verdad sencilla* (The Song of Simple Truth). In 1939, Julia de Burgos moved to New York City, where she became active in the Puerto Rican nationalist movement and was associated with the Juan Antonio Corretjer's liberationist newspaper *Pueblos Hispanos* (Hispanic Peoples), in which she published many of her most famous poems. She spent somewhat more than a year in Cuba and then returned to New York in 1942, where she experienced isolation, depression and alcoholism for the next eleven years. In 1946 she received the prize for journalism from the Puerto Rican Literature Institute for an editorial she wrote in *Pueblos Hispanos*. In 1953, her body was found on a New York City street without any identification. Today she is celebrated for her elegant lyricism, her commitment to freedom, women and her country.

Born in Dover, New Jersey, to an Italian American mother and a Cuban father, **Rafael Campo** (1964-) attained a prestigious and privileged education, not only earning the degree of medical doctor from Harvard Medical School (1992), but also serving as a Rhodes Scholar at Oxford University (1986). His career as a poet began as an undergraduate at Amherst College, where he created a collection of poems as a Creative Writing honors thesis, while also majoring in Neuroscience. From then on his career has been replete with writing awards, including a George Starbuck Writing Fellowship to Boston University (1990), the Agni Poetry Prize (1991) and

The Kenyon Review Writer of the Year award (1992). Campo has published his poems and belles letters in numerous magazines, including *The Paris Review*, *The Partisan Review* and *Prairie Schooner*. His first collection of poems, *The Other Man Was Me: A Voyage to the New World* (1990), explored Latino ethnicity, gay identity, the responsibility of doctors in the age of AIDS and the meaning of family. Campo's other poetry collections include, *What the Body Told* (1996), a Lambda Literary Award winner; *Diva* (1999), which was a finalist for the National Book Critics Circle Award and the Paterson Poetry Prize; *Landscape with Human Figure* (2002), which won the Gold Medal from *ForeWord*; *The Healing Art: A Doctor's Black Bag of Poetry* (2003) and *The Enemy* (2007). His latest work, *The Enemy*, conceived in the aftermath of 9/11, takes on some of the most tendentious issues in American cultural life, including the "War on Terrorism," AIDS, feminism, gay marriage and immigration. *The Poetry of Healing: A Doctor's Education in Empathy, Identity, and Desire* (1997) was also a Lamba Award winner. In addition, Campos' poetry has appeared in numerous anthologies, including *Best American Poetry 1995*, *Things Shaped in Passing: More "Poets for Life" Writing from the AIDS Pandemic* (1996), *Gay Men at the Millenium* (1997), and periodicals, including the *New York Times Magazine*, *The Nation*, *The Paris Review*, *The New Republic* and the *Washington Post Book World*.

Born in Chicago to working-class Mexican-American parents, **Ana Castillo** (1953-) made her way into print during the 1970s as a Chicana feminist poet, first in such magazines as *Revista Chicano-Riqueña* and later by self-publishing her own chapbooks, *Otro Canto* (1977, Another Song) and *The Invitation* (1979). In 1984, Castillo published her first full-length collection of poems, *Women Are Not Roses* with Arte Público Press. During the late 1980s and to the present, Castillo has developed into a respected fiction writer, publishing novels with the independent small press, Bilingual Review Press, and later with W. W. Norton: *The Mixquihuala Letters* (1986), *So Far from God* (1993), *Sapogonia: An Anti-romance in 3/8 Meter* (1994), *Peel My Love like an Onion* (2000). In 1991 and 1995, respectively, Castillo published two feminist tracts, *Massacre of the Dreamers: Essays on Xicanisma* and *The Sexuality of Latins* (with Cherrie Moraga and Norma Alarcón) which are often cited, along with her work on the Spanish version of *This Bridge Called My Back*, as a standard text on Chicana literary theory. Other works in various genres include *My Father Was a Toltec and Selected Poems* (poetry, 1995), *Ask the Impossible* (poetry, 2001), *Goddess of the Americas / La Diosa de las Américas* (essays, 1996) and *Loverboys* (short stories, 1996).

Sandra Castillo (1962-) is a poet, writer and professor. Born in Havana, Cuba, Castillo and her family fled to Miami in 1970 on one of President Lyndon B. Johnson's last Freedom Flights. Later graduating from Florida State University with an M.A. in Creative Writing, her published work includes the award-winning novel *My Father Sings to My Embarrassment* (2000), as well as poetry featured in journals including *Borderlands: Texas Poetry Review*, *Cimarron Review* and *PALABRA: A*

Magazine of Chicano & Literary Art, and the anthology *Cool Salsa: Bilingual Poems on Growing Up Latino in the United States* (1994). Castillo is currently a professor at Miami Dade College.

Carlota Caulfield is a poet, translator and literary critic. Born in Havana, Cuba, she holds an M.A. in Spanish Literature from San Francisco State University and a Ph.D. in Spanish and Latin American literatures from Tulane University. Her eleven published collections of poetry include works such as *At the Paper Gates with Burning Desire, The Book of Giulio Camillo (a model for a theater of memory), El libro de Giulio Camillo (maqueta para un teatro de la memoria) / Il Libro de Giulio Camillo (modello per un teatro della memoria)* and the award-winning *Movimientos metálicos para juguetes abandonados.* Her creative work has appeared in literary journals in the United States, Europe and Latin America. Caulfield is currently Professor and Head of the Spanish and Spanish-American Studies Program at Mills College.

Lorna Dee Cervantes (1954-) is a Mexican poet and writer. In 1992, Cervantes became the first Hispanic writer to win the prestigious Paterson Poetry Prize for her second book, *From the Cables of Genocide: Poems of Love and Hunger*, a collection that features the great themes of life, death, social conflict and poverty; she was also awarded the Latin American Writers Institute Award that same year. Lorna began writing poetry when she was six years old; poems written when she was fourteen were eventually published in a magazine after Cervantes had established her career as a writer. In 1990, she left her Ph.D. studies in Philosophy and Esthetics at the University of California-Santa Cruz, before finishing her dissertation. She then went on to teach Creative Writing at the University of Colorado in Boulder, where she is a tenured professor today. Cervantes' early career as a poet achieved recognition in 1974 when her work was published in *Revista Chicano-Riqueña*. In 2006, Cervantes published *Drive: The First Quartet,* a large volume of selected works covering a twenty-five year span.

Lucha Corpi (1945-), poet and writer, was born in the small tropical village of Jáltipan, Veracruz, Mexico, in 1945. Despite much hardship and poverty, she eventually earned both a B.A. and an M.A. in Comparative Literature. She is also a founding member of the cultural center, Aztlán Cultural, which later merged with a center for writers, Centro Chicano de Escritores. During the 1970s, Corpi began publishing Spanish poetry in small magazines and in 1976, a group of her poems, along with those of two other poets, were issued in book form in *Fireflight: Three Latin American Poets.* By 1980, Corpi's collected poems were published in her first book, *Palabras de mediodía / Noon Words,* along with their translations by Catherine Rodríguez-Nieto. In 1990, Corpi published a third collection, *Variaciones sobre una tempestad / Variations on a Storm,* again with translations of her poems by Rodríguez-Nieto. In the early 1980s, Corpi made the transition to prose and to writing in English with the publication of various short stories in magazines. In 1984, she published her first novel, *Delia's Song,* based on her involvement in the Chicano Movement and campus politics at the University of California. Later, in the 1990s, Corpi began to create an ongoing series of detective novels, including *Eulogy for a Brown Angel* (1992), *Cactus Blood* (1995), *Black Widow's Wardrobe* (1999) and *Crimson Moon* (2004). Described as a feminist detective novel, *Eulogy* was awarded the PEN Oakland Josephine Miles award and the Multicultural Publishers Exchange Best Book of Fiction award. She continues writing in both English and Spanish, and since 1977 she has been a tenured teacher in the Oakland Public Schools Neighborhood Centers Programs, where she specializes in adult education.

Carlos Cumpián (1953-) is one of the pioneers among Chicago Mexican and Mexican-American writers in identifying themselves as Chicano and presenting and publishing their work in the city during the 1970s. From San Antonio, Cumpián went to Chicago as a boy and attended school in the city. His interest in poetry was awakened by the presentations of Chicago Rican poet David Hernández and cultivated by contacts with other young writers, such as Carlos Morton, Ana Castillo, Sandra Cisneros and then his "spiritual father," Carlos Cortez. Starting as the poetry editor for *Abrazo* (Embrace), the small journal of the Movimiento Artístico Chicano (MARCH, Chicano Artistic Movement), Cumpián soon became the leading figure in the organization, shifting its emphasis from the arts to print media and poetry, developing chapbooks and small volumes of verse, and coordinating a group project of poetic performance. Cumpián also became a staff member of the campus journal, *Ecos,* while pursuing his B.A. at the University of Illinois at Chicago. The uncredited editor of MARCH's collection, *Emergency Tacos,* featuring his own work along with those of Sandra Cisneros and other writers, Cumpián went on to produce three volumes of his own: *Coyote Sun* (1990), *Latino Rainbow* (1994) and *Armadillo Charm* (1997).

Abelardo "Lalo" Delgado (1931-2005) is one of the most renowned and prolific Chicano poets, a pioneer of bilingualism in Hispanic poetry and a consummate oral performer of his works. At age 12 he and his mother immigrated to El Paso, Texas, from northern Mexico, where he lived in a poor Mexican barrio until 1969. During the height of the Chicano Movement in the late 1960s and throughout most of the 1970s, Delgado became one of the most popular speakers and poetry readers in the Southwest. Besides writing numerous poems, essays and stories that have been published in literary magazines and anthologies nationwide, Delgado is the author of some 14 books and chapbooks; many of these were published through his own small printing operation known as Barrio Press. Delgado's first book, *Chicano: 25 Pieces of a Chicano Mind* (1969), is his best known, containing many of the poems that were performed personally in the heat of the protest movement and that subsequently received widespread distribution through small community newspapers and hand-to-hand circulation throughout the Southwest. Other noteworthy titles include *It's Cold: 52 Cold-Thought Poems of Abelardo* (1974), *Here Lies Lalo: 25 Deaths of Abelardo* (1979) and his book of essays, *Let-*

ters to Louise (1982), which ponder the feminist movement and the social roles of women and men, and was awarded the Premio Quinto Sol, the national award for Chicano literature. In 2001, Delgado published a compilation of his favorite works in *Living Life on His Own Terms: Poetic Wisdom of Abelardo*. In all, Delgado was a remarkably agile bilingual poet, an outstanding satirist and humorist, an undaunted and militant protester and pacifist and a warmhearted and loving narrator and chronicler of the life and tradition of his people.

Poet **Martín Espada** (1957-) was born into a Puerto Rican family in Brooklyn, New York. After having studied law, passed the bar and exercised the legal profession for various years, Espada gave up the law for poetry. A prolific writer, Espada has published well-received collections of his highly crafted verse, somewhat in the Nuyorican tradition: *Trumpets from the Islands of Their Eviction* (1987); *Rebellion is the Circle of a Lover's Hands* (1990); *City of Coughing and Dead Radiators* (1993); *Imagine the Angels of Bread* (1996), winner of an American Book Award; *A Mayan Astronomer in Hell's Kitchen: Poems* (2000); and *Alabanza: New and Selected Poems* (2003), recipient of the Paterson Award for Sustained Literary Achievement and was named an American Library Association Notable Book. In 2004, Espada published a bilingual audiobook, *Now the Dead Will Dance the Mambo: The Poems of Martín Espada*, which captures his dramatic reading style. In 2007, Espada published *The Republic of Poetry*, in which he develops poems to celebrate politically engaged poets in Latin America, those engaged in liberation struggles throughout the world, such as Dennis Brutus of South Africa and his own works engaged with the politics of the United States. Among Espada's mentors and models are Federico García Lorca and Clemente Soto Vélez, whose poetry he has helped rescue. Espada published a prose collection, *Zapata's Disciple: Essays*, in 1998. In addition to the Paterson Award, Espada has received the PEN/Voelker Award for Poetry and two fellowships from the National Endowment for the Arts. He is an associate professor of English at the University of Massachusetts-Amherst.

Blas Falconer was born and raised in Virginia of a Puerto Rican mother from Salinas, Puerto Rico, is a poet and author of *The Foundling Wheel* (2012), *A Question of Gravity and Light* (2007) and *The Perfect Hour* (2006). In 2011 he was awarded the National Endowment for the Arts Fellowship; other awards include the Maureen Egen Writers Exchange Award from Poets & Writers, the *New Delta Review* Eyster Prize for Poetry and the Barthelme Fellowship. Falconer holds an MFA from the University of Maryland and a Ph.D. in Creative Writing and Literature from the University of Houston.

Born and raised in El Paso, Texas, **Alicia Gaspar de Alba** (1958-) is the quintessential bilingual/bicultural writer, penning poetry, essays and narrative with equal facility in English and Spanish. Gaspar de Alba holds an M.A. in English from the University of Texas at El Paso and a Ph.D. in American Studies from the University of New Mexico. Gaspar de Alba is professor and founding faculty member of the

César Chávez Center for Chicana/Chicano Studies at UCLA. In 2001, she was jointly appointed to the English Department. Gaspar de Alba is the author of a short story collection, *The Mystery of Survival* (1993), which won the Premio Aztlán, and the highly acclaimed historical novel *Sor Juana's Second Dream* (1999), which has been translated to Spanish and German. However, Gaspar de Alba's major fiction project bore fruition in 2006: *Desert Blood: The Juárez Murders*. *Desert Blood* was awarded the Lamba Literary Award and chosen to the Latino Literary Hall of Fame. In 1989, her poetry was featured in an anthology of the works of three poets: *Three Times a Woman: Chicana Poetry* and in 2003, she published her selected poems and essays in *La Llorona on the Longfellow Bridge: Poetry y Otras Movidas, 1985-2001*. Her incisive and controversial book-length essay, *Chicano Art Inside / Outside the Master's House: Cultural Politics and the CARA Exhibition* was published by the University of Texas Press in 1998. In 2002, she and Tomás Ybarra-Frausto co-edited a collection of essays on Chicano esthetics: *Velvet Barrios: Popular Culture & Chicana/o Sexualities*. In 1989, Gaspar de Alba received a Massachusetts Artists Foundation Fellowship Award in poetry; and in the Fall of 1999, she held the prestigious Roderick Endowed Chair in English at the University of Texas at El Paso, where she was a Distinguished Visiting Professor for one semester. In all of her work, Gaspar de Alba is one of the most eloquent exponent of a lesbian esthetic and a promoter of the empowerment of women.

Lourdes Gil is a poet, essayist and professor. She was born in Havana, Cuba, and left the island in 1961 as part of Operation Peter Pan, which rescued children from the Castro revolutionary government. Her poetry collections include *El cerco de las transfiguraciones*, *Empieza la ciudad*, *Blanca aldaba preludia*, *Vencido el fuego de la especie* and *Neumas*; her poetry has also appeared in anthologies such as *Burnt Sugar: A Cuban Anthology* and the poetry book *Indomitas al sol: cinco poetas cubanas de Nueva York*. She has also been the recipient of several fellowships, including The Ford Foundation, The Poetry Society of America and the Oscar Cintas Foundation, among others. Gil holds an M.A. from New York University and is currently a professor at Baruch College.

Rodolfo "Corky" Gonzales (1929-2005) was born in a Denver barrio to parents who were seasonal farmworkers. Because of the instability of migrant work, Gonzales received both formal and informal education. Gonzales used boxing to get out of the barrio, becoming the third-ranked featherweight in the world. During the Chicano Movement, Gonzales was also a prolific poet as well as a playwright whose plays were produced at the Crusade for Justice and elsewhere. Such plays as *The Revolutionist* and *A Cross for Maclovio* (1966-67) were an early call to militancy and nationalism for Chicanos. Gonzales authored the famous and influential epic poem, *I Am Joaquín / Yo Soy Joaquín*, which weaves myth, memory and hope as a basis for a Chicano national identity. The poem was reprinted in Mexican-American neighborhood newspapers across the Southwest, recited repeatedly at activist meetings and made into a film produced by El Teatro Campesino and recited by Luis Valdez, which made it one of the most well-known pieces of Chicano literature during and after the Chicano Movement. Gonzales also organized annual Chicano Youth Liberation conferences that sought to cultivate a national sense of cultural solidarity and to work toward self-determination. The first such conference resulted in *El Plan Espiritual de Aztlán* (The Spiritual Plan of Aztlán), a document that outlined the concept of ethnic nationalism for liberation. Gonzales' political and inspirational speeches can also be considered in the body of Chicano literature.

Ray Gonzalez was born and raised in the border town of El Paso, Texas, and this desert landscape permeates his writings. Gonzalez is primarily known as an award-winning poet, having authored numerous collections of poetry over the last two decades, beginning with *From the Restless Roots* (1985). Since then, Gonzalez has published at least nine additional collections of his poetry. His collection entitled *Twilights and Chants* (1987) won the Four Corners book award in poetry and, in 1996, *The Heat of Arrivals* earned him a PEN/Oakland Josephine Miles Book Award. His acclaimed collection *Turtle Pictures* (2000), a multi-genre poetic text, earned a Minnesota Book Award in Poetry along with widespread critical success. In addition to his many works of poetry, Gonzalez has written two collections of essays and two works of fiction. *Memory Fever* (1993) alternates between personal essay and short story to paint a moving portrait of growing up on the U.S. and Mexico border. His later collection, *The Underground Heart* (2002), written nearly a decade later, deals with the author's return to his early home. Where *Memory Fever* focused on the American Southwest as the backdrop for autobiography, *The Underground Heart* approaches this terrain after a long period of absence. In 2001, Gonzalez published his first work of fiction, *The Ghost of John Wayne*. Along with his own creative projects, Gonzalez has edited over a dozen anthologies, including *After Aztlán* (1992) and *Muy Macho* (1996). Gonzalez served as Assistant Professor of English and Latin American Studies and the University of Illinois at Chicago from 1996 to 1998. He most recently wrote *Consideration of the Guitar: New and Selected Poems* (2005). He currently serves as a Professor of English at the University of Minnesota, where he teaches Creative Writing and U.S. Latino Literature.

Franklin Gutiérrez is writer, poet and professor. A native of Santiago, Dominican Republic, Gutiérrez most recently authored the novel *El canal de la delicia* (2009) and is the co-author of works such as the *Diccionario de la literatura dominicana, bibliográfico y terminológico* and the *Antología histórica de la poesía dominicana del siglo XX (1912-1955)*. His awards include the National Essay Award from the Secretariat of State for Education and Culture for his book *Enriquillo: radiografía de un héroe galvaniano* and in 2008, Gutiérrez received the honor of Personalidad Cultural Dominicana in recognition of his contributions to Dominican culture and literature. He holds an M.A. and a Ph.D. from The City University of New York.

Victor Hernández Cruz (1949-) was born in Aguas Buenas, Puerto Rico. He moved with his family to New York's Spanish Harlem at the age of five. The Nuyorican poet who was discovered as a precocious street poet while still in high school in New York has become the most recognized and acclaimed Hispanic poet by the mainstream. Despite his early acceptance into creative writing circles, culminating with *Life* magazine's canonizing him in 1981 as one of the twenty-five best American poets, Hernández Cruz has resisted estheticism and academic writing to remain very much an oral poet, a jazz poet, a poet of the people and popular traditions, a bilingual poet, a poet of intuition and tremendous insight. In high school he began writing poetry, and in the years following graduation, his poetry began to appear in *Evergreen Review*, *New York Review of Books* and many other magazines. Beginning in 1970, he worked with poetry-in-the-schools programs in New York, such as the Teachers and Writers Collaborative. In 1973, Cruz left New York and took up residence in San Francisco, where he worked for the U.S. Postal Service and served as a visiting poet at area colleges. Hernández Cruz received fellowships from the National Endowment for the Arts and the Guggenheim Foundation in 1980 and 1991, respectively. Hernández Cruz's poetry books include *Papo Got His Gun* (1966), *Snaps* (1969), *Mainland* (1973), *Tropicalization* (1976), *By Lingual Wholes* (1982), *Rhythm, Content and Flavor* (1989) *Red* Beans (1994), *Panoramas* (1997) and *Maraca: New and Selected Poems, 1965-2000* (2001). Hernández Cruz's latest effort is *The Mountain in the Sea* (2006), extending his biculturalism and bilingualism to include words and phrases in Arabic and North African culture in an exploration of the deepest roots of Puerto Rican and Nuyorican identity. His most recent work is *In the Shadow of Al-Andalus* (2011).

Born in Havana, Cuba, **Carolina Hospital** (1957-) accompanied her family into exile in 1961, and was raised and educated in Florida. Hospital graduated from the University of Florida in 1979 with a B.A. in English and in 1983 with an M.A. in Hispanic American Literature. A poet from an early age, Hospital captures in her bilingual verse the transition of her community from exile to immigration to American identity. In 1989, Hospital compiled the first anthology of Cuban American literature, *Cuban American Writers: Los Atrevidos*, thus announcing the birth and acceptance of Cuban American literature as being other than a literature of exile and immigration. In this anthology, she declared that Cuban American writers were risk-takers, daring to belong to a future made up of a new reality. After publishing individual poems in numerous periodicals and anthologies, Hospital finally selected her best work from 1983 to 2003 and published *The Child of Exile: A Poetry Memoir.* Her awards include a 1995 Hispanic Women in Literature Award from the Coalition of Hispanic American Literature. Since 1979 Hospital has taught English at Miami-Dade Community College, holding the Endowed Teaching Chair from 1996 to 1999 and 2003 to 2005.

Angela de Hoyos (1940-2009) was born into a middle-class family in Coahuila, Mexico, the daughter of a proprietor of a dry-cleaning shop and a housewife who had an artistic bent. After a tragic burning as a young child, de Hoyos was forced to convalesce in bed for many months, during which she entertained herself by composing rhymes. While she was still a child, her family moved to San Antonio and her interest in poetry continued. In the late 1960s, de Hoyos began publishing poetry and entering her work in international competitions, for which she won such awards as the Bronze Medal of Honor of the Centro Studi a Scambi Internazionale (CSSI), Rome, Italy, 1966; the Silver Medal of Honor (literature), CSSI, 1967; Diploma di Benemerenza (literature), CSSI, 1968; the Diploma di Benemerenza , CSSI, 1969 and 1970. During the 1980s, de Hoyos also founded a cultural periodical, *Huehuetitlan,* which is still in existence. In addition to this intense literary life, de Hoyos developed a successful career as a painter. Her works, also inspired by Mexican-American culture, are widely exhibited and collected in Texas. De Hoyos's poetry is socially engaged while at the same time humanistic in the best sense of the word. Her most important book, *Woman, Woman,* deals with the roles that society has dictated for women and their struggle to overcome the limits of those roles. In *Woman, Woman,* de Hoyos has also perfected her bilingual style, innovatively mixing the linguistic codes of English and Spanish to reach beyond the merely conversational to the more philosophical—the choice of language and lexicon is not just a socio-linguistic one, it is also a deeply cultural one. Angela de Hoyos' other books and chapbooks include *Selecciones* (1976, Selections), *Poems / Poemas* (1975), *Chicano Poems from the Barrio* (1975), *Arise Chicano: and Other Poems* (1975) and *Linking Roots* (1993).

Gabriela Jáuregui (1979-) is an author of critical as well as creative work. A native of Mexico City, Jáuregui holds an M.F.A. in Creative Writing from the University of California–Riverside and a Ph.D. in Comparative Literature from the University of California–Irvine. A founding member of the sur+ publishing collective in Mexico, her work has been published in journals and anthologies in the United States, Mexico and Europe.

Wasabi Kanastoga (aka Luis E. López, 1962-) was born in Santiago de Cuba. Living in California since 1970, he is one of the few tri-cultural Latino-American writers. He is a poet and fiction writer whose poems and stories deal with the absurdities of the day-to-day life of Mexicans and Cubans living and dying in Los Angeles. His work has been featured in many literary reviews and anthologies, including *Iguana Dreams: New Latino Literature, Real Things: An Anthology of Popular Culture in American Poetry* and *Paper Dance:* 55 Latino Poets. He also authored a novel, *City for Sale.* He has a B.A. in Psychology from California State University-Long Beach and is a family counselor for El Centro in East Los Angeles.

Jesús Abraham "Tato" Laviera (1951-) became the first Hispanic author to win the American Book Award of the Before Columbus Foundation, which recognizes and promotes multicultural literature. Laviera is the best-selling Hispanic poet of the United States and he bears the distinction of still having all of his books in print. Born in Santurce, Puerto Rico, he migrated to New York City at the age of ten with his family, which settled in a poor area of the Lower East Side. Since 1980, Laviera's career has included not only writing but touring nationally as a performer of his poetry, directing plays he has written and producing cultural events. In 1980 he was received by President Jimmy Carter at the White House Gathering of American Poets. In 1981 his second book, *Enclave*, was the recipient of the American Book Award. Tato Laviera has said, "I am the grandson of slaves transplanted from Africa to the Caribbean, a man of the New World come to dominate and revitalize two old world languages." And, indeed, Laviera's bilingualism and linguistic inventiveness have risen to the level of virtuosity. Laviera is the inheritor of the Spanish oral tradition, with all of its classical formulas, and the African oral tradition, with its wedding to music and spirituality; in his works he brings both the Spanish and English languages together as well as the islands of Puerto Rico and Manhattan—a constant duality that is always just in the background. His first book, *La Carreta Made a U-Turn* (1979) uses René Marqués's *Oxcart* as a point of departure and redirects it back to the heart of New York, instead of to Puerto Rico, as Marqués had desired; Laviera is stating that Puerto Rico can be found here too. His second book, *Enclave* (1981) is a celebration of diverse heroic personalities, both real and imagined: Luis Palés Matos and *salsa* composers, the neighborhood gossip and John Lennon, Miriam Makeba and Tito Madera Smith, the latter being a fictional, hip offspring of a Puerto Rican and a Southern American black. *AmeRícan* (1986) and *Mainstream Ethics* (1988) are surveys of the lives of the poor and marginalized in the United States and a challenge for the country to live up to its promises of equality and democracy. Laviera has continued to write poetry and a number of plays, but in 2004 he became blind from diabetes. After a series of operations and rehabilitation, he learned to write and type in Braille. Despite having to submit to dialysis, he continues his life as a troubadour or poet on the road. In 2005, he became a spokesperson for Latinos with diabetes as part of the American Association for Diabetes. The Jesus A. Laviera One-Day with Diabetes Project promotes diabetic Sugar Slams, The Sugar Slammers and his musical play "DIABET-IT-IS." Laviera's latest play is "The Spark," which was commissioned for a cultural center in Chicago.

Caridad de La Luz (La Bru-j-a) was born in the Bronx of Puerto Rican parents and is a Nuyorican poet, actress, recording artist and activist. Her most well-known poems, "W.T.C." and "Lola" were performed on HBO's Def Poetry Jam, and "Nuyorico," which was featured in a Levi's print ad in magazines worldwide. La Bruja is also the author of a highly successful musical, *Boogie Rican Blvd.*

Activist, journalist and creative writer, **Demetria Martínez** (1960-) was born in Albuquerque, New Mexico. She received a bachelor's degree in Public Policy from Princeton University in 1982 and began publishing her poems in 1987. The very next year, she was indicted for smuggling refugee women into the United States, and the government attempted to use one of her poems against her as evidence: "Nativity for Two Salvadoran Women." Martínez was acquitted, based on first amendment rights. In 1990, she became a columnist for the *National Catholic Reporter* in Kansas City, but soon lost interest and returned to poetry and creative writing. Her plan soon came to fruition as her first novel, *Mother Tongue*, won the Western States Fiction Award; it is the tale of a young woman who comes to know herself through her love of a Salvadoran refugee smuggled into the United States during the Sanctuary Movement. Her two books of poetry, *Breathing between the Lines* (1997) and *The Devil's Workshop* (2002), address Good and Evil in the human condition. Her *Confessions of a Berlitz-Tape Chicana* (2005), winner of the 2006 International Latino Book Award, is a collection of passionate essays, newspaper columns, speeches and poems that reveal Martínez's ethos for activism: from prayer to social and political intervention. Martínez addresses a broad array of contemporary themes, from undocumented workers to the war in Iraq.

Puerto Rican poet, translator and academic, **Julio Marzán** (1946-) came to New York when he was four months old; despite receiving his education in English-dominant schools, Marzán maintained his Spanish and today is completely bilingual in his poetry and one of the few translators who can translate equally well from one language to the other. After graduating from Cardinal Hayes High School, Marzán went on to receive an B.A. from Fordham University (1967), an M.F.A. in Creative Writing from Columbia University (1971) and a Ph.D. from New York University (1986). He has taught English at Nassau Community College for many years, except for the 2006 school year, when he was a visiting professor at Harvard University. While Marzán has published poems and translations in magazines and anthologies far and wide, he has also published two books of poems, *Translations without Originals* (1986) and *Puerta de tierra* (1998, Gateway), which may not fit the mold of Nuyorican writing in its classical/canonical referents and command of craft as perfected in the academy. In 2005, Marzán published his first novel, *The Bonjour Gene*, dealing with a generational curse of womanizing among the members of the Bonjour family in both the island of Puerto Rico and New York. Marzán's first major translation project was *Inventing a Word: An Anthology of Twentieth-Century Puerto Rican Poetry* (1980). However, his greatest translation feat was that of taking the onomatopoetic works of poet Luis Palés Matos and rendering them in a sonorous English rendition in *Selected Poems / Poesía Selecta: The Poetry of Luis Palés Matos* (2001). As a scholar, he has published three very innovative works: *The Spanish American Roots of William Carlos Williams* (1994), *The Numinous Site: The Poetry of Luis Palés Matos* (1995) and *Luna, Luna: Creative Writing Ideas from Spanish and Latino Literature* (1997). Marzán, a life-long resident of Queens, New York City, was recently named Poet Laureate of Queens County, to serve from 2007 to 2010.

Pablo Medina (1948-) is a memoirist, poet and novelist whose works echo the loneliness and melancholia of exile. He was one of the first Cuban American writers to switch from writing in Spanish to English. Medina was born in Havana in 1948 into a middle-class family of Spanish descent. Growing up in Havana during the 1950s, events of the Cuban Revolution unfolded before him: sabotages, dictator Fulgencio

Batista's (1901-1973) henchmen rounding up suspects and dead bodies at a park. All of these images he depicts in his memoirs, *Exiled Memories: A Cuban Childhood* (1990). After Fidel Castro's triumph in 1959, Medina and his parents went into exile, settling in New York City. He attended public school for one year and then went to Fordham Preparatory School, a Jesuit institution located in the Bronx. After graduation, he matriculated at Georgetown University, where he earned a B.A. and an M.A. In 1975, Medina wrote, according to Virgil Suárez in *Little Havana Blues* (1996), the first collection of poems written directly into English by a Cuban-born writer; it was titled *Pork Rind and Cuban Songs*. This was followed by two poetry collections, *Archinginto the Afterlife* (1991) and *Floating Island* (1999). In 1994, he published his first novel, *The Marks of Birth*. Although he does not identify the country as Cuba, it is a novel about the revolution and Castro's dictatorship. In 2000, he published his second novel, *The Return of Felix Nogara*. Other titles include: *Todos me van a tener que oír / Everyone Will Have to Listen* (1990), translations, with poet Carolina Hospital, from the Spanish of Cuban dissident Tania Díaz Castro; *Puntos de Apoyos* (2002, Supporting Points), poems written in Spanish; a new and updated edition of *Exiled Memories* (2002); *The Cigar Roller: A Novel* (2005) and *Points of Balance,* a bilingual poetry collection (2005). Medina is a member of the Creative Writing faculty of the New School University in New York City.

Rubén Medina was born in Mexico and is one of the founders of the Movimiento Infrarrealista of Mexico City (1975-1978). He is a poet, translator, professor and scholar. His publications include *Autor, autoridad y autorización: Escritura y poética de Octavio Paz* and *Báilame este viento, Mariana* (1980), as well as poems such as "Amor de Lejos . . . Fools' Love" (1986) and "Nomadic Nation / Nación nómada." His poems have been included in numerous Mexican, Latin American and U.S. Latino anthologies. Medina is currently a professor at the University of California-San Diego.

Nancy Mercado (1959-) is a writer, educator and activist. She holds an M.A. from New York University and a Ph.D. in Creative Writing from Binghamton University-SUNY. Mercado, a writer of the Nuyorican Movement, is the author of many essays, anthologized poems, and the book *It Concerns the Madness* (2000), as well as several one-act plays including *Palm Trees in the Snow* (1989), *Chillin'* (1990) and *Forever Earth* (1991).

Pat Mora (1942-) has developed the broadest audiences for her poetry of all of the Hispanic poets in the United States. Her clean, crisp narrative style and the healing messages in her verse have allowed her poetry to reach out to both adults and young people. Mora was born in El Paso, Texas, where she received all of her higher education, including college. After graduating from the University of Texas at El Paso in 1963, she worked as an English teacher in public schools and college. A writer since childhood, Mora published her first, award-winning book of poems, *Chants* in 1984. It was followed by other poetry collections: *Borders* (1986), *Communion* (1991) and *Agua Santa / Holy Water* (1995) and *My Own True Name*

(2000). Mora is also well known for her children's picture books, including: *A Birthday Basket for Tía* (1992), *Listen to the Desert* (1993), *Pablo's Tree* (1994), *The Gift of the Poinsettia* (1995), *The Big Sky* (1998), *The Rainbow Tulip* (1999), *The Night of the Full Moon* (2000), The *Bakery Lady* (2001), *A Library for Juana: The World of Sor Juana Inés* (2002) and *Doña Flor* (2005). A number of her children's works, such as *The Desert Is My Mother* (1994), *Delicious Hullabaloo* (1999), *The Big Sky* (2002) and *Adobe Odes* (2004), are made up of poems as opposed to the narrative technique used in most of her other children's books. In 1993, she published autobiographical essays in *Nepantla: Essays from the Land in the Middle*. Mora's awards include fellowships from the Kellogg Foundation (1986) and the National Endowment for the Arts (1994), Southwest Book Awards (1985 and 1987) and the Skipping Stones Award (1995). In 2002, *A Library for Juana* was a "Commended" title of the Americas Award for Children and Young Adult Literature.

Born in Cuba and raised in the United States, **Elías Miguel Muñoz** (1954-) is one of the most accomplished bilingual novelists, penning original works in either English or Spanish, based on accommodation of Cuban immigrants to life in the United States. Within that overarching theme of culture conflict and synthesis is the conflict of homosexual identity with societal norms in Hispanic and Anglo-American cultures. After receiving his Ph.D. and becoming a professor of Spanish at Wichita State University, Muñoz gave up on the restricted world of university teaching in 1988 to become a full-time writer. He has been a prolific writer of poetry, stories and novels. His books include *Los viajes de Orlando Cachumbambé* (*The Voyages of Orlando Cachumbambé*, 1984), *Crazy Love* (1988), *En estas tierras / In This Land* (1989), *The Greatest Performance* (1991) and *Brand New Memory* (1998). In all, the joys and fears of sexual awakening are set to the backdrop of popular music and film during the time period evoked. In the 1990s, he began publishing textbook readers in various editions for learners of Spanish, such as *Ladrón de la mente* (Mind Thief), *Viajes fantásticos* (Fantastic Voyages) and *Isla de luz* (Island of Light), employing his usual poetically rich vocabulary and imagination. In his latest novel, Muñoz has returned to writing in Spanish. *Vida mía* (2006, Life of Mine) is a highly autobiographical novel of first love and a chronicle of life in Cuba during the 1960s, evoking the music and popular culture of the times.

Havana-born **Alicia Achy Obejas** (1956-) is a widely published poet, fiction writer and journalist. She and her family left Cuba clandestinely on a boat when she was only six years of age. After spending a brief time in Miami, she and her family were relocated to Michigan City, Indiana, where Obejas was raised. In 1979, she moved to Chicago, where she became a journalist for *The Chicago Sun-Times*. Before publishing her novels, Obejas published her poetry and short stories widely in small magazines and in anthologies. As a poet, she was the recipient of a National Endowment for the Arts Fellowship in 1986. For more than a decade, Obejas was the author of a weekly column, "After Hours," for the *Chicago Tribune* and contributed regularly to other Chicago periodicals, as well as such national, mainstream ones as *Vogue* and *The Voice*. In 1993, Obejas obtained a Masters of Fine Arts from Warren Wilson College with a collection of short stories for her master's thesis. In 1994, Obejas published her first book, *We Came All the Way from Cuba So You Could Dress like This: Stories,* which despite the title is made up of personal memoirs, essays and fiction; the book is held together by the constant perspective of the outsider, political exile or economic refugee. Her novels *Memory Mambo* (1996) and *Days of Awe* (2001) both were honored with the Lammy for Best Lesbian Fiction. In addition to her awards for fiction, Obejas has also received a Pulitzer Prize for team investigation for the *Tribune*, the Studs Terkel Journalism Prize and the Peter Lisagor Award for political reporting from Sigma Delta Chi/Society for Professional Journalists. She has also received a National Endowment for the Arts fellowship for poetry and earned residencies at Yaddo, Ragdale and the Virginia Center for the Arts. Obejas' most recent offering is her editing a collection of noir detective/mystery stories, entitled *Havana Noir*, in 2007.

Puerto Rican novelist, short story writer and poet **Judith Ortiz Cofer** (1952-) was born in Hormigueros, Puerto Rico, into a family that was destined to move back and forth between Puerto Rico and Patterson, New Jersey, due to her father's career in the Navy. After college, Cofer pursued further studies, obtaining an M.A. degree from Florida International University and receiving a fellowship for graduate work at Oxford University in England. Throughout her education, Cofer was a writer and, in 1980, began to receive recognition for her work, first with a fellowship from the Florida Arts Council, then other awards from the Bread Loaf Writers Conference (1981) and from the National Endowment for the Arts (1989). Cofer became the first Hispanic writer to receive a Special Citation from the PEN Martha Albrand Award for *Silent Dancing: A Remembrance of a Puerto Rican Childhood* (1990), which is a collection of autobiographical essays and poems. The book was also awarded the Pushcart Prize in the essay category, the New York Public Library System List of Best Books for the Teen Age and its title essay was chosen by Joyce Carol Oates for *The Best American Essays* (1991). Cofer was also the first U.S. Hispanic to win the O. Henry Prize (1994) for the short story. In 1994, she also won the Anisfield-Wolf Award in Race Relations for her novel *The Latin Deli*. Cofer's two major works of poetry are *Reaching for the Mainland* and *Terms of Survival*, both published in 1987. Her novel *Line of the Sun* (1990) is based on her family's gradual immigration to the United States and chronicles the years from the Great Depression to the 1960s. Her young adult story collection, *The Year of Our Revolution* (1999), picks up where *Silent Dancing* left off, examining a young Latina's coming of age in Patterson and beginning to rebel against the old ways of her Hispanic family. Her most recent works include *Call Me Maria* (2004); *Riding Low on the Streets of Gold: Latino Literature for Young Adults,* a young adult anthology edited by Cofer (2004); *The Meaning of Consuelo* (2003); *Woman in Front of the Sun: On Becoming a Writer* (2000). Judith Ortiz Cofer is currently the Regents' and Franklin Professor of English and Creative Writing at the University of Georgia.

Poet and painter **Ricardo Pau-Llosa** (1954-) was born in Havana into a middle-class family that had struggled to emerge from poverty in Cuba. After the Cuban Revolution, the family went into exile in 1960, when Pau-Llosa was just six years old, first to Chicago and later to Tampa. Although he was educated in American schools, Pau Llosa continues to cultivate the theme of exile in his poetry and art and to balance nostalgia for the homeland he barely knew with the overwhelming reality of a U.S. culture that has made him feel foreign since his childhood. His poetry collections include *Sorting Metaphors*, which won the national competition for the first Anhinga Poetry Prize (1983); *Bread of the Imagined* (1992); *Cuba* (1993); *Vereda Tropical* (1999); *The Mastery Impulse* (2003) and *Parable Hunter* (2008). He has also published individual poems in numerous magazines throughout the United States. In addition Pau-Llosa has published essays and short stories in magazines and anthologies, and is a renowned critic of the visual arts, particularly twentieth-century Latin American painting and sculpture. His essays in particular explore the exilic identity as experienced by all Cuban/Cuban American artists in the United States. In 1984, Pau-Llosa was awarded the Cintas Fellowship for Literature and, in 1998, *Miami News Times* named him "best local poet." He also won the *Linden Lane Magazine* English-Language Poetry Prize (1987). Pau-Llosa works as a professor of Creative Writing at Miami-Dade College.

Willie Perdomo was born in East Harlem of Puerto Rican parents and is a Nuyorican poet, children's book author and educator. A co-founder and publisher of Cypher Books and three-time fellow of New York Foundation for the Arts, he is the author of *Where a Nickel Costs a Dime* (1996), *Postcards of El Barrio* (2002) and the award-winning *Smoking Lovely* (2003), recipient of the PEN American Center Beyond Margins Award. Additionally, his first children's book, *Visiting Langston*, received the 2002 Coretta Scott King Honor. Perdomo currently teaches at Fordham University.

A poet, fiction writer and scholar, **Gustavo Pérez-Firmat** (1949-) is the author of ten books and over seventy essays and reviews. Pérez-Firmat was born in Havana, Cuba, and relocated with his family to Miami after Castro came to power in Cuba. The recipient of fellowships from the National Endowment for the Humanities, the American Council of Learned Societies and the John Simon Guggenheim Foundation, Pérez Firmat earned his Ph.D. in Comparative Literature from the University of Michigan (1979). His books of literary and cultural criticism include *Idle Fictions* (1982), *Literature and Liminality* (1986), *The Cuban Condition* (1989), *Do the Americas Have a Common Literature?* (1990) and *My Own Private Cuba* (1999). His groundbreaking book-length essay, *Life on the Hyphen: the Cuban-American Way* (1994) was awarded the Eugene M. Kayden University Press National Book Award for 1994 and the Latin American Studies Association's Bryce Wood Book Award. Themes of biculturalism are ever-present in Pérez-Firmat's three collections of poetry: *Carolina Cuban* (1987), *Equivocaciones* (1989) and *Bilingual Blues* (1995), which are full of code-switching and bilingual-bicultural double entendres and playfulness. In 2000, he published a novel, *Anything but Love*. His tour-de-force exploration of bilingualism and biculturalism as a critic and writer, *Tongue Ties: Logo-Eroticism in Anglo-Hispanic Literature*, was published in 2003. In his book-length memoir, *Next Year in Cuba* (1995), which was nominated for a Pulitzer Prize, Pérez-Firmat documents the tension his generation feels between identifying with other Americans their age and identifying with their parents, who always looked forward to returning to Cuba. True to form, Pérez-Firmat re-created the memoir in Spanish in 1997 as *El año que viene estamos en Cuba*. In 2005, Pérez-Firmat published a memoir, *Scar Tissue*, in prose and verse in which he chronicles his dealing with the death of his father and with his own prostate cancer. Pérez-Firmat is currently the David Feinson Professor of Humanities at Columbia University.

Pedro Pietri (1944-2004), writer and poet, was born in Ponce, Puerto Rico, just two years before his family migrated to New York. He was orphaned of both parents while still a child and raised by his grandmother. Pietri attended public schools in New York City and served in the Army from 1966 to 1968. Other than his having taught writing occasionally and participated in workshops, very little else is known about this intentionally mysterious and unconventional figure. Pietri published collections of poems and poetry chapbooks: *The Blue and the Gray* (1975), *Invisible Poetry* (1979), *Out of Order* (1980), *Uptown Train* (1980), *An Alternate* (1980), *Traffic Violations* (1983) and *Missing Out of Action* (1992). Nevertheless, it was his first book of poetry, *Puerto Rican Obituary* (1974), that brought him his greatest fame and a host of imitators, making him a model for the Nuyorican school of literature. In 1973, a live performance by him of poems from this book was recorded and distributed by Folkways Records. In 1980, Pietri's short story "Lost in the Museum of Natural History" was published in bilingual format in Puerto Rico. Pietri also had numerous unpublished, but produced, plays and two published collections: *The Masses Are Asses* (1984) and *Illusions of a Revolving Door: Plays Teatro* (1992). Pietri's work is one of a total break with conventions, both literary and social, and it is subversive in its open rejection of established society and its hypocrisies.

Miguel Piñero (1946-1988), the most famous dramatist to come out of the Nuyorican school, was born in Gurabo, Puerto Rico. He was raised on the Lower East Side of New York, the site of many of his plays and poems. Shortly after moving to New York, his father abandoned the family and the young Piñero had to live on the streets until his mother could find a source of income. Piñero was a gang leader and involved in petty crime and drugs while an adolescent; he was a junior high school dropout and by the time he was twenty-four he had been sent to Sing Sing Prison for armed robbery. While at Sing Sing, he began writing and acting in a theater workshop there. By the time of his release, his most famous play, *Short Eyes* (1975) had already been prepared in draft form. The play was produced and soon moved to Broadway after getting favorable reviews. During the successful run of his play and afterwards, Piñero became involved with a group of Nuyorican writers in the Lower East Side and became one of the principal spokespersons and models for the new school of Nuyorican literature, which was furthered by the publication of *Nuyorican Poets: An Anthology of Puerto Rican Words and Feelings*, compiled and edited by him and Miguel Algarín in 1975. During this time, as well, Piñero began his career as a scriptwriter for such television dramatic series as "Barreta," "Kojac" and "Miami Vice." In all, Piñero wrote some eleven plays that were produced, most of which are included in his two collections, *The Sun Always Shines for the Cool, A Midnight Moon at the Greasy Spoon, Eulogy for a Small-Time Thief* (1983) and *Outrageous One-Act Plays* (1986). Piñero is also author of a book of poems, *La Bodega Sold Dreams* (1986). Included among his awards were a Guggenheim Fellowship (1982) and the New York Drama Critics Circle Award for Best American Play, an Obie and the Drama Desk Award, all in 1974 for "Short Eyes." Piñero died of sclerosis of the liver in 1988, after many years of hard living and recurrent illnesses as a dope addict.

Born in San Antonio, Texas, from age two **Raúl Salinas** (raúlsalinas, 1934-2008) was raised in Austin. In 1957, he moved to Los Angeles and the next year he was sentenced to 15 years of imprisonment at Soledad State Prison. In Leavenworth penitentiary, Salinas founded and edited two journals: *Aztlán de Leavenworth* and *New Era Prison* Magazine. During this time and after his release, he became one of the most noteworthy self-taught prison poets, even elevating prison to a metaphor in his poetry; appropriately one of his most famous poems (originally published in *Aztlán de Leavenworth* in 1970) and the title of his first book reveal this esthetic: *Un Trip through the Mind Jail y Otras Excursions* (1980). Through assistance from students and professors at the University of Washington, Salinas was released early and in 1972, took courses at the university and became involved in the Chicano and Native American movements. In addition to publishing his work widely in magazines, Salinas is the author of a second book of poems, *East of the Freeway: Reflections de Mi Pueblo* (1995). In 1999, Arte Público Press of the University of Houston, re-issued *Un Trip* and hailed Salinas as a pioneer of Hispanic literature in the United States. Salinas was the owner and operator of Resistencia Bookstore in Austin, Texas, and the publisher of Red Salmon Press, which he founded in 1983. In 2006, with the assistance of editor Louis G. Mendoza, Salinas published *raúlrsalinas and the Jail Machine: My Weapon is My Pen*, his collection of journalism and personal correspondence, especially focusing on the years of his incarceration; the collection is important as a document linking the struggles for humane treatment of prisoners to the civil rights movement that was taking place outside the correctional facilities. That same year, he published *Indio Trails: A Xicano Odyssey through Indian Country*.

Alberto Álvaro Ríos (1952-), a native of Nogales, Arizona, is a writer and poet of several award-winning works and has been included in various major national and international literary anthologies. He is the author of numerous collections of poetry, including *Dangerous Shirt* (2009); *The Theater of Night* (2007), *The Smallest*

Muscle in the Human Body (2002) and *Whispering to Fool the Wind* (1982), which won the 1981 Walt Whitman Award. Ríos, a recipient of many awards, including six Pushcart Prizes in both poetry and fiction, is also the author of *Capirotada: A Nogales Memoir* (1999), *The Curtain of Trees: Stories* (1999), *Pig Cookies and Other Stories* (1995) and *The Iguana Killer: Twelve Stories of the Heart* (1984), which was honored with the Western States Book Award. Ríos is currently Regents Professor of English at Arizona State University.

Mexican-American novelist **Tomás Rivera** (1935-1984) is one of the principal founders of the Chicano literary movement. Born into a family of migrant workers in Crystal City, Texas, Rivera had to fit his early schooling as well as his college education in between the seasons of work in the fields. He, nevertheless, achieved an outstanding education, and became a college professor and administrator. Rivera most famously is the author of one of the foundational works of the Chicano literary movement . . . *y no se lo tragó la tierra / And the Earth Did Not Devour Him* (1971). In many ways, . . . *y no se lo tragó la tierra* came to be the most influential book in the Chicano's search for identity. Before his death in 1984, Rivera wrote and published other stories, essays and poems. Through his essays, such as "Chicano Literature: Fiesta of the Living" (1979) and "Into the Labyrinth: The Chicano in Literature" (1971), and his personal and scholarly activities, he was one of the prime movers in the promotion of Chicano authors, in the creation of the concept of Chicano literature and in the creation of Chicano literature and culture as legitimate academic areas in the college curriculum. In 1989 his stories were collected and published under the title of *The Harvest*, which was also the title of one of his stories, and in 1990 his poems were collected and published under the title of *The Searchers*. That same year, all of his works were collected and published in *Tomás Rivera: The Complete Works*, the only volume of a Chicano author's complete works published to date.

In 1993, **Luis J. Rodríguez's** (1954-) memoir of life on the streets, *Always Running: Gang Days in LA,* became the first Hispanic book to win the Carl Sandburg Award for Non-Fiction. It also won the *Chicago Sun-Times* First Prose book Award in 1994. Born in El Paso as the son of Mexican immigrants and raised in Los Angeles, where he became a gang member and petty thief, Rodríguez escaped the life on the streets out of the force of will and began working in heavy industry as well as keeping journals and writing. By the 1980s while living in Chicago, his articles and stories began to appear in mainstream magazines and newspapers. When he perceived the lack of access to publication for Latino and minority writers, in the late 1980s Rodríguez founded Tía Chucha Press, at first a publisher of chapbooks. He published his own *Poems across the Pavement* with Tía Chucha in 1989. His second book of poetry, *The Concrete River* (1993), won the PEN Oakland/Josephine Miles Award in 1991. These were followed by *Trochemoche* (1989, Helter Skelter), a mélange of various style of urban spoken word and more intimate and affecting verse, and *My Nature is Hunger: New and Selected Poems*

(2005), the latter being a compilation of some of his earlier poems, along with twelve new ones. In his *The Republic of East LA* (2003), he assembles twelve stories of diverse characters who struggle to survive crime, poverty and deprivation in the East Los Angeles barrio. In recent years, Rodríguez has turned to producing children's and young adult literature, including *America Is Her Name* (1998) and *It Doesn't Have to Be This Way: A Barrio Story* (2004), both of which deal with the evils and dangers of inner city life. His *Music of the Mill*, his first historical novel, received the Latino Book Award for fiction.

Born in the farm town of Old Picacho, New Mexico, **Benjamin Alire Sáenz** (1954-) is one of the few Mexican-American novelists to see many of his works published by major, commercial presses in the United States. Raised by devout working-class parents near Mesilla, New Mexico, Sáenz studied for the Catholic priesthood, earning a Master's degree in Theology in 1980 from the University of Louvain in Belgium and becoming ordained in 1981. Despite his life-long religiosity, Sáenz left the priesthood and decided to pursue a career in writing; he received a Master's degree in Creative Writing from the University of Texas at El Paso in 1988. In 1991, Sáenz published his first book, *Calendar of Dust*, a poetry collection commemorating the diverse peoples and their migrations in the borderlands. It immediately won the Before Columbus American Book Award and, based on this initial work, he was awarded a Lannan Poetry Fellowship in 1992. That same year, Sáenz published a collection of short stories, *Flowers for the Broken*, again exploring the peoples and culture of the U.S.-Mexico border. The prolific Sáenz went on to publish another poetry collection, *Dark and Perfect Angels* in 1995; the poems contained in this deeply spiritual and personal anthology eulogize deceased friends and relatives as well as fictionalized strangers. That same year, Sáenz broke into publishing with a commercial house, Hyperion, for his novel *Carry Me Like Water*. In *The House of Forgetting* (1997), Sáenz produced an even more commercially viable novel, this exploring the psychological thriller genre. Sáenz's latest novel, *In Perfect Light* (2005), the first also to be issued simultaneously in Spanish translation, enters the world of child molestation, the Juárez underworld and the breaking apart of an El Paso Chicano family. In 2002 and 2006, respectively, Sáenz returned to a small presses to issue his third and fourth books of poems, *Elegies in Blue* and *Dreaming the End of War*. In recent years, Sáenz has also published a number of bilingual picture books for children with El Paso's Cinco Puntos Press. Sáenz currently teaches in the bilingual Masters of Fine Arts Program at the University of Texas at El Paso.

Born in Robstown, Texas, close to the Mexican border, **Luis Omar Salinas** (1937-) spent some of his early years in Mexico and by age nine had moved to live with an aunt and uncle in California. He attended public schools and began college at Fresno State University, where he edited the literary magazine, *Backwash,* but never received his diploma. In 1970 he published his first book of poetry, *Crazy Gypsy,* a highly artistic work that became an anthem for Chicano activists. Many of the poems were included in the first anthologies of Chicano literature and have become canonized in U.S. Hispanic literature: "Crazy Gypsy," "Aztec Angel," "Nights and Days," "Mexico, Age Four" and others. In *Darkness Under the Trees: Walking Behind the Spanish* (1982), and in the works that follow, Salinas heightens the note of sorrow and melancholy as he attempts to rationalize his unjust fate. Salinas, who has supported himself with a variety of blue-color jobs, has won some of the most prestigious awards for writing, including the California English Teachers citation, 1973; Stanley Kunitz Poetry Prize (for *Afternoon of the Unreal*), 1980; Earl Lyon Award, 1980; General Electric Foundation Award, 1983. In 1986, Salinas' best poems were collected in a hefty volume entitled *The Sadness of Days*. His latest contribution is *Elegy for Desire* (1997), a collection of odes, elegies and cantos.

Ricardo Sánchez (1941-1995) was the first Chicano writer to have a book of poetry published by a mainstream commercial publishing house when Anchor/Doubleday issued his *Canto y grito mi liberación* (1973, *I Sing and Shout for My Liberation*). Sánchez was one of the most prolific Chicano poets, one of the first creators of a bilingual literary style and one of the first to be identified with the Chicano Movement. Much of his early life experiences of oppressive poverty and overwhelming racism, as well as his suffering in prisons and his self-education and rise to a level of political and social consciousness, is chronicled in his poetry, which although very lyrical, is the most autobiographic of all the Hispanic poets. Thus all of his books serve as a chronicle of the ups and downs of his life and his wide-ranging travels: *Hechizo Spells / Hechizospells* (1976), *Milhuas Blues and gritos norteños* (1980), *Brown Bear Honey Madness: Alaskan Cruising Poems* (1982), *Amsterdam cantos y poemas pistos* (1983), *Eagle Visioned / Feathered Adobes* (1990) and *Amerikan Journeys: Jornadas americanas* (1994). In 1985, Arte Público Press published a selection of his English-language poems in *Selected Poems*. In 1995, Washington State University issued a reprint edition of *Canto y grito mi liberación* and in 1997, a posthumous collection of Sánchez's love poems, many of which had never been published, were issued as *The Loves of Ricardo Sánchez* by Tía Chucha Press.

Gary Soto (1952-) is the Chicano poet who is most acclaimed in academic circles in the United States. After winning some of the most prestigious creative writing awards and achieving tenure at the University of California, Soto transformed himself into a highly commercial writer of children's and young adult literature. Born to Mexican-American parents in Fresno, California, Soto was raised in the San Joaquin Valley. In 1976, Soto earned his M.F.A. in Creative Writing from the University of California-Irvine, and thereafter began teaching at the University of California-Berkeley. For his poetry, Soto won the following awards: the Academy of American Poets Prize (1975), the Bess Hopkins Prize (1977), a Guggenheim Fellowship (1979) and the Levinson Award (1984), among others. His short story collections and children's books have also won awards, including the American Book Award (1984) and the Tomás Rivera Award (1998). Soto's poetry books include *The Elements of San Joaquín* (1977), *Where Sparrows Work Hard* (1981), *Black Hair* (1985) and *Who Will*

Know Us? (1990), *A Natural Man* (1999), among others. His most famous young adult novel is *Baseball in April* (1990). Among his children's picture books are *Boys at Work* (1995), *Chato's Kitchen* (1997) and *Big Bushy Mustache* (1998). In the new millennium, Soto began writing a series of novels around his recurrent protagonist, Silver Mendez, a thirty-nine-year-old unemployed poet: *Nickel and Dime* (2000), *Poetry Lover* (2001) and *Amnesia in a Republican County* (2003).

Chicana poet **Carmen Tafolla** (1951-) was born and raised in San Antonio. She began coming to prominence in the late Chicano Movement of the mid-1970s. She holds B.A. degrees in Spanish and French (1972) and an M.A. in Education (1973) from Austin College. After receiving her doctorate Ph.D. in Bilingual Education from the University of Texas, Tafolla began teaching Women's Studies at California State University-Fresno. Despite her educational accomplishments, Tafolla is an oral poet and performer who bases her work on the bilingualism and biculturalism of working-class Mexican-American neighborhoods. A folklorist at heart, she has preserved many of the folkways and much of the worldview of common folk in her verse. To date, she has published the following books: *Get Your Tortillas Together* (in 1976 with Cecilio Gracía-Camarillo and Reyes Cárdenas), *Curandera* (1983, *Faith Healer*) *To Split a Human: Mitos, Machos y La Mujer Chicana* (1985) and *Patchwork Colcha: Poems, Stories and Songs in English and Spanish* (1987). What comes to the fore in Curandera is a constant in Tafolla's esthetic, which derives directly from oral lore and wisdom passed on by women. In 1989, her *Sonnet to Human Beings* won the University of California-Irvine award for Chicano literature, and in 2001 she published a well-reviewed collection, *Sonnets and Salsa*. Tafolla has also written works for children, including *The Dog Who Wanted to Be a Tiger*, *Baby Coyote and the Old Woman / El coyotito y la viejita* (2000) and *My House Is Your House: Mi casa es su casa* (2000).

Gloria Vando (1934-) is the daughter of two Puerto Rican writers, Anita Vélez-Mitchell and Erasmo Vando. Born and raised in New York and educated in the United States and Europe, she ultimately received her B.A. from Texas A&M University in 1975. Vando is a contributing editor of *The North American Review*, and the co-editor of *Spud Songs: An Anthology of Potato Poems*, benefiting Hunger Relief. In 1977, Vando founded a literary magazine and press, Helicon Nine, which published outstanding literary and artistic works by women until 1992. While more than fifty anthologies contain her poems, it was not until 1993, that Vando published her first collection of poems, *Promesas: Geography of the Impossible*, which became the first Hispanic book to win the Thorpe Menn Award for literary achievement. In 2002, Vando published her second collection, *Shadows and Supposes*, winner of the 1998 Alice Fay Di Castagnola Award from the Poetry Society of America; the book was also a finalist for the Walt Whitman Poetry Contest. Other awards for her work over the years include the Billee Murray Poetry Prize (1991), the Stanley Hanks Memorial Award (1986) and various fellowships and grants from the Kansas Arts Commission. Three of her poems were adapted for the stage under the title, *Moving Targets: Three Interpretations of Murder,* and were showcased at the Women's Work Festival in New York City in 1999. Her work has also been included in presentations at Lincoln Center for the Performing Arts, New Federal Theatre and Latino Playwrights Theatre in New York City.

Sherezada "Chiqui" Vicioso (1948-) is a Dominican poet, playwright and essayist. She holds an M.A. in Education from Columbia University and completed postgraduate studies in Cultural Administration for the Getulio Vargas Foundation in Brazil. Her many works include *Viaje desde el agua* (1981), *Un extraño ulular traía el viento* (1985) and *Volver a vivir: imágenes de Nicaragua* (1986). Vicioso is also the author of many plays, including *Salomé U: cartas a una ausencia, Desvelos* (dialogue between Emily Dickinson and Salomé Ureña), *NUYOR/islas* and *Wish-ky Sour*, which was the 1997 recipient of the Premio Nacional de Teatro Cristóbal de Llerena.

Evangelina Vigil-Piñón (1949-) was born in San Antonio, Texas, the second of ten children of a very poor family that lived for years in public housing. Her first full-length collection of poems, *Thirty an' Seen a Lot* (1982), won the American Book Award of the Before Columbus Foundation. Despite the apparently natural vernacular of her writing, Vigil-Piñón's poetry is the product of great craftsmanship, obtained through extensive reading and self-education well as through formal study. She obtained a B.A. in English from the University of Houston in 1974 and took post-graduate courses at various institutions afterward. She also has served as an adjunct faculty member for the University of Houston since the mid-1980s. In 1977, Vigil-Piñón became the first Hispanic writer to win the National Literary Contest of the Coordinating Council of Literary Magazines for work published in a small magazine. Vigil-Piñón is the Chicana poet who has most sensitively portrayed and celebrated working-class culture. She is also one of the leading exponents of bilingual code-switching in poetry. Her work at the center of U.S. Hispanic literature as the poetry editor for the leading Hispanic literary magazine, *The Americas Review*, made her a leader in the Hispanic women's movement as a speaker and host of writers on tour. Vigil-Piñón's second poetry collection, *The Computer Is Down* (1987) explores how common folk must accommodate to or become displaced from the modern social and technological landscape. In 2001, Vigil-Piñón published a lyrical first book for children, *Marina's Muumuu.*

Alma Luz Villanueva (1944-) is a Mexican-American poet, short story writer and novelist. Her works include *Soft Chaos* (2009), *Luna's California Poppies* (2002), *Vida* (2002) and *Desire* (1998). The recipient of numerous awards, her collection *Poems* won the University of California at Irvine's Third Chicano Literary Prize in 1977, and her fiction novel *Ultraviolet Sky* won the 1989 American Book Award from the Before Columbus Foundation. Her most recent awards include the 1994 Latino Literature Prize for *Planet with Mother May I?* Villanueva also holds an M.F.A. in Creative Writing from Antioch University in Los Angeles, where she currently teaches.

Credits

Jack Agüeros

"Psalm for the Next Millennium": Reprinted from *Lord, Is This a Psalm* © 2002 by Jack Agüeros with permission of Hanging Loose Press.

"Sonnets for the Four Horsemen of the Apocalypse: Long Time among Us" : Reprinted from *Sonnets from the Puerto Rican* © 1996 by Jack Agüeros with permission of Hanging Loose Press.

Miguel Algarín

"A Mongo Affair": Reprinted from *Survival Supervivencia* © 2009 by Miguel Algarín with permission of Arte Público Press-University of Houston.

"El jibarito moderno": Reprinted from *On Call* © 1994 by Miguel Algarín with permission of Arte Público Press-University of Houston.

"Nuyorican Angel of Records": Reprinted from *Love Is Hard Work* © 1991 by Miguel Algarín with permission of Scribner Poetry.

Alurista (Alberto Baltazar Urista)

"Tarde sobria": Reprinted from *Floricanto en Aztlán* © 1971 by Alurista with permission of UCLA Chicano Research Center, Regents of the University of California. All rights reserved.

"do u remember": Reprinted with permission of *Revista-Chicano Riqueña* with permission by Arte Público Press-University of Houston.

"cornfields thaw out": Reprinted with permission of *Revista-Chicano Riqueña* with permission by Arte Público Press-University of Houston.

Julia Alvarez

"Homecoming" & "Dusting": Reprinted from *Homecoming* © 1984, 1996 by Julia Alvarez. Published by Plume/Penguin, a division of Penguin Group (USA). First published in *The George Washington Review* by permission of Susan Bergholz Literary Services, New York, NY, and Lamy, MN. All rights reserved.

"Bilingual Sestina" & "Exile": Reprinted from *The Other Side / El otro lado* © 1995 by Julia Alvarez. Published by Plume/Penguin, a division of Penguin Group (USA). First published in *The George Washington Review* by permission of Susan Bergholz Literary Services, New York, NY, and Lamy, MN. All rights reserved.